LC
213
E365
2002

EDUCATING *ALL* LEARNERS

ABOUT THE AUTHORS

Festus E. Obiakor is a Professor in the Department of Exceptional Education, University of Wisconsin-Milwaukee. He is a nationally/internationally known teacher, scholar, and consultant. Dr. Obiakor has served as Distinguished Visiting Professor at a variety of universities, and is the author or co-author of more than 100 publications, including books, articles, and essays.

Patrick A. Grant is a Professor in the Department of Special Education, Slippery Rock University of Pennsylvania. He earned his graduate degrees from the University of Oregon. Dr. Grant is a storyteller, an advocate for diversity, student retention, and minority student recruitment. He continues to work with first year students, mentoring them to stay in school, and complete their education.

Elizabeth A. Dooley is the Chair of the Department of Educational Theory and Practice, and an Associate Professor of Special Education at West Virginia University. She also serves as Program Coordinator, and Summer Program Director, for a statewide community/university program that promotes, and enhances academic excellence and achievement for underserved youth. Dr. Dooley has over 12 years experience in higher education teaching and administration, and over six years experience in the public schools.

EDUCATING *ALL* LEARNERS

Refocusing the Comprehensive Support Model

Edited by

FESTUS E. OBIAKOR

Department of Exceptional Education
School of Education
University of Wisconsin-Milwaukee

PATRICK A. GRANT

Department of Special Education
Slippery Rock University of Pennsylvania

ELIZABETH A. DOOLEY

Department of Educational Theory and Practice
West Virginia University

Published and Distributed Throughout the World by

CHARLES C THOMAS • PUBLISHER, LTD.
2600 South First Street
Springfield, Illinois 62704

This book is protected by copyright. No part of
it may be reproduced in any manner without
written permission from the publisher.

©2002 by CHARLES C THOMAS • PUBLISHER, LTD.

ISBN 0-398-07264-7 (hard)
ISBN 0-398-07265-5 (paper)

Library of Congress Catalog Card Number: 2001054017

With THOMAS BOOKS *careful attention is given to all details of manufacturing and design. It is the Publisher's desire to present books that are satisfactory as to their physical qualities and artistic possibilities and appropriate for their particular use.* THOMAS BOOKS *will be true to those laws of quality that assure a good name and good will.*

Printed in the United States of America
SR-R-3

Library of Congress Cataloging-in-Publication Data

Educating all learners : refocusing on the comprehensive support model / edited by Festus E. Obiakor, Patrick A. Grant, Elizabeth A. Dooley.
    p. cm.
  Includes bibliographical references (p.) and index.
  ISBN 0-398-07264-7 (cloth) –ISBN 0-398-07265-5 (pbk.)
    1. Educational equalization. 2. Inclusive education. I. Obiakor, Festus E. II. Grant, Patrick A. III. Dooley, Elizabeth A.

LC213 .E365 2002
379.2'6–dc21
                                                                               2001054017

To my wife, Pauline; to my children, Charles, Gina, and Kristen; to Mama, and all my family members in Nigeria, thank you for being there for me as always. To my well-wishers, friends, mentors, and mentees, thank you also for enriching my life immensely.

To my wife, and friend, Pauline; and to my pillars of strength, Nia, Zackiya, Nicolas, Patrice, and Guyon, thank you for your unconditional love, support, encouragement, and kindness. To my friends and family members in Jamaica and the U.S., thank you for understanding it takes a responsible village to raise a child.

To my parents, the late Fred, and Juanita Dooley; and my brother Fredrick Mark, thank you for strength. To my husband Cornell, thank you for your warm and loving spirit. Thank you to my sisters, my anchors, Freda, Debbie, Jacque and Kitty; to my nieces, Memori, Chanel, Delorean, Fredricka; and my great nephew Zyon, be encouraged. To the Dooley and Burks extended family members, thank you for the wealth of reunion memories and unwavering support.

CONTRIBUTORS

GREGORY F. ALOIA
College of Education
Florida Atlantic University
Boca Raton, Florida

STEPHEN F. ALOIA
Department of Special Education
California State University at Fullerton
Fullerton, California

JEFFREY P. BAKKEN
College of Education
Department of Special Education
Illinois State University
Normal, Illinois

FERNANDO ALMEIDA DINIZ
Department of Educational Studies
University of Edinburgh
Edinburgh, Scotland

ELIZABETH A. DOOLEY
Department of Educational Theory and Practice
West Virginia University
Morgantown, West Virginia

DON DRENNON-GALA
Correctional Treatment Specialist
United States Department of Justice
Federal Bureau of Prisons
Chattanooga, Tennessee

REGINA L. ENWEFA
Department of Communicative Disorders
School of Allied Health Services
Jackson State University
Jackson, Mississippi

STEPHEN C. ENWEFA
Department of Communicative Disorders
School of Allied Health Services
Jackson State University
Jackson, Mississippi

BRIDGIE ALEXIS FORD
Department of Counseling & Special Education
University of Akron
Akron, Ohio

PATRICK A. GRANT
Department of Special Education
Slippery Rock University of Pennsylvania
Slippery Rock, Pennsylvania

PAULINE B. GRANT
Reading Specialist
Slippery Rock, Pennsylvania

PAULINE HARRIS-OBIAKOR
Student Technology Services
University of Wisconsin–Milwaukee
Milwaukee, Wisconsin

JOSEPH NWOYE
Department of Curriculum & Instruction
Illinois State University
Normal, Illinois

SUNDAY O. OBI
Department of Education & Human Services
Kentucky State University
Frankfort, Kentucky

FESTUS E. OBIAKOR
Department of Exceptional Education
University of Wisconsin–Milwaukee
Milwaukee, Wisconsin

LORETTA P. PRATER
School of Family & Consumer Sciences
Lumpkin College of Business & Applied Sciences
Eastern Illinois University
Charleston, Illinois

RAMEL L. SMITH
Doctoral Candidate–School Psychology
University of Wisconsin–Milwaukee
Milwaukee, Wisconsin

CHRISTINE M. TOSCANO-NIXON
Doctoral Candidate–Special Education
West Virginia University
Morgantown, West Virginia

PEICHI TUNG
Doctoral Candidate–Administration, Planning & Social Policy
Harvard University Graduate School of Education
Cambridge, Massachusetts

CHERYL A. UTLEY
Juniper Gardens Children's Project
University of Kansas
Kansas City, Kansas

LYNN K. WILDER

Department of Counseling Psychology & Special Education
Brigham Young University
Provo, Utah

DARRELL WILLIAMS

Doctoral Candidate—Department of Administrative Leadership
University of Wisconsin–Milwaukee
Milwaukee, Wisconsin

FOREWORD

Working in developing countries in Latin America and Africa without financial resources and infrastructure, I saw the results of providing students with and without disabilities services that are not comprehensive. For instance, in countries where educators did not work with families, deaf students who had learned to sign could not return home because they could not communicate with their parents. In addition, where there was no collaboration between community agencies and educational programs, students with developmental disabilities who had completed educational programs could not be reintegrated into their communities because no provisions had been made for their lodging or employment. These problems were especially acute in countries where national and local governments had neglected to establish a plan for rational, orderly expansion of general and special education services.

The situation in the United States is not nearly as problematic as what occurs in many countries. However, even though we are the richest country in the world, the educational services for students with and without disabilities leave much to be desired because they do not result from a collaborative effort on the part of educators, community agencies, families, and local, state and national governments. What makes matters worse, is that educators, parents, community workers, and politicians each blame the other groups for the state of affairs.

Educating All Learners: Refocusing the Comprehensive Support Model tackles this problem. The contributors suggest that instead of pitting one group against another, a better method is to have all of these groups work together in an integrated, collaborative, multifaceted approach to assist **all** students to succeed. And, they describe in detail the roles that each of these groups can play in a comprehensive approach to improving the education our children receive.

The comprehensive support model that emerges from the 13 chapters of this book provides a road map for all concerned individuals who want to solve problems of educational inequality. Applying the comprehensive support model will help insure that **all** children in developed and developing countries receive the education they deserve.

In the end, this book provides a paradigm shift from the traditional way of looking at the role of education, family, community and government. It is an important book for this day and age—undergraduate and graduate students, parents and special educators, experienced and inexperienced scholars, minority and majority communities, and policy makers and lawmakers will find this book very useful. I recommend it highly for anyone interested in making a difference in the educational lives of **all** children.

DR. HERBERT GROSSMAN
Professor Emeritus
San Jose State University

PREFACE

The die is now cast! The paradigm has shifted! General and special educators are feeling the pressure to educate **all** learners in spite of their abilities, disabilities, socioeconomic backgrounds, racial identities, cultural differences, linguistic differences, and national origins. In direct response to demographic shifts in power, new ways of learning and teaching are now advocated to prevent misidentification, misassessment, miscategorization, misplacement, and misinstruction. It is now clear that we must educate **all** learners!

Our book, *Educating All Learners: Refocusing the Comprehensive Support Model* (CSM), makes it imperative to maximize the fullest potential of **all** students. It focuses on the premise that "we should leave no child behind." The objectives are to teach the unteachable and to reach the unreachable. In order to meet these objectives, this book advocates the use of the CSM to incorporate efforts of the "self," family, school, community, state, nation, and world. No one entity could do the job alone—all entities must collaborate and consult with each other in honor of the popular African concept of "It takes a whole village to raise a child." For inclusive education to work, general and special educators, parents, students, community leaders, and governments must understand their roles in building bridges and partnerships. We can no longer divorce any component from the whole process to properly educate our populace!

Educating All Learners has 13 chapters. We invited scholars and educators from across the nation and globe to contribute their unique perspectives. Chapter 1 presents the conceptual framework of the book. Chapter 2 discusses the role of the "self" in the educational process. In Chapter 3 and 4, the roles of families and schools are analyzed. Chapter 5 recognizes the homeless, a segment of the population that is frequently ignored in educational plannings and fundings. Chapters 6 and 7 discuss the impacts of teacher preparation and professional development in educating the child. In Chapter 8, community involvement in the educational process is synthesized. Chapters 9 and 10 evaluate state and federal roles in educating *all* learners. In Chapters

11 and 12, the impacts of technology and global education are described. And Chapter 13 summarizes future prospects of educating *all* learners in an increasingly complex society.

Rarely have other books addressed the comprehensive nature of the educational process. We believe *Educating All Learners* is a book for the new millennium. The blame game must be resisted! The "self" must be ready or be made ready; the school must be ready or be made ready; the community must be ready or be made ready; the state must be ready or be made ready; the nation must be ready or be made ready; and the world must be ready or be made ready. These are the central foci of the book. Hopefully, students, parents, school professionals, teacher educators, community leaders, policymakers, politicians, and development planners will find this book useful. As we move toward practicalizing "inclusive education" and "inclusive society," we need books that can advance this movement. Persons interested in advancing our society through "education" will find *Educating All Learners* to be very informative.

We thank the contributors for their dedication to excellence—their chapters contributed to the quality of this book. We especially thank Dr. Herbert Grossman for writing the Foreword of this book. In sum, we give special thanks to our family members, friends, and well-wishers for their wonderful support during the writing of this book.

FESTUS E. OBIAKOR
PATRICK GRANT
ELIZABETH DOOLEY

CONTENTS

Foreword by Herbert Grossman xi
Preface xiii

Chapter
1. THE COMPREHENSIVE SUPPORT MODEL FOR ALL LEARNERS: CONCEPTUALIZATION AND MEANING 3
   Festus E. Obiakor, Pauline Harris-Obiakor, and Ramel L. Smith
2. THE POWER OF THE "SELF" IN EDUCATION 18
   Festus E. Obiakor and Darrell Williams
3. FAMILY AND SCHOOLING 32
   Loretta P. Prater
4. SCHOOLS: THE ROLES THEY SHOULD PLAY 49
   Patrick A. Grant and Pauline B. Grant
5. THE HOMELESS ARE PEOPLE, TOO: INCLUDING HOMELESS STUDENTS IN EDUCATIONAL PROGRAMMING 64
   Lynn K. Wilder
6. PREPARING TEACHERS FOR ALL STUDENTS 84
   Jeffrey P. Bakken, Gregory F. Aloia, and Stephen F. Aloia
7. COMMUNITY INVOLVEMENT IN EDUCATION 99
   Elizabeth A. Dooley and Christine M. Toscano-Nixon
8. PROFESSIONAL DEVELOPMENT: AN ESSENTIAL COMPONENT FOR EDUCATING TEACHERS AS LIFELONG LEARNERS 113
   Cheryl A. Utley, Festus E. Obiakor, and Bridgie Alexis Ford
9. STATE GOVERNMENTS: THE ROLES THEY MUST PLAY 130
   Sunday O. Obi

10. FEDERAL EDUCATIONAL POLICIES AND
    INNOVATIONS: IMPACTS ON EDUCATING
    ALL STUDENTS 150
    Joseph Nwoye and Peichi Tung
11. THE ROLE OF TECHNOLOGY IN THE EDUCATION
    OF ALL CHILDREN 166
    Stephen C. Enwefa, and Regina L. Enwefa
13. EDUCATING ALL CHILDREN GLOBALLY 179
    Fernando Almeida Diniz
14. EDUCATING ALL CHILDREN: FUTURE PROSPECTS 191
    Don Drennon-Gala, Festus E. Obiakor, and Patrick A. Grant

Author Index 199
Subject Index 206

EDUCATING *ALL* LEARNERS

Chapter 1

THE COMPREHENSIVE SUPPORT MODEL FOR ALL LEARNERS: CONCEPTUALIZATION AND MEANING

FESTUS E. OBIAKOR, PAULINE HARRIS-OBIAKOR, AND RAMEL L. SMITH

Issues of educational reform, redesign, and reconstruction have been at the forefront in the United States (Boykin, 2000). During the pre Civil Rights era, education was designed for the dominant culture, and the curriculum was dominated by Anglocentric values and themes formulated to acculturate immigrants into the homogenous society. In fact, schools became gatekeepers to eliminate those who failed to assimilate into the American mainstream. To a large measure, learners were disallowed to reach their maximum potential by being indoctrinated into a style conducive to traditional Eurocentric institutions. Boykin argued that the goals of school were to socialize a labor force that met the demands of the dominant society. However, current demographic changes have witnessed some shifts in powers and paradigms on how issues of *quality* and *equity* are addressed. We are now in a technological and informational age, and it seems clear that our world is getting smaller. To compete in this age of change, America must revamp its educational policies and practices to facilitate a comprehensive approach that operationally integrates the "self," families, schools, communities, and government agencies.

With legislative reformations and great technological advances, it would appear that the United States' traditional educational problems would have been resolved. To the contrary, there is a plethora of evidence to suggest that savage inequalities still exist (Kozol, 1991). Schools appear to have deviated from the landmark case of *Brown v. Board of Education of Topeka* and almost regressed back to the *Plessy v. Ferguson* era. Kozol explained how several of the nation's school systems are shamefully equivalent to systems during the Jim Crow era. Though certain school districts have made great strides to meet educational and social needs of students from different ethnic groups, apparent problems continue to exist. As a result, efforts must be proactively made to correct educational inadequacies and inequities (Boykin, 2000; Kozol; Obiakor, 1994). One suggested method throughout this chapter and this book is the Comprehensive Support Model (CSM) designed to educate all of our children and empower all of our citizenry. The flexibility of the CSM is ideal for a society with great heterogeneity and puts together energies of individual students, families, schools, communities, and governments. In this chapter, we discuss the conceptualization and meaning of the CSM as they relate to the education of all learners. Embedded in our discussion are cases that enhance the functions of the CSM.

THE CSM: OPERATIONAL DEFINITION

With the multidimensional nature of problems that confront America's children and youth, it seems logical to tackle these problems in an integrative manner that combines collaborative strategies with multifaceted interventions. In an effort to look for magic solutions, the *blame game* has flourished. In reality, students are not only to blame; parents are not only to blame; schools are not only to blame; and local, state, and federal governments are not only to blame. In this chapter (and throughout this book), we are not interested in placing blame, but in recommending ways for removing obstacles that keep children from reaching their potential. We propose the CSM because it has its roots from the "whole village" African concept of educational service delivery that values all societal entities (Obiakor, 1994).

Based on the CSM, the "self," family, school, community, and government are collaboratively involved. The "self" is involved because without the personal powers of persons involved in learning, self-responsibility may not be maximized. The family is important because it is the cornerstone of the student and the bridge that connects the student with the school. The school is a part of the CSM because it has teachers and professionals who have the power to shift their paradigms regarding demographic changes. The community is an important part of the CSM because it provides a variety of opportunities and choices for children and youth, parents, schools, and governmental entities to come together. In addition, local, state, and federal governments are important because they generate equitable policies that strengthen the multiple voices of the citizenry. Evidently, a reasonable government cannot divorce itself from happenings in families, schools, and communities.

The CSM is sequential, yet it is a mutually inclusive phenomenon. Its elements are operational, especially when:

1. The development and use of identification, assessment, and instructional strategies function within the context of cultural competence.
2. The creation of a collaborative system of community support for families has its guiding principle in the eradication of social stereotyping based on race, ethnicity, national origin, gender, and socioeconomic status.
3. The development of an awareness and appreciation for the many family forms that value individual differences and strengths.
4. The thwarting of conditions leading to violence in the home or the community cultivates a sense of safety for children and families.
5. The advocacy for economic policies and human services attest to being pro-family by virtue of proven outcomes.
6. The promotion of culturally competent practices in schools and in the larger society respects differences in worldviews and learning styles among individuals.
7. The advocacy for expanded services provides for affordable quality childcare to meet the varied needs of all families and children (e.g., infant and adolescent 24-hour care and weekend care).
8. The development of collaborative community approaches to problem solving involves students, parents, schools, and community leaders.
9. The recognition that the focus of the problem in situations of risk is not only in the individual but also in institutional barriers in the environment.
10. The reconfiguration of curricula eliminates the hidden curriculum and other culturally insensitive curricula variables.
11. The reinstitution of rites of passage and service opportunities cultivates a sense of belonging and resiliency in youth.
12. The broadening of visions in educational reform includes economic reform and the investment in human capital.

The intensity and integrity in which the aforementioned steps function determine the efficacy of this model. The CSM enhances reciprocity and creates a win-win situation for everyone involved in the educational process. Each possible entity of the CSM is dependent on another entity within the system. It is operationally essential that each entity in the CSM execute its part with fidelity; therefore, each individual or group must be motivated as well as properly trained.

FUNCTIONAL COMPONENTS OF THE CSM

The components of the CSM are inextricably interwoven; however, the isolation of each category is designed to affirm that there is accountability on each level. In this section, we delve specifically into each component of the CSM (a) "self," (b) family, (c) school, (d) community, and (e) government agencies.

Self

Educational systems are designed to intellectually and socially develop all students into tomorrow's leaders (Davis & Jordan, 1995). The "self," in essence, represents individuals involved (in this case, students). The centerpiece of the CSM revolves around students. We believe the critical role that students play must not be downplayed. Students have to learn to survive and thrive in impoverished homes, ill-equipped schools, dilapidated neighborhoods, and seemingly uncaring governments (Kozol, 1991; Wilson, 1996). It is unrealistic to expect children to flourish when they are deprived of the basic necessities of life (Comer & Poussaint, 1992; Shafer, 1996). Students who thrive in such conditions have been classified as resilient. Resiliency has been defined as (a) the ability to thrive, mature, and grow in the face of adverse conditions (Gordon, 1995); and (b) the successful adaptation to life tasks in the face of social disadvantage or highly adverse conditions (Finn & Rock, 1997). Interestingly, many multicultural students have to be "resilient" to make it through the educational system. As a consequence, changes in curriculum, instruction, and preservice training are needed to increase the educational success of all students.

Many laws have been passed to open doors that were previously closed to many students from multicultural backgrounds. While these laws have failed in their quest to produce a perfect system, the role of students can help to further the full intent of these laws. Students must be educated to be responsive to the environment and take proactive steps to maximize their learning potential. The CSM encourages students to be active and responsible members of the support system. Consider Case 1 below:

Case 1

Student X was an intelligent student who was often involved in off-task behaviors in class. Initially, his teacher permitted these behaviors because he was likeable and completed his work. As time went on, his behaviors grew worse and his grades began to suffer. Several interventions were implemented over a three-year timeframe to help him. They included (a) selecting him to participate in a "young leaders" group, (b) employing services of a volunteer mentor who worked with him twice a week; and (c) placing him in a smaller classroom to improve class performance. Despite the efforts of his mother, school, and mentor, he failed to take advantage of the services and eventually was expelled from school.

Case 1 illustrates the importance of the student in developing his/her self-responsibility. Student X was granted opportunities that are not afforded to many students; nevertheless, he was expelled from school because of his inability to carry his share of the load. The student must demonstrate self-efficacious and self-empowerment attitudes. Even with a great support system, the student must be self-knowledgeable, self-loving, and self-empowered (Obiakor, 1998a, 1998b).

Families

Although the student is the centerpiece of the CSM, families act as the cornerstone of this model. Families are responsible for the care, love, support, and development of the child (Shafer, 1996). The CSM elucidates the importance of the family creating a solid foundation for the child since many factors that influence the child are based on external events that take place before he/she reaches the compulsory age for public education. The substantial contributions of the family both genetically and environmentally aid and assist in shaping the child (Kozol, 1991; Stevenson, 1998; Wilson, 1996). It is common knowledge that the family serves as the bridge that connects the student with the school (Strickland & Ascher, 1992). It can never be divorced from educational and social duties and responsibilities after the child reaches compulsory age. It is essential that the family participates in schools, classrooms, sporting events, field trips, school performances, and Parent Teacher Association (PTA) meetings (Epstein, 1992; Slavin, 1997).

When the family is actively involved in school, potential problems are handled expeditiously, and comprehensive preventive and proactive techniques can be designed to create more culturally responsive classrooms. Family empowerment extends a family atmosphere into the school and creates a home away from home as depicted by Case 2 below:

Case 2

Teacher A was a long-term substitute teacher who was recruited to fill a vacancy left by a colleague recovering from surgery. One of the students in the classroom had family members who were very active in the school.

On the first day of class, Parent X came into the classroom and welcomed Teacher A to the school and offered his assistance. Although Teacher A rarely employed the services of Parent X in the classroom, a friendship blossomed. According to Teacher A, "Just knowing I had someone who was on my team made all the difference. Upon my arrival in the school, I immediately recognized a sense of community and family in the building and it was nice to be accepted immediately and unconditionally. In fact, because of the kindness I have received I am even more motivated to educate and inspire these children."

Case 2 illustrates how families can directly influence their children's education. Parent X was there to help Teacher A get acclimated to the system. Parent X's involvement was successful because he understood his role and respected the boundaries of the teacher. Because of this friendly involvement, he felt empowered, his child felt empowered, and Teacher A felt empowered.

Schools

What does it really take for a student to be successful in school? The choice of curriculum, instruction, and discipline styles can be the difference between success and failure. Many children are forced to endure teaching styles that do not maximize their educational potential (Goor & Porter, 1999). Consequently, some scholars and educators (Obiakor, 1999; Rotatori & Obi, 1999) have argued that some multicultural learners are often misunderstood, misidentified, misassessed, miscategorized, and as a result are misinstructed. It is no surprise that culturally diverse students are overrepresented in special education programs and underrepresented in programs for students with gifts and talents. These disproportionate numbers are attributed to Eurocentric interpretations and sometimes illusory conclusions (Chang, Lai, & Shimizu, 1999; Delgado & Rogers-Adkinson, 1999).

Many colleges and universities have failed to satisfactorily prepare educators for today's classroom (Haberman, 1995; Seidman, Allen, Aber, Mitchell & Feinman, 1994; Yeo, 1997). For instance, Haberman asserted that upon completion of traditional teaching programs teachers are as prepared for urban classrooms as a swimmer who prepared for the English Channel by training in the university swimming pool. Shortly after the Supreme Court decision in the *Brown v. Board of Education of Topeka* in 1954, teachers began to express interest in being prepared to teach all children (Ladson-Billings, 1999). Almost half a century later, these cries are still tacitly heard among our educators. Not long ago, Guillaume, Zuniga-Hill, and Yee (1995) emphasized that teachers of diverse students should:

1. Develop a knowledge base about diverse ethnic groups and have multiple opportunities to examine personal attitudes toward students of color.
2. Develop culturally and linguistically supportive strategies and approaches that make learning available and equitable for all students.
3. Have ample exposure to students of diverse backgrounds and to teachers who can model appropriate instructional approaches.
4. Commit to professional growth regarding issues of diversity. (p.70)

To correct current school problems, efforts must be made to proactively promote progressive multicultural thinking. It is essential that institutions of higher learning design more classes to respect the growing demographic shifts of the U.S. and equip teachers with multicultural pedagogical techniques. Educators must be willing to leave their comfort zones and learn to reach out to families and communities (McAllister & Irvine, 2000; Obiakor, Harris-Obiakor, Obi, & Eskay, 2000). The school must keep its pulse on community and family activities, especially as they become increasingly diverse (Coley, 1998; Delgado & Rogers-Adkinson 1999; McLoyd, Jayarante, Ceballo, & Borquez, 1994; Sparks, 1999; Taylor, 1996; Taylor & Roberts, 1995; Wakschlag, Chase-Lansdale, & Brooks-Gunn, 1996). By utilizing resource persons from the home and community, the school reduces cultural ignorance, fosters a working relationship between the two entities, and provides learning environments that facilitate success for all children. Consider Case 3 below:

Case 3

Teacher A, an African-American woman, was confused on how to teach the history of Native Americans. She watched movies and read books, but felt it did not adequately describe the true essence of Native Americans. At the height of her frustration a friend introduced her to Del, a Native American who coached wrestling at a local community center. Teacher A invited Del to her class. In turn, he felt excited about the class—he captivated the students with his tribal stories, authentic food, and clothing. At the conclusion of the session, Teacher A presented Del with letters and pictures from students. Since then, Del has continued to be a guest speaker in Teacher A's class. It is now an annual event.

Case 3 exemplifies the beauty of the CSM model. This case showed how a teacher decided to get the real facts about Native Americans rather than to perpetuate negative stereotypes. She moved out of her comfort zone to acquire the service of a resource person who could best help her students. More importantly, her students learned the history about Native Americans from a Native American. Teachers can help to advance the culture of all students—they can take advantage of resource persons in the community through school. Progressive educators can connect themselves to students, colleagues, and communities.

Community

The community is a macrocosm of the family. This relationship has been described not only as intertwined, but reciprocal (Watts-Jones, 1997). A neighborhood without a positive foundational support is without expectations, obligations, and moral codes (Wilson, 1996). The connection between the environment and school generally is ignored in most discussions about reform and improvement (Noguera, 1996). In fact, Noguera stated that improvements in schools are not possible unless improvements in the environment are designed. We believe many school reform and restructuring programs have failed because they have not fully utilized the resources within the student's environment. Resources such as clergy and community members should be incorporated into reform plans. In two independent studies, Coley (1998) and Stevenson (1998) collected data that revealed interactions between the school and community are highly correlated with high academic development and lowered social deviant behaviors among adolescents. Neighborhoods and communities have proven to have great impacts on determining the child's academic achievement, depression level, emotional development, social behavior, and self-esteem (Coley; Gauze, Bukowski, Aquan-Aassee, & Sippola, 1996; Royse, 1998; Stevenson; Watts-Jones).

The whole village must be responsible to raise a responsible child. The Milwaukee Catalyst (1998) reiterated this idea in its quest for effective educational reforms based on research. This organization highlighted five essential support systems that must be in place to improve school-community relationships, namely:

Effective school leadership.
Family-community partnerships.
A school environment that supports learning.
Effective staff development and collaboration.
A quality instructional program. (p.1)

As the Milwaukee Catalyst concluded "Making practices like these a reality requires major changes—not only in the classroom but also in the way the entire school is run and in its ties with students, families, and the community. Making these changes allows schools to focus their resources and attention on improving teaching, learning, and student achievement for all children" (p. 2). Earlier, Peterson (1992) noted that "community in itself is more important to learning than any method or technique. When community exists, learning is strengthened—everyone is smarter, more ambitious, and productive. Well-formed ideas and intentions amount to little without a community to bring them to life" (p. 2). Educators can ill-afford to divorce themselves from the community, and vice versa. Obstacles that face communities will continually manifest themselves in schools, and the way educators address these challenges will have life lasting implications (Obiakor, Karr, Utley & Algozzine, 1998). Consider Case 4 below:

Case 4

> An African American superintendent of a school district was hired to respond to multicultural issues confronting the schools and community. For some reason, he had the habit of not inviting African American specialists on multicultural issues. He consistently invited White women and ignored African American resource persons in the community to appeal to the powers-that-be in that city.

Case 4 accurately depicts *fraudulent multiculturalism* that lends itself to multiple deficiencies and dangerous ramifications. The problem with this scenario is not the invitation extended to White women, but the blatant exclusion of other prominent resource persons in the community to please the powers-that-be (Obiakor, 1994). Case 4 is a prototype of the façades that are frequently employed in school districts to show collaboration between the school and community. The impetus behind the CSM is to remove such fraudulent multicultural paradigm employed in many schools and the society as a whole. Fraudulent multiculturalism creates fraudulent sense of community where problems are swept under the rug. Communities that want to grow will grow, and those that do not will remain retrogressive. Communities that reflect twenty-first century changes will be willing to deal with sociocultural demographic problems.

Government

The landmark Supreme Court case of *Plessey v. Ferguson* in 1896 mandated that races could be separated as long as facilities for each group were commensurate. This era known by many as the Jim Crow era blatantly disregarded the law because institutions were separate, but unequal. The critical question is, How much has the government done to change these injustices over the past century? In 1954, *Plessey v. Ferguson* was ruled unconstitutional with the *Brown v. Board of Education of Topeka* decision that led the initiative to desegregate public schools. Although schools were being desegregated, it was evident that children from multicultural backgrounds were being systematically removed from the general classroom. The legislative branch of the government stepped in to prevent children with linguistic and cultural differences from being disproportionately placed in special education classes based on the use of intelligence test alone. Many exemplary litigations (e.g., the 1967 *Hobson v. Hanson* case, the 1970 *Diana v. State Board of California* case, and the 1972 *Larry P. v. Riles* case have fostered equality in educational programming. These litigations frequently result in legislation.

Through important legislative mandates (e.g., the 1975 Education for All Handicapped Children Act, the 1990 Individuals with Disabilities Education Act, and the 1997 reauthorization of the Individuals with Disabilities Education Act), the government has tried to enhance possibilities for a free and appropriate education for all students. Though these legislative efforts are progressive and helpful, they are not in themselves the cure-all. The spirits of these laws have been sometimes missed, and as a consequence, savage inequalities continue to exist in many of our schools (Kozol, 1991). In addition, many of these government laws have guaranteed school funding on local, state, and federal levels; but ironically, inadequate funding continues to be a problem.

It is essential to note that government initiatives, such as Goals 2000 have allowed school districts to receive resources at local, and state levels to help implement divergent educational programs for all students. In addition, governments have funded and awarded grants to various institutions of higher learning and community organizations that aspire to design innovative programs geared toward bridging economic and social gaps between people. For instance, institutions such as Charter, Voucher, and Choice Schools have been supported at some levels to create opportunities for all students. We believe the government can be a primary and prominent change agent. Additionally, we believe governmental agencies can hold institutions accountable and mandate subsequent allocation or non-allocation to foster the compliance of rules, regulations, and results. Even as unpopular as race-based government remedies (e.g., affirmative action regulations) may be, they have been used by governments to frequently buttress equality of citizens. Consider Case 5 below:

Case 5

Ethnic minority students at the University of California-Berkeley stated publicly their disgust with the Regents of the university for removing affirmative action regulations from this school. The ban on affirmative action was viewed by many as a blatant attack on minority students and employees, and a step back toward the promotion of equality in the United States.

As a result of the ban, very few minorities have been admitted to the university, and the impact is already being felt at the state's institutions.

Case 5 depicts a case where the government could circumvent unconstitutional efforts to remove rights guaranteed by previous legislation. Since education is important to all Americans, the government must respect and enforce the legislation passed to ensure equality for all its citizenry. As it appears, the CSM acknowledges the government as an inevitable force to fight injustices and enhance educational *equality* and *quality* for all learners.

CONCLUSION

In this chapter, we have addressed the meaning and importance of the CSM. We believe it is imperative that students, families, schools, communities, and governments understand their roles in making the world a better place. It is easy to play the *blame game*, but we are in this together! As a matter of urgency, components of the CSM must be infused in all educational levels and programs. The CSM must be free-flowing and mutually inclusive. Families, both traditional and nontraditional, must continue to be central stakeholders in the planning of educational services to meet their individual needs. Educators and other service providers must employ family advocates whose primary work would be to forge educational partnerships with students and the greater community. Local, state, and federal governments should be utilized for continual funding and for holding institutions accountable to ensure that all our children receive quality and appropriate education. In the end, educational services must be provided in an atmosphere of respect for the family and an environment where communication is an ongoing priority.

The CSM has a global implication. If we can work together in our classrooms, families, communities, and governments, we can work together in our world. Shifting paradigms and powers can be a painstaking process, and as educators, we have to be willing to step outside of our comfort zones to take risks. In a school where the CSM is implemented with integrity and fidelity, "culture" will become a noncontroversial phenomenon that increases the goodness and quality of classroom activities (Obiakor, 2000, 2001). In the spirit of the common good, we are convinced that such a comprehensively supported school will:

1. Be located in all neighborhoods (i.e., suburb, urban, rural, and inner city areas).
2. Be dedicated to excellence, believe in "quality with a heart," and have teachers with "soul."

3. Have minority and majority students and teachers to reflect demographic changes.
4. Hire administrators who care for children.
5. Create and maintain learning communities.
6. Empower parents and community members in all their activities.
7. Work collaboratively, consultatively, and cooperatively with parents.
8. Have culturally competent teachers who help produce culturally competent children.
9. Go beyond traditions and be creative.
10. Address issues of students' learning styles and multiple intelligences.
11. Encourage all students to maximize their potential.
12. Try to educate all children and not get rid of them indiscriminately.
13. Respond to student stressors and individual differences.
14. Prepare students to be responsible, nationally and globally aware, and productive citizens through self-knowledge, self-esteem, and self-empowerment.
15. Have truly good teachers who teach reality.

REFERENCES

Boykin, A.W. (2000). Talent development, cultural deep structure, and school reform: Implications for African immersion initiatives. In D.S. Pollard & C.S. Ajirotutu (Eds.), *African-centered schooling in theory and practice*. Westport, CT: Bergin & Garvey.

Coley, R.L. (1998). Children's socialization experiences and functioning in single motherhood households: The importance of father and other men. *Child Development, 69*, 219–230.

Chang, J., Lai, A., & Shimizu, W. (1999). Educating the Asian-Pacific exceptional English-language learners. In F.E Obiakor, J.O Schwenn, & A.F. Rotatori (Eds.), *Advances in special education: Multicultural education for learners with exceptionalities* (pp. 33–52). Stamford, CT: JAI Press.

Comer, J.P. (1997). *Waiting for a miracle*. New York: Penguin Group.

Comer, J.P., & Poussaint, A.F. (1992). *Raising black children*. New York: Penguin Group.

Davis, J.E., & Jordan, W.J. (1995). The effects of school context, structure and experience on African-American males in middle and high schools. *Journal of Negro Education, 63*, 570–587.

Delgado, B.M., & Rogers-Adkinson, D. (1999). Educating the Hispanic-American learner. In F.E. Obiakor, J.O. Schwenn, & A.F. Rotatori (Eds.), *Advances in special education: Multicultural education for learners with exceptionalities* (pp. 53–72). Stamford, CT: JAI Press.

Epstein, J.L. (1992). School and family partnerships. In M. Alkin (Ed.), *Encyclopedia of educational research* (pp.1139–1151). New York: Macmillan.

Finn, J.D., & Rock, D.A. (1997). Academic success among students at risk for school failure. *Journal of Applied Psychology, 82,* 221–234.

Gauze, C., Bukowski, W.M., Aquan-Assee, J., & Sippola, L.K. (1996). Interactions between family environment and friendship and associations with self-perceived well-being during early adolescence. *Child Development, 67,* 2201–2216.

Goor, M.B., & Porter, M. (1999). Preparation of teachers and administrators for working effectively with multicultural students. In F.E Obiakor, J.O. Schwenn, & A.F. Rotatori (Eds.), *Advances in special education: Multicultural education for learners with exceptionalities* (pp.183–204). Stamford, CT: JAI Press.

Gordon, K.A. (1995, August). Self concept and motivational patterns of resilient african-american high school students. *Journal of Black Psychology, 2,* 239–255.

Guillame, A.M., Zuniga-Hill, C., & Yee, I. (1995). Prospective teachers' use of diversity issues in a case study analysis. *Journal of Research and Development in Education, 28,* 69–78.

Haberman, M. (1995). *Star teachers of children in poverty.* West Lafayette, IN: Kappa Delta Pi.

Kozol, J. (1991). *Savage inequalities: Children in American schools.* New York: Crown.

Ladson-Billings, G.J. (1995). Preparing teachers for diverse student populations: a critical race theory perspective. In A. Iran-Nejad & P.D. Pearson (Eds.), *Review of research in education* (pp. 211–247). Washington, DC: American Educational Research Association.

McAllister, G., & Irvine, J.J. (2000). Cross cultural competency and multicultural teacher education. *Review of Educational Research, 70,* 3–24.

McLoyd, V.C., Jayarante, T.E., Ceballlo, R., & Borquez, J. (1994). Unemployment and work interruption among African-American single mothers: Effects on parenting and adolescent socioemotional functioning. *Child Development, 65,* 562–589.

Milwaukee Catalyst (1998). *Facts: A resource guide.* Milwaukee, WI: Author.

Noguera, P.A. (1996). Confronting the urban school reform. *The Urban Review, 28,* 1–19.

Obiakor, F.E. (1994). *The eight-step multicultural approach: Learning and teaching with a smile.* Dubuque, IA: Kendall/Hunt.

Obiakor, F.E. (1998, August 24). Make your own destiny. *The Emporia State University Bulletin, 98,* 17.

Obiakor, F.E. (1999a). Multicultural education: Powerful tool for educating learners with exceptionalities. In F.E. Obiakor, J.O. Schwenn, & A.F. Rotatori. (Eds.), *Advances in special education: Multicultural education for learners with exceptionalities* (pp.1–14). Stamford, CT: JAI Press.

Obiakor, F.E. (1999b, Fall). Teachers expectations of minority exceptional learners: Impact on "accuracy" of self-concepts. *Exceptional Children, 66,* 34–50.

Obiakor, F.E. (2000, October). *Transforming teaching-learning to improve student achievement.* Position paper presented at the Best Practice Conference, Institute for the Transformation of Learning, Marquette University, Milwaukee, WI.

Obiakor, F.E., (2001). *It even happens in "good" schools: Responding to cultural diversity in today's classrooms.* Thousand Oaks, CA: Corwin Press.

Obiakor, F.E., Harris-Obiakor, P., Obi, S.O., & Eskay, M. (2000). Urban learners in general and special education programs: Revisiting assessment and intervention issues. In F.E. Obiakor, S.A. Burkhardt, A.F. Rotatori, & T. Wahlberg (Eds.), *Advances in Special Education: Intervention techniques for individuals with exceptionalities in inclusive settings* (pp.115–131). Stamford, CT: JAI Press

Obiakor, F.E., Karr, S., Utley, C., & Algozzine, B. (1998). The requirements and demands of being an educator. In R.J. Anderson, C.E. Keller, & J.M. Karp (Eds.), *Enhancing diversity: Educators with disabilities* (pp. 142–154). Washington, DC: Gallaudet University Press.

Peterson, R. (1992). *Life in a crowded place: Making a learning community.* Portsmouth, NH: Heinemann.

Rotatori, A.F., & Obi, S.O. (1999). Directions for the future: empowering the culturally diverse exceptional learners. In F.E. Obiakor, J.O. Schwenn, & A.F. Rotatori (Eds.), *Advances in special education: Multicultural education for learners with exceptionalities* (pp. 233–242). Stamford, CT: JAI Press.

Royse, D. (1998). Mentoring high-risk minority youth: evaluation of the brothers project. *Adolescence, 33,* 145–158.

Seidman, E., Allen, L., Aber, J.L., Mitchell, C.C., & Feinman, J. (1994). The impact of school transitions in early adolescence on the self-esteem and perceived social context of poor urban youth. *Child Development, 65,* 507–522.

Shafer, D.R. (1996). *Developmental psychology: Childhood and adolescence* (4th ed.). Pacific Grove, CA: Brooks/Cole.

Slavin, R.E. (1997). *Educational psychology: Theory and practice* (5th ed.) Needham Heights, MA: Allyn and Bacon.

Sparks, S. (1999). Educating the Native-American learner. In F.E. Obiakor, J.O. Schwenn, & A.F. Rotatori. (Eds.), *Advances in special education: Multicultural education for learners with exceptionalities* (pp.73–90). Stamford, CT: JAI Press.

Stevenson, H.C. (1998). Raising safe villages: Cultural-ecological factors that influence the emotional adjustment of adolescents. *Journal of Black Psychology, 24,* 44–59.

Strickland, D.S., & Ascher, C. (1992). Low-income African-American children and public schooling. In P.W. Jackson (Ed.), *Handbook of research on curriculum: A project of the American Educational Research Association* (pp. 609–625). New York: Macmillan.

Taylor, R.D. (1996). Adolescents' perceptions of kinship support and family management practices: Association with adolescent adjustment in African-American families. *Developmental Psychology, 32,* 687–695.

Taylor, R.D., & Roberts, D. (1995). Kinship support and maternal and adolescent well-being in economically disadvantaged African-American families. *Child Development, 66,* 1585–1597.

Wakschlag, L.S., Chase-Lansdale, P.L., & Brooks-Gunn, J. (1996). Not just "ghosts in nursery": Contemporaneous intergenerational relationships and parenting in young african-american families. *Child Development, 67,* 2137–2147.

Watts-Jones, D. (1997). Toward an African-American genogram. *Family Process, 36,* 375–383.

Wilson, W.J. (1996). *When work disappears: The world of the new urban poor.* New York: Vintage Books.

Yeo, F. (1997). Teacher preparation and inner-city schools: sustaining educational failure. *The Urban Review, 29,* 127–143.

Chapter 2

THE POWER OF THE "SELF" IN EDUCATION

FESTUS E. OBIAKOR AND DARRELL WILLIAMS

In recent years, there has been a vociferous outcry for schools to do a better job in educating all learners. While educators acknowledge the critical role they play in shaping the future of America's youth, this task is not theirs alone. The society has come to realize that a child who is only educated at school is an uneducated child. To address the educational needs of the whole child, a comprehensive support model (CSM) must be employed (Obiakor, 1994, 1996a, 2001). In this approach, several key players including the "self" must be involved to build a strong foundation, yet the role of the "self" (i.e., the individual student) is rarely recognized as being a factor in determining future success. Today, how the "self" survives in school, family, and community has become a critical dimension in the educational process. In other words, the "self" can be built or destroyed, and the "self" can be very resilient. In this chapter, we discuss the power of the "self" and how this dynamic power interacts with the family, school, and community.

Defining the "Self"

The role of the "self" in determining educational success has been overlooked. Obiakor (1996b) and Osborne (1996) noted that the "self" is a dynamic structure that develops in a way that continuously reconfirms itself. The concept of "self" is not an entity in itself, it is composed of several constructs such as self-knowledge, self-esteem, self-determination, self-perception, self-ideal, self-empowerment, and self-responsibility. Sometimes these constructs are used synonymously by educators and researchers, and sometimes they mean different things to them. In all, the power of the "self" cannot be downplayed. Osborne defined self-concept as the sum total of attributes, attitudes, and values that a person believes define who he/she is. The "self" may become more or less positive or negative as a person encounters life's successes or failures. Self-knowledge is defined as being formed as a person comes to know his/her own attitudes, emotions, and overall internal state of being from observation of his/her own visible behavior and the circumstances in which that behavior occurs (see Osborne). The "self" can be holistically or multidimensionally viewed. According to Osborne, the "self" centers around a person's beliefs and how those beliefs influence behavioral actions. As a result, the "self" can be very active (see Obiakor).

The "self" can be measured, and its potential can be optimized (Obiakor, 1994, 1996b, 1999, 2001). Within our schools, students are faced with many situations that may attempt to damage their "self." In many cases, students fall into the mode of self-fulling prophecy or learned helplessness because of negative encounters. Viewed from such a perspective, students' perceptions of themselves become their reality (Osborne, 1996). As Osborne pointed out, if students perceive themselves as not being smart or intelligent, they may begin to engage in behaviors that confirm that perception. A student may choose not to complete certain tasks deemed as difficult because he/she feels not smart enough. Such a negative view yields damaging results for a student's self-concept. Hence, the concept of the "self" must be enhanced if students are to be prepared to encounter difficult situations and respond appropriately. There are many aspects underlining the development of the "self." As it appears, the "self" is a dynamic entity. How the "self" influences and is impacted by the family, school, and community are explored in the following sections.

The "Self": An Integral Part of the Family

The family plays a unique role in influencing future decisions of their children. Field and Hoffman (1999) confirmed that many children are growing up in substandard living conditions, single parent homes with limited family resources, and within families operating in the uninvolved parenting style. As well, many parents have shifted the responsibility of rearing their children to their own parents. In spite of such circumstances, children can still maximize their potential. Though children's dreams and goals can be realized, many have no dreams or ideas of what they want to become and how they can contribute to the greater society. Consider the experience of the second author of this chapter who grew up in rural Mississippi during the 1970s. He remembers that in those days, elders would often ask children what they wanted to be when they grew up, and they would respond, "I want to be a doctor or a lawyer." Today, when similar questions are asked, many children, especially poverty-impacted children, tend to respond, "I don't know." This is a dangerous phenomenon!

Children must begin to dream again; however, families must work with educational professionals to help children to take the steps necessary to turn their dreams into reality (Obiakor, 1996b). Growing up in poverty or a single parent home is not an excuse for not realizing one's full potential. Children must be taught to be resilient, self-determined, and to have a well defined sense of "self." According to Brown, Caston, and Benard (2001), children who are resilient, self-determined and have a strong sense of self strive to rise above the darkness of life's injustices to the light of life's joys. Through their efforts and character, these children ultimately define themselves and determine their own destiny (Osborne, 1996). Furthermore, they realize the dysfunctional family situation they may have been subjected to does not define them or their character as individuals. There have been several cases where children have risen above unfortunate life circumstances to become successful contributing adults within the society. Consider Cases 6 and 7 below:

Case 6

> Rosie was a young lady born in a small rural town in Mississippi. Most of the residents in this town earned a living by picking cotton or peas. She was born and reared in wood shack. There was no running water or indoor plumbing. As she went to school, she often wore the same tattered but clean clothing three times a week. Her mother was the proud single parent of six children. At 36 years of age, her mother had difficulty meeting the basic needs of her children even while receiving government assistance. Rosie would often reflect on how hard a time her mother had rearing her and her siblings. She decided that she did not want to live her life in the same manner as her mother. She started to focus her attention on her goal on becoming a lawyer. After years of study, she accomplished her goal. She is currently practicing law with a major law firm in Memphis, Tennessee. She is also a frequent speaker in schools across the South as she provides encouragement to students and assures them that they can reach their goals and turn their dreams into realities, in spite of their circumstances.

Case 6 reveals the power of the "self" to survive. The conditions and circumstances in which Rosie was reared is very similar to how many children are being reared today. However, this case illustrates how she was self-determined to change her destiny from that of her mother. In spite of her living conditions and family situation, she was resilient. She did not allow those circumstances to determine her fate, but used those circumstances as fuel to burn her internal desire to reach her goal and to maximize her potential. In this case, Rosie exhibited confidence in her abilities and took steps toward achieving her goal. She did not allow her circumstances to cloud her view of what she wanted and knew she could become. She did not view poverty as a never ending cycle, but as a state of mind. Although, in the materialistic sense, Rosie was poor, but her mind was rich with knowledge of "self" and her heart was filled with desire and self-determination to succeed. This is the type of resiliency that parents must foster within their children, and that children must exhibit to break the psychological chains on their minds. Families must begin to help children to develop their own "self" and maximize their full potential.

Case 7

> Trina was born in a housing project located in Chicago. She always wanted to become a doctor. She lived in a small one-bedroom apartment along with her three younger siblings. Her mother who was addicted to drugs worked at a local McDonalds. The money she earned usually went to support her habit, thereby leaving very little money to buy food and other basic necessities for her children. To help support the family, she was forced to get a job. Although she had to get a job, she stayed focused on her goal. Therefore, Trina got a job at the local hospital, as a nurse's assistant during the day while she went to school at night. The money she earned was stretched to support her family. She graduated with honors, was admitted into college, and was later accepted into medical school in Nashville, Tennessee. Today, she is a medical doctor.

In Case 7, in spite of her mother's drug habit, Trina did not lose focus of her goal. She did not develop the "victim mentality." Rather, she showed great self-determination toward achieving her goal and did not let her mother's drug habit or her family situation to limit what she wanted to become. She believed in herself and her abilities. She had the self-confidence to pursue her goal against the odds. She exhibited great resilience, self-sacrifice, and self-determination to overcome adversity and achieve her goals.

There is no doubt that the family plays a critical role in developing the "self." The family is a place in which children learn to interpret the realities of life (Brown, 2000). Hence, parents serve as their children's interpreters in making sense of the information they receive and their given abilities. According to Kerka (2000), family functioning and parent-child relationships have great influence in career development than family structure or parent's educational and occupational status. In addition to family functioning, another major influence is parenting style. The manner in which parents' rear their children heavily persuade future decisions their children will make. Kerka described parenting styles as broad patterns of childrearing practices, values, and behaviors. For families to increase the likelihood of children maximizing their full potential while positively contributing to society as a whole, greater parent-child relationships must be formed. In addition to the need for stronger parent-child relationships, families must become more functional. In their study, Way and Rossman (1996) found that students identified proactive family interactions as engines behind their successful career choices. As Kerka noted, proactive families (a) are well organized, cohesive, and expressive; (b) are extroverted and manage conflict positively; (c) seek out ways to grow; (d) are sociable; (e) make decisions through the democratic process; (f) encourage individual development; and (g) are emotionally engaged. These descriptors are invaluable in helping to develop the "self" in children and in helping families to become stronger and more functional. Hence, the role of the family in helping children develop themselves is very important.

Like the CSM (Obiakor, 1994), the self-determination model (SDM) (Field & Hoffman, 1999) provides direction for parents to assist children in becoming more self-determined. The SDM model, like the CSM, recognizes the role that parents, schools, and communities play in fostering self-success in children. The SDM has five components critical to fostering self-determination in children, namely: (1) know yourself, (2) value yourself, (3) plan, (4) act, and (5) experience and learn. These five components emphasize the need for a person to know himself/herself and to recognize his/her strengths and weaknesses. Thus, a person must build upon his or her strengths and weaknesses in a self-determined manner. In consonance with self-determination is self-reflection (Ellis, 1999). Self-reflection requires an individual to take a deep look inside himself or herself. Through self-reflection of actions taken to become more self-determined, a person can assess his/her own growth. Children's self-responsibility behaviors may be enhanced through increased intimacy with parents (Taylor & Field, 1997). Parents must utilize the many opportunities they have to interact with their children to instill in them a sense of responsibility and self-worth, help them build their self-esteem, and motivate them to become self-sufficient. These are critical skills which parents must develop in their children along with the knowledge and skills necessary to become independent self-determined individuals. The "self" will always be a part of the family, and the family can always help to build the "self."

Building the "Self" is Building the Community

Like the family, the community plays a key role in developing the "self." However, the role of the community is as important as the role of the "self." While the community may house a wealth of resources, it is up to individuals to access those resources for academic and social development. The "self" initiative of the individual is the key to success. In addition to accessing community resources, individuals must take advantage of the many learning opportunities that are available within the community (i.e., library, museum, schools, jobs, and entrepreneurial offers). It is counterproductive for individuals to sit and wait for opportunities to knock at their doors. Goals must be set, and actions to foster self-completion must be taken (Osborne, 1996).

Many communities are frequently viewed negatively by those who reside in them and outsiders who are ignorant of what happens in them. For instance, in neighborhoods where crime, drug, prostitution, unemployment are commonplace, the community may not be viewed as a place of hope for many of its residents. However, the desperate conditions that may be present within a particular community should not be used as an excuse for an individual not to maximize his/her potential. Hence, it is the responsibilities of each "self" to seek out needed resources and take the necessary steps to grow. Consider Cases 8 and 9 below:

Case 8

> Barry was a student from a small town in Mississippi. In this town, there were no libraries, museums, or factories, only cotton fields. Each day after school, he would pick cotton until dark, then do his homework, eat, and go to bed. However, this was not the life he wanted to live. He wanted to be a teacher. His mother always told him that education was the key to knowledge and that key would open many doors to future success. Hence, Barry worked very hard in school. He never missed a day of school. When the teacher assigned projects that required the use of the library, he would walk up town to use the library and get a ride home when he finished. Eventually, he finished high school, college, and is currently in graduate school pursuing a doctorate degree.

The above case illustrates Barry's self-determination. Although the town where he lived did not have the resources needed to help him complete given tasks; he did not become a "victim." He did not allow his circumstance to impede his ability to complete given assignments. He took initiative and sought after resources that would allow him to complete his assignment. He knew that completing this simple task would take him one step further toward reaching his goal of becoming a teacher.

Case 9

> Willie and Robert were from a small rural town located on the Tennessee-Kentucky border. In this town, there was one store and one factory where

most of the residents worked. They both were pretty good students with very good grades. Willie and Robert were very aware of what they wanted to do when they finished college. They both wanted to be doctors. Throughout the school year, Willie and Robert would go to the local college to meet professors and students to learn as much as they could about their future profession. They would also go to the library to access information about doctors seeking information on what it takes to become a doctor. Upon finishing high school and college, these two friends were accepted into medical school. Currently, the two friends are working as pediatricians in Atlanta, Georgia.

In Case 9, the importance of goal-oriented behavior is clearly demonstrated. Willie and Robert knew what they wanted to do to pursue professional lives. Besides knowing and saying verbally what they wanted to do in their professional lives, they took steps to make their goal a reality. They exhibited great resilience by breaking the status quo of working in the factory, as most people in their town, to reach their goal. Furthermore, this illustrates how proper utilization of resources in the community can contribute to future career exploration.

One of the most effective ways in which community establishments can assist students in becoming more community-minded while helping them develop a sense of self-confidence and pride is by providing students with service learning opportunities (Brown, 1998). Service learning is a work-based learning experience through which students learn, develop, and apply academic and vocational skills to address the real life needs of their local communities (see Brown). During the 1990s, many school districts implemented school-to-work programs in an effort to link what was being taught in the classroom to real world situations. However, service learning differs from school-to-work. While school-to-work programs are more focused on school-based learning and learning about work-related issues, service learning is work-based and actively engages students in the process. However, school-to-work and service learning are both initiatives designed to connect students to their communities and give them opportunities to apply learned skills in real-life settings while helping them develop attitudes, values and behaviors that will lead them to become contributing members of society (see Brown).

It is apparent that the community can be a great resource to assist individuals to develop themselves. However, it is also apparent that the community can act as an unwilling agent to destroy the "self." Hindrance of access to resources within the community through racist practices seeks to destroy individual self-concept and self-development. For instance, police racial profiling, the disproportionate incarceration of African American males, and the disproportionate representation of minorities in special education programs can destroy self-confidence and self-esteem. In addition, the massive amount of negative advertisement in various media surrounding the less fortunate paints false perceptions in the minds of many Americans. Such negative perceptions turn into attitudes, acts, or practices that seek to destroy the "self." These acts and practices may manifest themselves in school in the form of low teacher expectations, labeling, and miscategorization (Obiakor, 1996b, 1999, 2001; Osborne, 1996). The communities' negative perceptions concerning the race and class of people are a reality. Many cultures, particularly African Americans have received much criticism about their state of being in society. However, the negative perceptions of others must not become the perceptions individuals have of themselves. To overcome these barriers, individuals must develop a strong sense of "self" and resiliency to injustices they confront. Additionally, they must develop the necessary knowledge, skills, and higher expectation to "fight the battle and win the war" in a community that cares.

Fortifying Bridges: The "Self" and Education

Each morning, millions of students across the nation enter school walls. These students come from different cultural, racial, and socioeconomic backgrounds. Along with differences in backgrounds are variances in self-interpretations, self-perceptions, and self-views embedded within particular cultures. For example, the concept of "self" is viewed differently among ethnic groups. To Westerners, the concept of "self" means being independent, while to Asians and Africans, the "self" is viewed as being interdependent and connected within a social context (Katz, 1993). The recognition of students' differences by educators is critical in providing them the necessary skills to maximize their potential (Obiakor, 1994, 1996b, 1999, 2001).

While students' motivation may be cultivated at home and community, one of the most effective avenues for engendering student motivation is a school's environment (Renchler, 1992). The school can increase student motivation, by implementing policies that promote (a) goal setting and self-regulation, (b) offering of student choices, (c) recognition of student achievements, (d) teamwork and cooperative learning, and (e) utilization of self-assessment models rather than social comparisons (see Renchler). Researchers (e.g., Eccles, Midgeley, Adler, & Renchler, 1984, 1992) asserted that proper implementation of such policies would increase students' personal motivation and promote students to have greater autonomy and control over their lives and learning as they pursue higher academic goals. As well, teachers can enhance students' intrinsic motivation by allowing them to feel in control of their own learning (Dev, 1997). However, all schools do not implement or have policies such as these that promote the "self." Therefore, it is imperative for students to look within themselves for the fortitude to succeed in school despite their flaws.

In schools that are especially located within large urban school districts, there are several factors that impact upon students' ability to reach their potential. Teachers often form perceptions and judgments about students based upon their race, data found in personal records, and the environments where they live. For example, a student from an affluent area of town may be perceived as being smart and well-behaved, while a student who may come from the poorest area of town may be viewed as not being smart with behavior problems (Obiakor, 1999, 2001). In his works, Obiakor noted that these problems have contributed greatly to unwarranted generalizations, miscategorizations, and stereotypical tendencies prevalent in schools and communities. Such perceptions undergird the ability and self-concept of students. Tauber (1998) noted that teachers form expectations and assign labels on students based on their body build, gender, race, ethnicity, name, attractiveness, dialect, and socioeconomic level. If the teacher perceives the student as being smart, he/she will expect more work from the child. On the other hand, if the teacher perceives the student as not being smart, he/she will expect less from the child. Students who are perceived to be low in ability are rarely given opportunities to learn new materials—they are called upon in class less, get little praises, and provided less informative feedback (Lumsden, 1997). Embedded in such perceptions is the notion that poor students cannot do well in school because they lack the ability. Such beliefs are fostered within students and contribute to the inaccurate self-concept they form of themselves (Obiakor, 1999). While the expectations of teachers are critical, researchers (e.g., Brophy, 1986; Lumsden) found that teacher expectations are usually self-fulling. Thus, teachers are encouraged to assess their own attitudes, beliefs, and expectations.

In today's schools, poor performance is often attributed to lack of ability and viewed as being irreversible no matter how much effort a person puts forth. Therefore, many students begin to develop what Brophy (1998) called the "failure syndrome." He contended that students who exhibit failure syndrome tend to approach tasks with low expectations for success and give up when there are early signs of difficulty. However, such behaviors can be reversed and success can be achieved. In many cases, students believe the amount of control they have over their own learning is determined by the teacher (Dev, 1997). The reality is students are in full control of their own learning! Although many teachers form negative perceptions of students, the perceptions that students have of themselves also affect their learning. To achieve in school, students must be self-motivated—they must seize the opportunity to learn as much possible, utilize the knowledge gained as building blocks for their own personal and academic development, and develop a strong sense of "self" (Obiakor, 1996b). Through gaining knowledge of "self," students become aware of their abilities as well as areas that need improvement (Osborne, 1996). Upon acquiring such knowledge, students must take steps toward improving in areas of need. However, self-knowledge is not enough; self-love and self-empowerment are also critical in this process (see Obiakor). To have high self-esteem, students must like themselves for who they are. Within the subset of self-esteem, the individual evaluates self characteristics relative to how he or she values those characteristics. Another major contributor to students' ability to achieve in school is their self-ideal. Usually, self-ideal indicates self-qualities which the student desires to achieve or maintain through personal effort (see Obiakor). Self-ideal is a critical element in a person's own personal development. A person with strong self-ideal sets his/her goal and is willing to put forth the necessary energy toward achieving that goal. However, many times, students appear to have a sense of high self-ideal, but when situations get difficult, their self-ideal is lowered. Consider Cases 10 and 11 below:

Case 10

> Janice, a senior in high school, was determined to pass her proficiency test. She had studied prior to the test and felt prepared to take it. After taking the test, she discovered that she did not score as well as she initially anticipated. She became so upset that she considered not taking the test again. This affected her college education and career in life. Today, she admits working in an environment that does not help her to maximize her fullest potential in life.

In this case, Janice began with a high sense of self-ideal. She exerted energy toward studying for her test. However, when she did score well, her sense of self-ideal decreased. Janice, being so upset about the matter, considered not taking the test again. She viewed not taking the test as the initial method to resolve this issue. With increased self-ideal, Janice would have considered studying even harder to make a higher score on the test. Many times, students develop the frame of thinking that they cannot achieve because of the pathology of failure or self-fulling prophecy (see Osborne). Hence, students begin to rationalize that they lack the inability to perform well academically.

Case 11

> Andre wanted to be become a professional football player as well as a pediatrician upon finishing high school and college. He was the star football player at his high school. However, within the classroom, Andre did

not perform so well. He rarely passed his tests and seldom turned in homework. After school, Andre spent three hours of football practice. When he got home he would spend an hour or two reviewing football tapes or old game tapes he had played in. Unfortunately, Andre missed playing football the latter part of his senior year due to the school "no pass, no play" policy.

The above scenario is played out in many high schools across the country. At any rate, in this case, Andre spent a considerable amount of time and energy on football-related tasks. Thus, the amount of time he spent on academic work suffered. Andre's grades did not suffer because he lacked the ability to perform well. Rather, his grades suffered because he did put forth the effort and energy into completing his assignments and studying for his tests. Students must realize that their lack of achievement may be attributed more to lack of personal effort rather than to lack of ability.

There are many other factors that contribute to students entrapment in the "failure syndrome." Societal factors such drug abuse, teen pregnancy, child abuse, and violence influence students' ability to achieve in school. Such factors influence teachers' actions and expectations for certain students and has led to many groups of students being tracked, stereotyped, and discriminated against, especially in large urban schools (Benard, 1997). Unfortunately, these factors are realities of life. Yet, through education and appropriate action, change can occur. Earlier Lifton (1994) noted that "resilience is the human capacity of all individuals to transform and change, no matter what their risks; it is an innate "self-righting mechanism" (p. 2). Students who are resilient exhibit the social competence to form relationships, the metacognition to problem-solve, the autonomy to develop a sense of identity, and a sense of purpose to plan and hope for the future (see Benard; Brown et al., 2001). However, the quality of such resilience lies on how students respond to life's challenges and ultimately, what they do about their situations (see Brown et al.,). These concepts are essential in helping students to manipulate and overcome the social and academic barriers they may encounter in life. Students must be well prepared to face such barriers as they arise in order to make choices that will facilitate the maximization of their educational potential. In the words of Obiakor (1998), "show me a successful person and I will show a person who has taken charge of his/her life! Show me a person who is a failure in life and I will show you someone who blames other people for his/her pitfalls" (p. 7). He added, "we must take charge of our lives to succeed in life. We must make frantic effort–that is the difference between winners and losers. Winners try to take charge of their lives and losers try to change others for their lives" (p. 7).

CONCLUSION

In this chapter, we have focused on several aspects of the "self" and education. The school, the family, and the community are critical components that influence the development of the "self." Fostering development of the whole child requires school, family, and community collaboration; and creating a healthy and democratic educational community is crucial to the development of the "self." In fact, the "self" is the foundation upon which the student's development is facilitated. Although the school, family, and community play important roles, ultimately, the "self" plays a more critical role in fostering personal and academic development. We cannot afford to have a country of "victims." The first step is for us to believe in ourselves as we develop the ability to achieve in the face of adversity.

Poverty, poor living conditions, drug-infested neighborhoods, single parent homes, racism, negative expectations, and illusory conclusions are endemic societal problems that deserve our attention. While it has been acknowledged that many of us do not have "boots" and "straps," it has also been acknowledged that most successful people are those who pulled themselves up by *their own bootstraps*. Our experiences have confirmed that a strong sense of "self" is a powerful tool that could directly influence our ability to succeed not just in school, but also in life. Since the "self" is dynamic, we must develop success-oriented behaviors. As Conrad N. Hilton (1987), the founder of Hilton Inn, wrote in his classical book, *Be My Guest,* our successes depend on our ability to:

1. Find our own particular talent.
2. Be "Big"–Think "Big," Act "Big," and Dream "Big."
3. Be honest with others and ourselves.
4. Live with enthusiasm.
5. Not let our possessions possess us.
6. Not worry about our problems.
7. Not cling to the past.
8. Look up to people when we can and look down to no one.
9. Assume our full share of responsibility for the world in which we live.

REFERENCES

Benard, B. (1997). Turning it around for all youth: From risk to resilience. *Urban Education, 126,* 1–4.

Brophy, J. (1996). Enhancing students' socialization: Key elements. *Elementary and Childhood Education,* pp. 1–3.

Brophy, J. (1998). Failure syndrome students. *Elementary and Childhood Education*, pp. 1–3.

Brown, B. L. (1998). Service learning: More than community service. *Career Education, 198,* 1–4.

Brown, J. H., Caston, M. D., & Benard, B. (2001). *Resilience education.* Thousand Oaks, CA: Corwin Press.

Dev, P. C. (1997). Intrinsic motivation and academic achievement. *Remedial and Special Education, 18,* 12–20.

Ellis, M. (1999). Self assessment: Discovering yourself and making the best choices for you! *Black Collegian, 30,* 1–4.

Field, S., & Hoffman, A. (1999). The importance of family involvement for promoting self-determination in adolescence with autism and other developmental disabilities. *Focus on Autism and Other Developmental Disabilities, 14,* 36–42.

Harvey, A. R., & Coleman, A. A. (1997). An Afro-centric program for African American males in the juvenile justice system. *Child Welfare, 76,* 197–212.

Hilton, C. (1987). *Be my guest.* New York: Prentice Hall.

Katz, L. G. (1993). Self-esteem and narcissism: Implications for practice. *Elementary and Childhood Education,* pp. 1–4.

Kerka, S. (2000). Parenting and career development. *Career Education, 214,* 1–5.

Lewis, A. (1992). Urban youth in community service: Becoming part of the solution. *Urban Education, 81,* 1–3.

Lifton, R. (1994). *The protean self: Human resilience in an age of fragmentation.* New York: Basic Books.

Lumsden, L. (1997). Expectations for students. *Eric Clearinghouse on Educational Management, 116,* 1–4.

Maqsud, M., & Coleman, M. F. (1993). The role of parental interaction in achievement motivation. *Journal of Social Psychology, 133,* 859–862.

Obiakor, F. E. (1994). *The eight-step multicultural approach: Learning and teaching with a smile.* Dubuque, IA: Kendall/Hunt.

Obiakor, F. E. (1996a). Collaboration, consultation, and cooperation: The "whole village" at work. In N. Gregg, R.S. Curtis, & S.F. Schmidt (Eds), *African American adolescents and adults with learning disabilities: An overview of assessment issues* (pp. 77–91). Athens, GA: The University of Georgia/Roosevelt Warm Springs for Rehabilitation Learning Disabilities Research and Training Center.

Obiakor, F. E. (1996b). Self-concept: Assessment and intervention for African-American learners with problems. In N. Gregg, R.S. Curtis, & S.F. Schmidt (Eds), *African American adolescents and adults with learning disabilities: An overview of assessment issues* (pp. 15–29). Athens, GA: The University of Georgia/Roosevelt Warm Springs for Rehabilitation Learning Disabilities Research and Training Center.

Obiakor, F. E. (1998, August 24). Make your own destiny. *Emporia State University Bulletin, 98,* 17.

Obiakor, F. E. (1999). Teacher expectations of minority exceptional learners: impact on "accuracy" of self-concepts. *Exceptional Children, 66,* 39–53.

Obiakor, F. E. (2001). *It even happens in "good" schools: Responding to diversity in today's classrooms.* Thousand Oaks, CA: Corwin Press.

Osborne, R. E. (1996). *Self: An eclectic approach.* Boston, MA: Allyn and Bacon.

Renchler, R. (1992). School leadership and student motivation. *Educational Management, 71,* 1–5.

Shumer, R. (1999). Service, social studies, and citizenship: Connections for the new century. *Social Studies/Social Science Education,* pp. 1–5.

Tauber, R. T. (1998). Good or bad, what teachers expect from students they generally get! *Teacher Education,* pp.1–4.

Taylor, S., & Field, T. (1997). Adolescents' perceptions of family responsibility-taking. *Adolescence, 32,* 969–977.

Way, W., & Rossman, M. (1996). *Learning to work: How parents nurture the transition from school to work.* Berkeley, CA: National Center for Research in Vocational Education.

Chapter 3

FAMILY AND SCHOOLING

LORETTA P. PRATER

What is parental or family participation and interaction? Coots (1998) described parental participation as encompassing activities that are mostly undertaken at school or in the home, which have a direct connection to improved school functioning or improved basic cognitive, socioemotional, and motor functioning. Parental participation or involvement in education is not new. For years schools have explored strategies at the local, state, and national levels to include such an involvement (Epstein, 1991). After all, parents and other family members are children's first educators, responsible for children's early socialization, and for setting a mental and emotional foundation upon which the school and community will build (Kelley-Laine, 1998).

There was a time when families were solely responsible for the education of children. The absolute place for education was in the home, when educators were then family members. When formal systems of education were established, schools were viewed as an extension of the home. As society changed throughout the years, education became more and more removed from the home. More responsibility for educating children was transferred to the school (Banks, 1989). Currently, except for an increasing number of parents who elect to home school their children, the school has assumed a significant role for the responsibility of educating youth. With increasing role expectations of school professionals, some educators may complain that they are literally taking the place of parents. This is impossible! Granted, there may be responsibilities assumed that were not discussed in the teaching methods classes, but teachers enter the life of the child at a later stage, in comparison to family members. The role of family members is an in-depth collection of dynamic entities and multivariables. In order to develop intellectually, emotionally, socially, and morally, a child requires participation in complex activities over a period of time with one or more persons with whom the child develops a strong emotional attachment (Horn, 1993). Students gain knowledge, values, and beliefs from parents, who directly or indirectly, help shape their orientation toward learning (see Banks).

Schools and families have a natural predisposition to form partnerships. In keeping with the teachings of Goodlad (1984), these components help form what he described as the necessary coalition of contributing groups. The school is only one component. According to Murphy (1993), the school occupies only 9% of children's lives. Parents and other community institutions are the custodians of children during 91% of their lives. A lot of learning can take place during the out of school time. Other scholars (e.g., Comer, 1992; Obiakor, 1994) have noted the importance of parents in the educational process. For instance, Comer viewed children within the context of the family and included parents as an integral part of the plan in educating children. In his school plans, he developed methods to include parents in a variety of activities to help design the school climate. Obiakor illustrated the importance of the family in the development of his Comprehensive Support Model (CSM) for the educational success of students from prekindergarten to the university. He proposed the process for educational success to be in stages that connect the family and self with schools and preparations. In effect, consultation with parents and guardians is a component of Obiakor's inclusive classroom educational model.

REFOCUSING THE CONCEPT OF FAMILY

Families are structured very differently today than in the past, which is one reason that general and special educators must refocus the comprehensive model. The comprehensive model was originally designed for the ideal *Leave it to Beaver* family. The family structure that best suits the organization and expectation of schools is the traditional nuclear family, with a stay-at-home wife and mother, and a breadwinner father (Smith & Griffith, 1990). This model does not fit many families today! The list of ways that families of school children differ is unlimited. To name a few, families of school children differ in socioeconomic status, number and educational level of parents in the household as primary caregivers, and in the primary language spoken in the household. All of these factors influence the likelihood of family involvement with the child's schooling. Schools increasingly are being asked to serve a diverse student population and give attention to improving the academic and social outcomes of racial-ethnic minority and low-income students (Desimone, 1999).

Who then, are family members? Family members, with whom the school interacts, may be the biological parents. Increasingly, however, schools are interacting with family members other than two biological parents of the child. This may be especially true of minority families, who often exist within an extended family household (Taylor, Chatters, Tucker, & Lewis, 1990; Vega, 1990). Additionally, one of the most dramatic changes in American family life during the past 20 years has been the growth in the number of single parents with children, representing approximately 29% of all families with children under the age of 18. These children will spend an average of 6 years within a single parent family structure (Lino, 1995). This represents a significant portion of their K-12 schooling years. In a primary single parenting situation, one parent assumes major physical and psychological care of the child. In most instances involving single parents, school and family interaction translates into school and mother interaction. This is a significant variable related to school and family interaction, because the absence of a father in the home contributes to lower levels of school involvement on the part of both mothers and fathers (Bogenschneider, 1997). Although the anticipated school parental contact is usually the mother, this practice is shifting with new family configurations, where fathers, grandparents, foster, or adoptive parents also fulfill the primary nurturing role (Hanson, Heims, Julian & Sussman, 1995; Pinson-Millburg, Schlossberg, & Pyle, 1996). More recent research by Waggoner and Griffith (1998) reported that caregivers who work in schools as volunteers are still primarily women: mothers, aunts, grandmothers, and older sisters. There are some fathers and grandfathers who are involved with children and their schooling, but their numbers are small and their contribution is usually evidenced by participating in fund-raising or school repairs.

In many families, especially African American families, students are more likely to be in mother-only families (Desimone, 1999). Single parenting on the part of unmarried mothers is much higher within the Black than White community, as evidenced by two-thirds of White children living with both biological parents, and only one-quarter of Black children who do so (Bianchi, 1995). Some of the single mothers were never married, which usually places these mothers, and subsequently their children, in a different economic category from the widowed or divorced. Some of these mothers were parents as teenagers, which accounts for a significant proportion of the growth of female-headed households over the past two decades (Prater, 1995). Children living with never-married mothers are the most economically disadvantaged group of children in single parent families (see Bianchi). Other disadvantages related to family structure and schooling include school outcomes and behavior management. For example, approximately 12 percent of children with both biological parents had repeated a grade in school compared with 16 percent of children from disrupted marriages and 20 percent of children with a never-married mother. Furthermore, children in single parent families and stepparent situations were more likely to have been suspended or expelled from school or to have required a nonroutine parent-teacher conference (see Bianchi).

The work of maternal involvement required of mothers by schools is difficult under conditions of sole supporting mothering, accompanied with full-time employment that often has inflexible hours. The traditional aim of parental involvement initiatives is for mothers to be active partners, supporters, and participants in school. The standard typology of school involvement does not acknowledge the gender, class, and race of parents, family structure, nor the possible involvement of other adults (Standing, 1999). In other words, the outdated model for family participation in schools has not changed, whereas the family structures and lifestyles have changed. This factor alone should stimulate an urgency to refocus!

INCLUSIVENESS IN EDUCATIONAL PROGRAMMING

Current visibility of people from different social classes and ethnic groups forces schools to interact with families from diverse cultures as they redesign their programs. This fact must be recognized and respected when working with students and planning their educational experience to provide parity of opportunities. It is from this long-held position that emerged the term, multicultural education, a reform movement with the goal of changing schools so that students from all social class, gender, racial, and cultural groups have an equal opportunity to learn (Banks, 1989; Neill, 1997). According to Neill, "Students come from many cultures and languages. Instruction and assessment should connect to the local and the culturally particular and not presume uniformity of experience, culture, language, and ways of knowing" (p. 36).

School governing bodies tend to be overwhelmingly male, White and middle class, and with a knowledge of the educational system shaped by their own professional knowledge or personal experience (Deem, 1991). More specifically, in school settings in the United States, most of the educators are females of Euro-cultural backgrounds. Whites represent 89.6% of the teachers in public schools (Obiakor, 1994). African Americans, Hispanics, Asian/Pacific Islanders and American Indians/Alaskan Natives represent 6.9%, 1.9%, 0.9% and 0.6% of the teachers respectively. In institutions of higher education, where K-12 teachers receive training, the situation is not any better. Less than 11% of university faculty is members of minority groups

(Green, 1989). Consequently, teachers who are asked to teach in multicultural settings and interact with families of different cultures may have very little experience, personal or professional, in multicultural environments. The cliché, "You don't know what you haven't been taught," applies very well to this situation!

It is even a challenge for teachers to read information that will be helpful to them in identifying strategies to stimulate parental participation of all cultures. When reviewing the literature, they will find that parental school involvement has been studied primarily in white populations (Bogenschneider, 1997). Moreover, most of the research reported in the literature has revolved around four themes: conformity between families and schools; improving student achievement; traditional forms of parent involvement in education; and school reform programs. In reality, debates in the critical literature should be organized in three themes: parent involvement and inequality; alternative definitions of parent involvement in education; and research on the social construction of mothering and schooling (Waggoner & Griffith, 1998). This void in the literature is a limitation for educators seeking professional development in working with diverse populations, including varying income levels of students and family members. Although teachers may not be wealthy, there is probably socioeconomic dissonance between them and their students whose family income is below the poverty level. Also, Turnbull and Turnbull (1997) noted that there are disadvantages of using Euro-cultural perspectives in working with parents who come from different cultures. In educating with a multicultural approach, the ethnic-racial identity of the teacher or students in a particular school is not the determining factor of whether to go beyond teaching Euro-cultural perspectives. The crucial factor is the commitment to providing multicultural education for all!

Parents of all economic levels should perceive that they have the opportunity for participation in some form of school activity. Why is social class an issue? The economic status of parents is of concern because parents of lower incomes may not have the flexibility of time to attend school functions. Because of low wages, some of these parents work more than one job to survive. Social stratification has resulted in many of these parents having children in the same schools, which may result in a high rate of nonparticipation, in comparison to high family participation rates of schools in middle and high income neighborhoods. These inequities impact students. According to Persell (1989), children of different social classes are likely to attend different types of schools, to receive different types of instruction, to study different curricula, and to leave school at different rates and times. As a result, when children end their schooling, they are more different from each other than they were when they entered. Persell further proposed that these differences may be seen as legitimating the unequal positions people face in their adult lives.

Even if one is to enter the nature versus nurture debate, it is evident that children are born into certain groups. Their family lineage determines race and ethnicity, for example. Children have no control over their social class status, a determination that impacts educational opportunities. For example, children in poverty inherit a complexity of risk factors, including those conditions related to health, safety, and housing (Devaney, Ellwood, & Love, 1997). Educators and family members are partners, with each having a significant, yet different, role. Youth receive the maximum benefit when family members and educators have a positive and reciprocal relationship. Children are seriously disadvantaged when family members and educators develop an antagonistic relationship. In small communities void of private schools and with only one elementary, middle and high school for children of all residents, the socioeconomic lines are not as immediately identifiable. Therefore, all of the students receive the benefits of school resources available. In metropolitan and surrounding suburban areas, that is not the case. The mere location of the school signifies an anticipated income level of students enrolled in that school, often accompanied by a stereotyped array of expectations from students and their family members.

Regardless of the social class status or family structure, there are common characteristics of school success as influenced by the home. Solo (1997) studied case studies of families with children who succeeded in school. The families were from varying income levels and marital structures. He reported several common family conditions that helped promote children's success in school, namely:

1. Parental high expectations of children's schooling.
2. Development of an intense drive as active agents of their own success.
3. Encouragement of children to deal with challenges, especially in school.
4. Close family relationship, which helped to build a positive self-image.
5. Encouragement of reading at home.
6. Parental involvement with the school.
7. Child's involvement in extracurricular activities.
8. Early exposure to cultural activities, such as libraries and museums.
9. Parental authority with clear and established standards of behavior.
10. Requirement of chores or household responsibilities.

Based on Solo's research, one would tend to wonder if there are other factors impacting the status of parental participation, because most parents probably want their children to succeed in school. Other than the implication of time, there are other variables contributing to the level of family interaction with schools. Attitudes and perceptions can serve as powerful forces to discourage or encourage participation.

PROFESSIONAL ATTITUDES: IMPACT ON EDUCATION

School professionals may view lack of parental involvement as a reflection of the level of parental interest. This may be a very inaccurate perception! For example, Epstein (1987) found that single-parent families were less likely to interact with the school and the teacher, but were as interested in their children's education and were as likely to work with their children at home as were other parents. Also, social class plays an important part in the formation of an individual's attitudes toward education. It is apparent that schools collect demographic information on members of the student's household. Therefore, educators are initially aware of some of these differences among their students. Could the self-fulfilling prophecy be a factor in anticipation of the nature and quantity of family and school interaction? Scholars have already proposed that if teachers expect less of students and teach them less, the children will likely learn less (Persell, 1989). Do educators expect less of parents with low incomes in comparison to those with high incomes? Are these attitudes formed even before teachers meet the family members or before they meet the students? These questions are not raised in an effort to establish blame, but merely to challenge educators to seriously reflect to determine if there are some preconceived attitudes influencing their behaviors toward family members. Is it possible for an African American male from a government subsidized housing development to go to Harvard, graduate in 4 years, go on to receive a Master's degree from the University of Southern California, and become a very successful investment broker? If the answer is "yes," as I assume it might be for some people, we have to ask the question "why?" The fact remains that teacher expectation and/or thinking influences how professionals and parents interact (Obiakor, 1999).

Some parents may feel inadequate to contribute to school initiatives. For example, parents with lower levels of education may be less involved in their adolescents' schooling. However, when they are involved, the outcome is a positive association with grades that is just as potent as that of parents with more education (Bogenschneider, 1997). Also, when parents identified as high risk or parents with limited English proficiency are nurtured to become involved in the schooling of elementary or high school students, the outcome is benefits to child's school performance (Simich-Dudgeon, 1993). Parent's choice of involvement is a function of their perceived skills and abilities, their employment and other demands, and invitations and opportunities presented by the school (Hoover-Dempsey & Sandler (1995). Unfortunately, some teachers believe that the quality of mothering is linked to deviancy and problem children. In some strange fashion, some teachers believe they must teach parents how to prepare and help their children. This is an attitude that may serve to limit participation from these mothers. Parents interpret this action as a "big brother is watching you" role by inviting parents to workshops to teach them how to be good parents. Parents may internalize a feeling that school officials are saying they are "bad" parents. In addition, they may ask themselves, "if I attend these sessions will others think I am a bad parent." Parents of children with behavior or academic concerns may be especially sensitive to these workshops. This approach makes parents feel that they are the cause of their children's failure in school (C. Banks, 1989). Attitudes can be helpful or damaging. It does not help when some educators feel that they have the training to know how best to educate another's child, or when they view the family as an unnecessary external force (Elliott & Sheridan, 1992). Input from family members is vital because families understand the culture in which the child lives. According to Bullivant (1989), teachers should learn something about the subjective cultures of children from different ethnic groups in the class. Developing and embracing a pattern of open communication with family members is one way to accomplish this goal. Grant (1991) noted that one of the main challenges facing schools is to change the school staff's attitudes and help educators develop a knowledge base in multicultural education.

THE SCHOOL CLIMATE: POSITIVE EFFECT ON LEARNING

According to Calabrese (1991), the school climate can endorse racial, sexual, and socioeconomic myths. Based on my experience as a K-12 secondary education teacher for 15 years, I believe the school climate, more than socioeconomic status, can determine the interest level or willingness of active participation from parents. In my first K-12 teaching assignment, I taught in an urban junior high school setting. Students primarily resided in two government supported residential housing complexes. One complex and surrounding neighborhood primarily served white families and was within walking distance of the school. The other complex was several miles from the school, but African American children were bused to the school for the purpose of court ordered integration. Although from different neighborhoods and racial/ethnic backgrounds, both groups were from families with low incomes and primarily single-mother-headed households. As a Home Economics teacher, I was very sensitive to the importance of including families as educational partners. After all, at one time, Home Economics teachers were required to make home visits. In that teaching assignment, I created numerous opportunities for parent participation, and I was pleased with the response. Those parents did not have wealth in dollars, but they had a wealth of interest and support for education. In my experience at that school, parents seemed to have an intensity of concern for their children to succeed, because most of them had very little formal education. The school climate was welcoming and encouraging of parental involvement!

In a later teaching assignment, I taught high school Home Economics/Family Life Education in an upper middle class suburban community with mostly two parent households. With a school enrollment of approximately 1200 students, there were less than 1 percent of minority students. Again, I started with high expectations of parental involvement and was pleased with the results. In comparing parental involvement between the two schools, one of the differences noted was that in the suburban school setting, many of the parents were the owners of the businesses that made donations of requested items. In the junior high school setting in the urban community, parents served as the broker to solicit items from business owners. Interestingly, the results were the same! Parental involvement in establishing partnerships with schools resulted in accomplishment of goals and benefits to the students. I wonder what would have been the results had my perceptions been negative or racially motivated! It has been proven that perceptions of racial bias have served to prohibit some African American parents from participating in school activities and facilitated negative attitudes toward educators and school administrators (Ogbu, 1978). Research has revealed how some African American parents, deeply concerned about the historical legacy of discrimination against African Americans in schooling, approach the school with open criticisms (Lareau, Horvat, & McNamara, 1999). This is also true of middle class African Americans. Although they benefit from their class position, they still face an institutional setting that they feel privileges white families (Fordham & Ogbu, 1986).

REFOCUSING PARTICIPATION OPTIONS FOR EDUCATIONAL ENHANCEMENT

There are numerous ways in which parents may become involved. It could range from working in booths at the school carnival to being guest speakers in classroom settings. There are other ways that schools can involve parents in off-site activities. One school in a metropolitan mid-western community allows parents to serve as volunteer school bus monitors. This program has been termed successful in that there are fewer disruptions on the bus during times the parent monitors are present. At it appears, some school districts have highly structured parent involvement programs, including employing persons to coordinate volunteer activities of parents. For instance, in a mid-size city in the southeast in which I previously resided, the district had an urban magnet school that requires a specified number of hours for parents, or other family members, to devote to school activities and various other needs. If parents did not meet the required number of hours, their children could be dismissed from the school and sent to the school for which they are zoned, based on residential boundaries. Students attending this magnet school achieved higher scores on benchmark tests, in comparison to students attending other urban schools in the district. Therefore, families were diligent about contributing their time to school events; they wanted their children to remain at that school. In this school setting, if parents were less than diligent in participation, the parental involvement coordinator monitored their behavior and reminded them of their commitment and the consequences of noncompliance.

It is important to note that there has been a rather narrow view of activities identified as parental involvement. Educators, as well as parents, can broaden their thinking regarding school and family interaction. When Waggoner and Griffith (1998) asked parents and teachers to describe parent involvement in education, most of the teachers' examples were bounded by the walls of the school. The majority of the teachers discussed parent involvement in terms of parents assisting teachers in classrooms, joining the Parent Teacher Association, or working one-on-one with children for remedial purposes. Parents can raise money for schools and can assist with field trips, coaching responsibilities, and as teacher-aides. Parents can also serve on policy-making bodies, such as school boards. On the other hand, not all parents are seeking involvement in schools. Chavkin and Williams (1993) reported that low-income minority parents often have different beliefs about parents' role in school involvement and are less involved in school activities than higher income, nonminority parents. This may be more of a factor of educational level and the related advantages or disadvantages, rather than ethnicity. Stevenson and Baker (1987) found a recurring theme to be that better-educated parents are more involved in activities that supplement their children's education, in contrast to the report of Brody, Stoneman, and Flor (1985) that less-educated parents are less willing or able, as implied earlier, to become involved in their children's education. Some parents feel they lack the skills to be involved in their children's education (Banks, 1989). For example, some parents assume the role of teacher in assisting with homework, but the homework assignments may be too difficult for them to understand. Teachers should consider the difficulty of the assignment and the educational level of parents when suggesting that parents assist with homework (Cooper, Lindsay, & Nye, 2000).

As C. Banks (1989) pointed out, groups of parents who tend to not be involved in school activities include parents with special needs, single-parent families, and families with low incomes. C. Banks suggested that teachers do the following:

1. Provide flexible times for conferences, such as early mornings, evenings, and weekends.
2. Provide baby-sitting service for activities at the school.
3. Work out procedures for acknowledging and communicating with noncustodial parents.
4. Use the parents' correct surname. Students will sometimes have different names from their parents. (p. 310)

Schools can seek to provide opportunities for parents to be active participants, rather than passive ones. Many schools tend to limit parental involvement to the role of consent giver (Harry, 1992). Others tend to establish interaction with parents within a negative context, such as when the child is in trouble (Prater & Tanner, 1995). Although unfortunate, these negative contacts may be the only communication parents receive from the school. This is no way to nourish trust and facilitate active participation. If schools want to build parental trust, they must begin by listening to parents, helping them to feel comfortable, and allowing the expertise of all parents to be recognized (Wells, 1992).

It is not uncommon to see that some parents elect to curtail or severely limit their involvement with schools. These are the growing number of parents who elect home schooling. These parents tend to be better-educated, white and higher income. With the rise of violence in schools, more parents may consider this option as an alternative to institutionalized public or private schooling.

POSITIVE STRATEGIES FOR PARENTAL INVOLVEMENT

Regardless of challenges, schools must seek to involve parents (Henderson, Marburger, & Ooms, 1986). In gaining parental involvement, teachers can be proactive in designing outreach initiatives through the establishment and maintenance of two-way communication. There are benefits in reaching out to parents, because school efforts to involve parents have resulted in improved parental attitudes and expectations toward their children and the school (Epstein, 1984). Educators may need assistance in establishing positive relationships with parents. C. Banks (1989) listed the following 7 strategies for accomplishing this relationship, namely:

1. Welcome parents to visit the classroom.
2. Send written information home about school assignments and goals and encourage parents to send notes to the teacher.

3. Talk to parents by phone.
4. Report problems to parents before it is too late for remedial action.
5. Get to know the students' community.
6. Have in-person conferences with parents.
7. Solicit information from parents on their views on education. (pp. 313–314)

Technology has provided other avenues for communicating with parents. Parents who have computers in the home and are Internet users can interact with schools through this resource. Rather than talking on the phone with parents, teachers and parents can e-mail each other. Educators can post information on web sites for parents. Homework can be coordinated electronically. Even though there is a digital divide and not all homes have computers, in an increasingly large numbers of homes, computers are as common as televisions. Area public libraries and some public schools have computers available for use by community residents. This resource is available for those who do not have computers in the home.

Parents who can navigate the political and educational system are empowered to get the best services for their children (Prater & Ivarie, 1999). Schools that seek to empower parents assume that parents are capable of influencing the outcome of their child's educational process (Espe-Sherwindt, 1991). Unfortunately, these assumptions are not all applied equally. In some instances, the practices of school officials communicate to parents that they have little worth in contributing to their child's education. Replacing negative communication with positive communication is another way to facilitate family participation. Sometimes, school officials have no struggle in getting parents involved, because involvement is also a goal of parents. According to Kelley-Laine (1998), parents' reasons for wanting to be involved in school can be categorized as follows:

1. Student achievement by identifying ways to improve achievement.
2. Parental education through participation in classes at the school.
3. Communication with school officials.
4. Influence of the curriculum.
5. Support for the school through assisting with activities.
6. Support from the school in assisting the family.

In a related fashion, Hoover-Dempsey, Bassler, and Brissie (1992) reported that school volunteering for white and middle-income students, compared with other racial-ethnic and income groups, is more likely to be associated with other unmeasured variables such as parents' sense of efficacy in contributing to their child's education and having parents who support the culture of the school system. Also, parents of middle-income children tend to enjoy lifestyles and careers with more flexibility to allow involvement in schools during regular school hours. Schools should seek to identify the type of involvement that works best for families not fitting the model of the ideal middle class family.

On the whole, to address educational outcomes, it is important to understand that parental involvement can have positive and not so positive outcomes. According to research reported by Cooper, Lindsay, and Nye (2000), over 40% of parents said that their involvement made homework harder, at least some of the time. These researchers further suggested that an active teaching role for parents may be most appropriate for students in early grades who may be experiencing difficulty in school. Some parents may be less helpful if they express frustration with their children's lack of understanding of concepts, which seem so natural to them. Parents can also display annoyance in trying to accept their child's lack of perfection, as witnessed so much on ball fields when observing the coach's behavior toward his/her own child's performance. This leads to the point that there can be advantages of parents not helping with homework, including the fact that some caregivers have to sacrifice time and energy to relearn the curriculum in preparing to assist with homework (Waggoner & Griffith, 1998). Schunk and Zimmerman (1994) reported that one of the major benefits of homework is its ability to help students develop time-management and study skills and to become autonomous, lifelong learners outside of the classroom. Parents who take over the homework responsibility may be robbing students of a valuable opportunity to establish independency and demonstrate self-reliance. In addition, parents' help with homework can also have a negative outcome for student achievement (Muller, 1993).

Much research has reported a positive relationship between academic attainment and good home-school relations (Baker & Stevenson, 1986; Bogenschneider, 1997; Kelley-Laine, 1998). There is even a lower likelihood of dropping out of school for students whose parents are involved with schooling (Rumberger, Ghatak, Poulos, Ritter, & Dornbusch, 1990). Much of this research has focused in investigating relationships between middle class families and schools in middle class neighborhoods. Research has also reported that children from families with low income and from racial minority backgrounds do not have the same educational opportunities as middle-income children (Kozol, 1991). Disparities exist between parents as well. Parents of minority children may not have the same opportunities for involvement as parents of nonminority children. Interestingly, Desimore (1999) found that PTO involvement was a stronger predictor of grades of Black students than for any other racial-ethnic minorities or for low-income students. Furthermore, PTO involvement allowed participation on advocacy and decision-making levels that may be especially important for traditionally disempowered Blacks. Unfortunately, the student's peers may undermine the involvement of African American parents of adolescents. African American adolescents are less likely to have peers who support academic achievement (Steinberg, Dornbusch, & Brown, 1992).

CONCLUSION

As formal education becomes ever more important, its methods more diverse and its purposes more complex, there is a growing recognition that family, school, and community each have a role to play in the process of educating children (Kelley-Laine, 1998). At carefully selected moments, politicians like to recite the phrase "Leave no child behind." I propose that not only are we leaving the children behind, but we are leaving the families of these children behind as well. The school must become more inclusive of families and respect the family's pivotal position of influence. We must refocus and reposition families as active, equal partners in schooling. We are in a new century with projections of more diversity than ever before. Now is the time to move from the position of maintaining the status quo!

In reflecting on the idea of refocusing the comprehensive model, as indicated in Chapter 1, it occurs to me that the model employed for years by schools was established with little or no diversity considered, not even diversity of gender. Now that there is the recognition of more diversity in our society than ever before, with parents from a multiplicity of ethnicities and cultures within common school settings, we must stop applying old techniques to new environments and situations. This strategy simply will not work! It is comparable to trying to put a square peg in a round hole. School professionals must end the "easy way out" of blaming and labeling parents; they must assume the leadership role of soliciting parents to join them in seeking solutions to the challenge of increasing school and parent interaction.

REFERENCES

Baker, D. P., & Stevenson, D. L. (1986). Mothers' strategies for children's school achievement: Managing the transition to high school. *Sociology of Education, 59,* 155–166.

Banks, C. A. (1989). Parents and teachers: Partners in multicultural education. In J. A. Banks & C. A. Banks (Eds.) *Multicultural education: Issues and perspectives* (pp. 305–322). Boston: Allyn & Bacon.

Banks, J. A. (1989). Multicultural education: Characteristics and goals. In J. A. Banks & C. A. Banks (Eds.), *Multicultural education: Issues and perspectives* (pp. 2–26). Boston: Allyn & Bacon.

Bianchi, S. M. (1995). The changing demographic and socioeconomic characteristics of single parent families. *Marriage and Family Review, 20,* 71–97.

Bogenschneider, K. (1997). Parental involvement in adolescent schooling: A proximal process with transcontextual validity. *Journal of Marriage and the Family, 59,* 718–733.

Brody, G. H., Stoneman, Z., & Flor, D. (1995). Linking family processes and academic competence among rural African American youths. *Journal of Marriage and the Family, 57,* 567–579.

Bullivant, B. M. (1989). Culture: Its nature and meaning for educators. In F. A. Banks & C. A. Banks (Eds.) *Multicultural education: Issues and perspectives* (pp. 27–45). Boston: Allyn & Bacon.

Calabrese, R. (1991). Public school policies and minority students. *The Education Digest, 56,* 17–21.

Chavkin, N. F., & Williams, D. L. (1993). Minority parents and the elementary school: Attitudes and practices. In N. F. Chavkin (Ed.), *Families and school in a pluralistic society* (pp. 73–84). Albany, N.Y: State University of New York Press.

Comer, J. P. (1992, September). Parents + school = success. *Parents,* p. 242.

Cooper, H., Lindsay, J. J., & Nye, B. (2000). Homework in the home: How student, family, and parenting-style differences relate to the homework process. *Contemporary Educational Psychology, 25,* 464–487.

Coots, J. J. (1998). Family resources and parent participation in schooling activities for their children with disabilities. *Journal of Special Education, 31,* 498–521.

Deem, R. (1991). Governing by gender? School governing bodies after the Education Reform Act. In P. Abbott & C. Wallace (Eds.), *Gender, power and sexuality.* London, England: Macmillan.

Desimone, L. (1999). Linking parent involvement with student achievement: Do race and income matter? *Journal of Educational Research, 93* (1), 11–31.

Devaney, B. L., Ellwood, M. R. & Love, J. M. (1997). Programs that mitigate the effects of poverty on children. *The Future of Children, 7,* 88–112.

Dawson, D. A. (1991). Family structure and children's health and well-being: Data from the 1988 National Health Interview Survey on child health. *Journal of Marriage and the Family, 53,* 573–584.

Elliott, S. N., & Sheridan, S. M. (1992). Consultation and teaming: Problem-solving among educators, parents and support personnel. *Elementary School Journal, 92,* 315–339.

Epstein, J. (1984). School policy and parent involvement: Research results. *Educational Horizons, 62,* 70–72.

Epstein, J. (1987, July). Parent involvement: State education agencies should lead the way. *Community Education Journal,* pp.4–10.

Epstein, J. (1991). Paths to partnership: What we can learn from federal, state, district, and school initiatives. *Phi Delta Kappan, 72,* 344–349.

Espe-Sherwindt, M. (1991). The IFSP and parents with special needs/mental retardation. *Topics in Early Childhood Special Education, 11,* 107–120.

Fordham, S., & Ogbu, J. U. (1986). Black students' school success: Coping with the burden of "Acting White." *Urban Review, 18,* 176–206.

Goodland, J. I. (1984). *A place called school: Prospects for the future.* New York: McGraw Hill.

Gorman, T. J. (1998). Social class and parental attitudes toward education: resistance and conformity to schooling in the family. *Journal of Contemporary Ethnography, 27,* 10–45.

Grant, C. A. (1991). Desegregation, racial attitudes, and intergroup contact: A discussion of change. *Phi Delta Kappan, 72,* 25–32.

Hanson, S. M., Heims, M. L., Julian, D. J. & Sussman, M. B. (1995). Single parent families: Present and future perspectives. *Marriage and Family Review, 20,* 1–25.

Harry, B. (1992). Restructuring the participation of African-American parents in special education. *Exceptional children, 59,* 123–131.

Henderson, A. T., Marburger, C. L., & Ooms, T. (1986). *Beyond the bake sale: An educator's guide to working with parents.* Washington, D C: National Committee for Citizens in Education.

Hoover-Dempsey, K. V., Bassler, O. C., & Brissie, J. S. (1992). Explorations in parent-school relations. *The Journal of Educational Research, 85,* 287–294.

Hoover-Dempsey, K. V., & Sandler, H. M. (1995). Parental involvement in children's education: Why does it make a difference? *Teachers College Record, 97* (2), 310–331.

Horn, W. F. (1993). Government can't buy you love: The best children's program is to put parents first. *Policy Review, 64,* 72–77.

Kelley-Laine, K. (1998). Parents as partners in schooling: The current state of affairs. *Childhood Education, 74,* 342–345.

Kozol, J. (1991). *Savage inequalities: Children in America's schools.* New York: Crown.

Lareau, A., & Horvat, E. M. (1997). Moments of social inclusion and exclusion race, class, and cultural capital in family-school relationships. *Sociology of Education, 72,* 37–53.

Lino, M. (1995). The economics of single parenthood: Past research and future directions. *Marriage and Family Review, 20,* 99–114.

Muller, C. (1993). Parent involvement and academic achievement: An analysis of family resources available to the child. In B. Schneider & J. S. Coleman (Eds.), *Parents, their children, and schools* (pp. 77–114). Boulder, CO: Westview.

Murphy, J. (1993). What's in? What's out? American education in the nineties. *Phi Delta Kappan, 74* (8), 641–646.

Neil, D. M. (1997). Transforming student assessment. *Kappan, 79,* 34–58.

Obiakor, F. E. (1994). *The eight-step multicultural approach: Learning and teaching with a smile.* Dubuque, IA: Kendall/Hunt.

Obiakor, F. E. (1999). Teacher expectations of minority exceptional learners: Impact on "accuracy" or self-concepts. *Exceptional Children, 66,* 39–53.

Ogbu, J. U. (1978). *Minority education and caste: The American system in cross-cultural perspective.* New York: Academic Press.

Persell, C. H. (1989). Social class and educational equality. In J. A. Banks & C. A. Banks (Eds.), *Multicultural education: Issues and perspectives* (pp. 68–86). Boston: Allyn & Bacon.

Pinson-Millburg, N. M., Schlossberg, N. K., & Pyle, M. (1996). Grandparents raising grandchildren. *Journal of Counseling and Development, 74* (6), 548–555.

Prater, L. P. (1995). Never married biological teen mother headed household. In S. M. Hanson, M. C. Heims, D. Julian, & M. Sussman (Eds.), *Single parent families* (pp. 305–323). New York: Haworth.

Prater, L., & Ivarie, J. (1999). Empowering culturally diverse parents in special education programs. In F. E. Obiakor, J. O Schwenn, & A. F. Rotatori (Eds.), *Advances in Special Education: Multicultural education for learners with exceptionalities* (pp. 149–166). Stamford, CT: JAI Press.

Prater, L., & Tanner, M. (1995). Collaboration with families: An imperative for managing problem behaviors. In F. E. Obiakor & B. Algozzine (Eds.), *Managing problem behaviors: Perspectives for general and special educators* (pp.178–206). Dubuque, IA: Kendall/Hunt.

Rumberger, R. W., Ghatak, R., Poulos, G., Ritter, P. L., & Dornbusch, S. M. (1990). Family influences on dropout behavior in one California high school. *Sociology of Education, 63,* 283–299.

Schnunk, D. H., & Zimmerman, B. J. (1994). *Self-regulation of learning and performance.* Hillsdale, NJ: Erlbaum.

Simich-Dudgeon, C. (1993). Increasing student achievement through teacher knowledge about parent involvement. In N. F. Chavkin (Ed), *Families and schools in a pluralistic society* (pp. 189–203). New York: State University of New York Press.

Smith, D., & Griffith, A. (1990). Coordinating the uncoordinated: Mothering, schooling and the family wage, *Perspectives on Social Problems, 2,* 25–43.

Solo, L. (1997). School success begins at home. *Principal, 77,* 29–30.

Standing, K. (1999). Lone mothers/ involvement in their children's schooling: Towards a new typology of maternal involvement. *Gender and Education, 11,* 57–74.

Steinberg, L., Dornbusch, S. M., & Brown, B. B. (1992). Ethnic differences in adolescent achievement: An ecological perspective. *American Psychologist, 47,* 723–729.

Stevenson, D. L., & Baker, D. P. (1987). The family school relation and the child's school performance. *Child Development, 58,* 1348–1357.

Taylor, R. J., Chatters, L. M., Tucker, M.B., & Lewis, E. (1990). Developments in research on black families: A decade review. *Journal of Marriage and the Family, 52,* 993–1014.

Turnbull, A. P., & Turnbull, H. R. (1997). *Families, professionals, and exceptionality: A special partnership* (3rd ed). Columbus, OH: Merrill.

Vega, W. A. (1990). Hispanic families in the 1980s: A decade of research. *Journal of Marriage and the Family, 52,* 1015–1024.

Waggoner, K., & Griffith, A. (1998). Parent involvement in education: Ideology and experience. *Journal for a Just & Caring Education, 4,* 65–77.

Wells, L. A. (1992). Getting parents involved in the classroom. *Contemporary Education, 64* (1), 46–48.

Chapter 4

SCHOOLS: THE ROLES THEY SHOULD PLAY

PATRICK A. GRANT AND PAULINE B. GRANT

America's concern about public schools is not new. More than two decades after the national report, *A Nation at Risk* and in its proposed solutions, the nation responded to an inadequate schooling system that failed miserably in international educational achievement. Today, the nation has permitted an inordinate amount of television viewing by children, lamented on failed family life, and ignored the powerful and often corrosive influence of the student peer group. As a result, the society has witnessed increasing childhood and adolescent pathologies of violence, depression, alcohol, and other drug abuse, as well as the abject failure of millions of youngsters to gain even basic literacy.

This new century has actually seen the United States at greater risk because schools are not performing their role in enhancing democratic citizenship, social justice, and individual as well as collective economic security in a global and technologically sophisticated world. It is logical to argue that individuals, who cannot read or write well, think critically or act morally on major human questions. As a result, individuals who show little in continuing to learn will be highly disadvantaged in the future and in the greater community (Boykin, 2000; Obiakor, 1994). In this chapter, we explore the role that schools should play in educating all our children. Grounded in our exploration are historical perspectives and the Comprehensive Support Model that help educators think deeply about children in our schools and the responsibility of our society.

THE UNITED STATES PUBLIC SCHOOL PHILOSOPHY: HISTORICAL PERSPECTIVES

Nation-states, such as the United States have shared common ideologies. Groups exist because they share an ideology, identity, purpose, and mode of action. A philosophy consists of a body of ideas, values, and preferences–these make up a cultural consensus that groups hold in common. This commonly shared culture is generally transmitted through a common language, which carries values along with a version of the past that explains the group's history. This sense of the past, which is important in forming cultural images and identity, often merges the historical with the mythic. However, whether mythical or historical, it is meaningful for the members of the group. In other words, ideologies are used to justify, rationalize, and explain national policies and programs (Gutek, 1988; Edel, 1985; & Pratte, 1977). Consequently, to become a participant in the groups concept of life, the young has to be deliberately taught and conditioned in the knowledge, values, and behaviors prized by the group.

Historically in the United States, public schools were viewed as agencies to create a national ideological consensus. They were referred to as common schools, which sought to build a commonly shared sense of national land and cultural identity (Gutek, 1993). From the ratification of the constitution in 1789 until the end of the civil war in 1865, the United States was involved in nation building. In this process of nation building, the emergent common or public school played an important role in enculturating or bringing the young into a new republican culture by imposing the dominant ideology on them (see Gutek). The educational practices of early America were direct expressions of the emerging culture. In the rural, preindustrial world of colonial and early national America, religious indoctrination was a main purpose of elementary schooling. Children learned to read in order to read the Bible; practically anything else that most people needed to know was learned in daily life in the community. Miller (1997) contended that schools played an intriguing role in early American life to ensure the continuity of Protestant moral values.

The common or public school movement began in the 1930s in New England. Educational historians have often used efforts of Horace Mann in Massachusetts as the model for illustrating the rise of common schooling. Horace Mann and Henry Bernard were the leaders of common schools in Connecticut followed by other proponents who developed a consensus ideology that served as the movement's rationale. This ideology rested heavily on the version of the American experience. First the new republic, the United States, has been created through efforts and genius of the revolutionary generation and the founding fathers that drafted the Constitution. Second, the formal representative institutions of government—the division of powers into legislative, executive, and judicial branches represented an ideal fusion of the thinking of the Enlightenment and the puritan Protestant heritage. Third, the dominant culture was English, White, and Protestant and its language and value were to be transmitted to all citizens of the republic, including those of other ethnic and language groups. Fourth, the common school would create a new American nationality, but one modeled on the heritage and values of the dominant group. The model of common schooling extended from New England across the United States and became the basis of the state-sanctioned but locally controlled public school system. By the 1870s, public school extended upward to include high schools at the secondary level (Gutek, 1993).

The period in which the public school system developed coincided with the waves of the massive immigration to the United States from Europe. In the 1840s and 1850s, new immigrants arrived with religion and language different from the descendants of the original colonists who were largely English, Scots, or Scots-Irish. The Irish, though English speaking, were Roman Catholics, the Germans, who spoke their own mother tongue, were Catholic, Lutheran, or Evangelic. The new immigration caused apprehension among members of the dominant group who feared that basic republican institutions might be undermined (Gabert, 1973). The educational strategy that developed was that the new immigrants should be assimilated into the dominant culture and its language. Assimilation meant that they were to take on the dominant group's knowledge and values. Research has shown that the German and the Irish, especially those who were Roman Catholic, however, resisted assimilation. These individuals sought to preserve their own culture and language by creating alternative parochial schools.

The defeat of the secessionist confederate states in the civil war freed thousands of African Americans who had been slaves in the south. Although there were some initial attempts to create what were called "mixed" or integrated schools, a dual system of separate schools segregated by race was established in the south and in the border states. The history of segregated schooling and its eventual ending by the Supreme Court decision in the 1954 *Brown v. Board of Education of Topeka* are a familiar part of American educational history. The ideology that came to govern the education of minorities (e.g., African Americans), became an important part of the history of public schooling. After the Civil War and during the Reconstruction era, from 1864 to 1877, a transfer of the New England common school ideology shaped educational policy for African Americans in the south through the theory and process of industrial education. Developed by General Armstrong of the Hampton Institute and his protégé Booker T. Washington, industrial education meant that African Americans should concentrate on learning the trades, agriculture, and domestic service. The values stressed were a kind of Black Puritanism that emphasized hard work, diligence, and a passive acceptance of the status quo. As with the immigration of the 1840s and 1850s, the dominant culture was imposed on African Americans, but according to a policy of racial segregation designed to create a mentality of servitude as opposed to professionalism and leadership.

Banks and Banks (1989) reported that by the mid-twentieth century, especially in the 1960s, the unidimensional view of the American character was challenged by those who wanted a more culturally pluralistic view of American culture. In effect, the advocates of cultural pluralism or multiculturalism wanted to broaden the educational mainstream so that it reflected the diversity of the population of the United States and the various cultures of the groups that composed it. In the 1950s, a serious challenge was mounted against racial segregation in the United States. The African American mobilization in the civil rights movement that led to the (a) Brown decision ending school segregation in 1954; (b) continued efforts to secure political and economic rights; and (c) work of Dr. Martin Luther King, Jr.,–these have become important series of episodes in American history. The civil rights movement also mounted a challenge against the inherited concept of African American education derived from the industrial education concept of General Armstrong and Booker T. Washington. In terms of attitudes and values, the legacy of industrial education reinforced the imitation of dominant group behavior. Along with the change in attitude came a change in racial designation and terminology.

Gutek (1993) reported that academic scholars fashioned a new and more accurate version of the African American experience. Kindred movements for Black pride and Black power were also developed. On many college and university campuses, black studies programs were established. At elementary and secondary levels, history, literature, and the social studies included the contributions of African Americans to the American culture. An important point that has come to be accepted is that Americans are connected culturally in terms of their heritage to people in other places throughout the world. Multiculturalism has become a bridge to internationalism. While African Americans were organizing to gain their cultural, economic, political, social, and educational rights, Hispanic Americans were also reaffirming their cultural heritage and uniqueness. For Hispanic Americans, those who share the Spanish language and culture, the educational goals was bilingual and bicultural education, which meant instruction that was conducted in both Spanish and English and emphasized both Hispanic and American cultures. Along with the renaissance of African American and Hispanic American consciousness and identity came a renewal of Euro-American ethnicity. Gutek contended that sociologist such as Moynihan and Novak found it an overstatement to say that the European ethnic groups who were contained in the massive immigration of the late nineteenth and early twentieth centuries had melted into a homogenized America. Once again a reasserted cultural pluralism contributed to the entry of multiculturalism into American education.

SCHOOLS AND THE COMPREHENSIVE SUPPORT MODEL

In 1935, W.E.B. Du Bois posed the question, "Does the Negro need separate schools?" The question came about as a result of Du Bois's assessment that the quality of education that African Americans were receiving in the nation's public schools was poor, an assessment that is still true today. Ironically, we are asking a similar question today–What does it really take for *all* students to be successful in school? One suggested method throughout this chapter and this book is the Comprehensive Support Model (CSM). Based on the working definition in Chapter 1, the school is an integral part of CSM because it has teachers and professionals who have the power to shift their paradigms regarding demographic changes. It is imperative that school administrators and everyone responsible for the education of all students work collectively to ensure that they are successful in their entire endeavor at school. Glasser (1969) reported that the role of the school in teaching children self worth, is giving them the knowledge and tools necessary to succeed in the society.

Critics of public education have become extremely good fishermen in the river called "accountability." These fishermen have hooked a number of red herrings: zero tolerance, no child left behind, vouchers, grade-level testing, and all children can learn. While these schemes and slogans are part political and part nonsense, together they are rapidly being established as criteria for evaluating school effectiveness (Thomas & Bainbridge, 2000). The late Ronald R. Edmonds who was acknowledged as the "father of the effective-schools movement suggested that all children can learn the basic curriculum of the school" (pp. 34–35). He further stated that schools need state and community support. As Thomas and Bainbridge noted, all children can learn if the following also happens:

- State legislatures provide adequate financial support for schools as required by a number of current State Supreme Court decisions.
- Every child has adequate health care, as required for appropriate cognitive development.
- A certified teacher with adequate salary staffs every classroom.
- Every child attends a school that meets the life-safety codes established by the states.

- Every child is cared for in a high-quality child-care facility.
- Each child has the opportunity to learn according to his or her developmental needs.

All children can learn the basic curriculum of the school *if given equal opportunity to do so,* and if provided the opportunity to learn in accordance with standards written into the Goals 2000: Educate America Act of 1994 (U. S. Department of Education, 1994). Unfortunately, most states do not provide these fundamental conditions. Hill (1999) contended that today many children with special health care needs, including those who would be considered by many to have "profound" problems and who in the past would have been cared for in hospitals and other institutions are living at home and being integrated at school with their "normal" peers.

Based on the CSM, public education provides a collective experience for building and maintaining a basic commitment to the values of a democratic system of government. A strong public education system is vital to America's well being. While we are committed to the elaboration of the American public education, we support effective schools that provide education excellence so that **all** children will have the opportunity to achieve academically at the highest level. Additionally, they will become responsible citizens, attain economic self-sufficiency, and maintain a sense of self through their own cultural heritage. We also believe parents, school personnel, community members, and government officials must work together to assure that **all** children have an opportunity to receive a quality education.

RESOLVING ISSUES: EDUCATING ALL LEARNERS

To buttress the school's role in educating all learners, many educational issues must be resolved. These issues are addressed in the following subheadings.

Funding and Financial Management

Many state boards of education solicit help the same way that Africans and Latin American nations beg for grants from agencies like Agencies for International Development. Kozol (1991) questioned why the educating of minorities has been reduced to begging. All levels of government—federal, state, and local—must share in the responsibility of providing adequate and equitable funding for public schools. The operation of an effective school requires strong and sustained financial investment. A CSM school uses resources to respond to educational challenges and assumes responsibility for investing in essential components of a quality program. These include, but are not limited to:

- Curriculum.
- Opportunities for professional development.
- Safe and well-maintained school buildings.
- Adequate media and technology.
- Before- and after-school child-care programs.
- Recreational facilities
- Nutrition programs.
- Availability and accessibility of transportation.
- Financial decisions based on programmatic needs and a commitment that sustains a strong system of education.
- Adequate funding for education and related support services that meet the needs of all students and teachers.

Academic Programs

It is important to note that in planning successful academic programs, school professionals and student families are important links in the success of the student's opportunities in general education curriculum issues. Most students bring their family issues with them to class and take their school issues home (O'Shea, O'Shea, Algozzine, & Hammitte, 2001). The CSM school should include academic programs that provide opportunities for all students to develop academic and life skills. These include sound reading and functional mathematical abilities; oral, written, and electronic communication skills; civic education; the arts; and the ability to collect and critically analyze information. In addition, a school's academic precedence must:

- Be determined through a collaborative process involving parents, staff, students, and community.
- Address the individual educational needs of all students.
- Include regular assessment of individual and grade-level student achievement with timely and easily understood reports to parents.
- Assure early diagnosis of student learning problems and provide prompt intervention.

Assessment

The CSM school should use assessment programs that identify how instruction can be improved and learning can be increased. Valid assessment does not consist of a single test score. For assessment to be successful, it must be pragmatic and involve the use of culturally reliable and valid instruments and techniques, depending on the specific purpose for the assessment (Hilliard, 1980; Samuda, Kong, Cummins, Pascual-Leone, & Lewis, 1991). Grant and Grant (2000) reported that it is unfortunate that many school districts delay identification until the middle grades because of intelligent tests that cannot accurately identify young gifted children, and that many children. A reliable assessment program must:

- Use instruments that are culturally and racially bias-free and in a language that the student understands.
- Measure what has been taught.
- Utilize multiple measures that are performance-based and reflect the different kinds of knowledge and skills a student is expected to acquire.
- Provide special remedial and other instructional support for students falling below standards and expectations.
- Have understandable procedures and information.
- Provide for maximum local and state control regarding the determination of tests to be given.
- Test new assessment models.
- Involve parents and students at all levels, but particularly at the local level, in the design, development, implementation, and evaluation of any student assessment and testing program.

Parental and Family Involvement

Talbot (1997) suggested that if parents are committed to their child's education, they must be willing to give their time to help create a learning environment at school. Earlier, Simich-Dudgeon (1987) supported the importance of parent involvement and cooperative relationship between parents and schools. Parental involvement is the participation of parents in every phase of the education and development of children from birth to adulthood, recognizing that parents are the primary influence in children's lives. Broadly interpreted, parental involvement includes adults who play an important role in a child's daily and family life. When parents are involved, students achieve more, regardless of socioeconomic status, ethnic and racial backgrounds, or the parent's educational level. Manning and Baruth (2000) contended that educators working with Europeans Americans usually work with the mother and father. Culturally diverse children and adolescents, however, often perceive the roles of grandparents, aunts, and uncles as similar to those of the mother and father. Howard, Williams, Port, and Leppert (2001) asserted that extended family members may also be an important part of the family unit as well as a family support. This is especially true in many minority cultures. For example, in African American families, the grandmother may be the family matriarch who provides shelter, care, and advice on a daily basis. Parental involvement includes parents' participation in organizations such as the Parent Teacher's Concerned with Children (PTCC) and/or Parent Teacher's Association (PTA), which reflect the community's collaborative aspiration for all children. Every school should promote partnerships that increase parental involvement and participation in the social, emotional, and academic growth of children.

In the CSM school, a parent-involvement program should include the National Standards for Parent/Family Involvement Programs, established by the National PTA (1998) in cooperation with education and parent-involvement professionals. The CSM school must:

- Ensure that communication between home and school is regular, two-way, and meaningful.
- Promote and support parenting skills.
- Allow parents to play an integral role in assisting student learning.
- Welcome parents in the school and seek their support and assistance.
- Ensure parents are full partners in the decisions affecting children and families.
- Encourage collaboration with the community.

Teachers and Staff

Members of different ethnic groups must be an integral part of the school's instructional, administrative, and supportive staff. School personnel–teachers, principals, cooks, custodians, secretaries, students, and counselors make contributions as important to multicultural environments as do the courses of study and instructional materials (Banks, 1988). The CSM school must provide opportunities for staff and certified teachers to enhance skills regularly to insure the individual academic success of all students. In specific terms, teachers and service providers must:

- Be culturally responsive.
- Display a belief that all children can learn and assist them by evaluating and monitoring individual abilities, assigning tasks that hold students accountable, provide clear and immediate feedback, and evaluate progress regularly.
- Respect and seek parents' cooperation and involvement in their children's education.
- Be models of good conduct.

- Be committed to shared learning.
- Create high expectations and seek ways to maximize achievement.
- Establish a classroom and school atmosphere in which students are encouraged to perform appropriately and are rewarded for their success.
- Utilize professional development opportunities.
- Be evaluated by a process that is regularly reviewed and evaluated.

Students

Not long ago, Collins (1990) argued that educators and facilitators of learning should provide children with the right environment, the right motivation, and the right material to help them to excel. The CSM school should support each student's individual needs and encourage student responsibility so each student develops into a life-long learner and a good citizen. As a result, the CSM school should:

- Have high expectations and values for **all** students and believe students have the ability to learn and develop their own individual strengths and talents.
- Place a high worth on individual student progress and monitor this progress by means of a carefully devised assessment program.
- Teach students according to a strong set of expectations for positive behavior and performance.
- Accept all students at the level of readiness at which they enter school and prepare them for learning.
- Prepare students to be productive citizens and members of their communities.
- Teach students to apply knowledge and skills inside and outside the school.
- Encourage flexibility and guidance so students develop powerful new learning tools and techniques as they put challenging new concepts to the test.

Community and Support Services

The CSM school should foster community and business involvement that results in positive partnerships that support education. The CSM school must:

- Establish and maintain clear methods of communication with the community.

- Work with the community to provide a safe environment for children and youth.
- Identify resources and services the community and business can provide in cooperation with the school.
- Provide an organizational structure that encourages community involvement, participation, decision making, and volunteerism in the schools.
- Encourage the use of school facility for community events.

No school exists as an island; all schools serve the interests of the communities in which they are located. For this reason, partnerships with the community improve school effectiveness. Unfortunately, there are some school officials who see low income communities as part of the problem (Kuykendall, 1992). The CSM school should integrate comprehensive services that address the needs of the whole child—emotional, intellectual, physical, social, and spiritual. Policies and goals regarding support services should be established by local school boards in partnership with parents, students, educators, community providers, and others. Support services must include:

- Health services.
- Food services/nutrition program.
- Counseling/social services.
- Health-promotion programs.
- Preschool child-development services.
- Literacy programs.
- Mentor programs.
- Before- and after-school child cares.

The School Environment and Accommodations

The school environment includes all experiences with which learners come in contact: content, instructional methods, the actual teaching and learning process and environment, the professional staff and other staff members, as well as the actions and attitudes of other students. This definition of environment is synonymous with curriculum itself (Baruth & Manning, 1991). The school environment should support school learning and socialization for all students. Tyler (1989) suggested that a supportive school environment is one in which the morale of both teachers and students is high. Teachers believe in their mission to help guide and stimulate the learning activities of all their students and are pleased with their students' responsive behavior. The philosophy of a CSM school welcomes students, staff, parents, and community and promotes cooperative efforts to develop the best educational environment. In a CSM school, settings are safe and encourage the highest level of student learning and achievement and diversity of cultures is recognized and respected. The CSM philosophy requires policies that:

- Prevent disruptive behavior.
- Determine appropriate discipline.
- Create awareness of gang activity and membership.
- Have zero tolerance for drug use, including tobacco and alcohol.
- Have a gun-free environment.
- Include safety-education programs in the curriculum.
- Prohibit corporal punishment.
- Develop with parent and community involvement, character-education programs.
- Establish alternative educational settings for students who violate safe climate policies.

The term accommodation was used by Piaget to describe the adaptation of an individual to the environment (Drew & Hardman, 2000). Adequate, up-to-date school buildings are critical to providing quality learning opportunities for children. Buildings and grounds must be well maintained and safe, regardless of the age of the building. The CSM environment must:

- Provide barrier-free access for individuals with disabilities.
- Be free of health and environmental hazards.
- Offer adequate space and size for low pupil/teacher ratios.
- Provide appropriate space for education-related services.
- Be equipped with appropriate technology for classroom and instructional use.

Governance

The governance structure of an effective school has a statement of philosophy based on current, recognized research with clear goals and objectives set by the governing board(s) as representatives of the community. To create an educational structure that serves the needs of all children, the CSM school must:

- Ensure parents are partners at all decision-making levels, including site-based management committees, specific issue committees, district-wide committees.
- Have the governing board(s) responding to and representing the community, setting clear policies based on the needs of all children.
- Ensure that the governing board(s) supports sufficient development opportunities for all staff.

- Ensure that the superintendent is a strong academic leader and an effective manager.
- Ensure that the principal is an instructional and administrative leader who requires all staff members to carry out prescribed instructional strategies.
- Ensure that the principal is accessible to parents, teachers, students, and community.

CONCLUSION

In this chapter, we have discussed the public school philosophy, examined the historical perspective in early American education, and analyzed how common schooling took on a solid cultural design. Encapsulated in our examination is the role of school. For years, educators have pointed an accusing finger at parents, television, schools, lack of funds, children home life and background, as what the National Education Association describes as "the distraction" which characterized American life in the past decade or so (Kuykendall, 1992, p. 107). Based on the CSM, parents, school personnel, community members, and government officials must work together to assure that **all** children in this country should have an opportunity to receive a quality education. We must never forget that prevailing conditions affecting activity influences the classroom climate. Through the school and classroom climate, students are inspired, nurtured, supported, and comforted. It is imperative that as we advance in this new century, the philosophy that **all** children can learn must become the new foundation for the twenty-first century education model. School officials must encourage businesses, hospitals, and/or other public service institutions to "adopt" their schools. We believe businesses have a stake in the education and socialization of students. With this model, we can create successful teaching/learning environments that enhance multicultural education and facilitate the needs of all our children.

REFERENCES

Banks, J. A. (1988). *Multiethnic education: Theory and practice*. Needham Heights: Allyn and Bacon.

Banks, J. A., & McGee Banks, C. (1989). *Multicultural education: Issues and perspectives*. Boston: Allyn and Bacon.

Baruth, L. G., & Manning, M. L (1991). *Multicultural counseling and psychotherapy: A lifespan perspective*. Upper Saddle River, NJ: Prentice-Hall.

Boykin, A. W. (2000). Talent development, cultural deep structure, and school reform: Implications for African immersion initiatives. In D. S. Pollard & C. S. Ajirotutu (Eds.), *African centered schooling in theory and practice*. Westport, CT: Bergin & Garvey.

Collins, M., & Tamarkin, C. (1990). *Marva Collins' way: Returning to excellence in education*. New York: G. P. Putnam's Sons.

Drew, C. J., & Hardman, M. L. (2000). *Mental retardation: A life cycle approach* (7th ed.). Upper Saddle River, NJ: Prentice Hall.

Dubois, W.E. B. (1935). Does the Negro need separate schools?" *Journal of Negro Education, 4,* 328–335.

Edel, A. (1985). *Interpreting education: Science, ideology and value*. New Brunswick, NJ: Transaction Books.

Gabert, G. (1973). *In Hoc Signo? A brief history of Catholic parochial education in America*. Port Washington, NY: Kennifat Press.

Glasser, W. (1969). *Schools without failure*. New York: Harper & Rowe.

Grant, P. A., & Grant, P. B. (2000). Teaching students with gifts and talents in inclusive settings. In F. E. Obiakor, S. A. Burkhardt, A. F. Rotatori, & T. Wahlberg (Eds.), *Intervention techniques for individuals with exceptionalities in inclusive settings: Advances in special education* (pp. 149–172). Stamford, CT: JAI Press.

Gutek, G. L. (1988). *Philosophical and ideological perspectives on education*. Englewood Cliffs, NJ: Prentice-Hall.

Gutek, G. L. (1993). *American Education in a global society: Internationalizing teacher education*. White Plains, NY: Longman.

Hill, J. L. (1999). *Meeting the needs of students with special physical and health care needs*. Upper Saddle River, NJ: Prentice Hall.

Hillard, A. G. (1980). Cultural diversity and special education. *Exceptional Children, 46,* 584–589.

Howard, V. F., Williams, B.F., Port, P. D., & Leppert, C. (2001). *Very young children with special needs: A formative approach for the twenty-first century* (2nd ed.). Upper Saddle River, NJ: Prentice Hall.

Kozol, J. (1991). *Savage inequalities: Children in American schools*. New York: Crown.

Kuykendall, C. (1992). *From rage to hope: Strategies for reclaiming Black and Hispanic students*. Bloomington, IN: National Educational Services.

Manning, M. L., & Baruth, L. G. (2000). *Multicultural education of children and adolescent,* (3rd ed.). Needham Heights: Allyn & Bacon.

Miler, R. (1997). *What are schools for?: Holistic education in American culture*. Brandon, VT: Holistic Education Press.

National PTA (1998). Components of an effective school: Executive summary. [14 paragraphs]. *Children First: The web site of the National PTA*. [On-line] Available: http://www.pta.org/programs [1998].

Obiakor, F. E. (1994). *The eight-step multicultural approach: Learning and teaching with a smile*. Dubuque, IA: Kendall/Hunt.

Pratee, R. (1977). *Ideology and education*. New York: David McKay.

O'Shea, D. L., O'Shea, L. J. Alogozzine, R., & Hammitte, D. J. (2001). *Families and teachers of individuals with disabilities: Collaborative, orientations and responsive practices.* Boston: Allyn and Bacon.

Samuda, R. J., Kong, S. L., Cummins, J., Pascual-Leone, J., & Lewis, J. (1991). *Assessment and placement of minority students.* Toronto, Canada: Hogrete.

Simich-Dudgeon, C. (1987). Involving limited-English-proficient parents as tutors in their children's education. *ERIC/CLL News Bulletin, 10* (2), 3–4.

Talbott, E. M. (1997). *The joy and challenge of raising African American children.* Montgomery, AL: Black Belt Press.

Thomas, M.D., & Bainbridge, W. L. (2001, December). The truth about 'all children can learn' [11 paragraphs] *The bookshelf: Education week on the WEB.* [On-line] Available: http:///edweek.org [2000, December].

Tyler, W. (1989). Educating children from minority families. *Educational Horizons, 67,* 114–118.

U. S. Department of Education (1994). *Goals 2000: Educate America Act of 1994.* Washington, DC: Author.

Chapter 5

THE HOMELESS ARE PEOPLE, TOO: INCLUDING HOMELESS STUDENTS IN EDUCATIONAL PROGRAMMING

LYNN K. WILDER

One group that teachers rarely think about and may not even realize exists is the group of students who are homeless. No at-risk group is more likely to be denied access to school or to fail in school when enrolled than homeless students (Stronge, 1995). Young homeless children may live in shelters with their parents, in tents or campers, or under bridges. Homeless adolescents may fend for themselves in cars, move constantly from one friend's house to another's, sleep in shelters for runaway youth, or live in abandoned buildings. It is not unusual for students and parents to conceal their homeless status from teachers, especially since teachers seldom visit student homes. Tragically, this group of "invisible" students is at high risk of school failure because their needs are frequently overlooked.

Attention may be drawn to homeless students when their families move, which many homeless do repeatedly after losing their latest temporary residence. After the move, transportation to the child's old school or enrollment in the new neighborhood school can be problematic. A school district sacrifices time and money to send a bus across district boundaries to transport the homeless student to the former school. Enrollment in the new neighborhood school may be difficult since homeless students may not have birth certificates, immunization records, or an address with which to enroll. The Stewart B. McKinney Homeless Assistance Act of 1987 (P. L 100-77) forbids schools to exclude homeless students when they fail to immediately produce these records; however, the reality is that schools still do (Lively & Kleine, 1996;

Olian, 2001). Homeless students, then, are "invisible" humans, either because teachers may be unaware of their living conditions and educational needs or because many simply do not attend school. The critical question is whether homeless students have special needs requiring the attention of school personnel. This chapter examines the issue of including the homeless in an educational environment by applying the Comprehensive Support Model (CSM), which integrates the strengths of "self," families, schools, communities, and government agencies in educational solutions. Embedded in my examination are pertinent cases and experiences that buttress the need for an integrative educational program.

HOMELESS STUDENTS

Young homeless students often live with their parents in shelters that only allow them to stay a restricted amount of time, or the family may live briefly with relatives. These living conditions are not likely to be permanent, and such transient living negatively affects school performance (Linehan, 1992). Moving is a stressor, and moving frequently detracts from students' abilities to focus on learning academics. With each move, emotional effort is expended adjusting to new teachers, new peer relationships, and new behavioral expectations, as well as new living conditions. For instance, one homeless shelter where I worked housed parents who previously had their children removed by the courts for abuse or neglect. The parents lived in the shelter with their children who had been returned to them conditionally. The local judge mandated that the families live in this homeless shelter for 6 months. During this time, the parents were required to attend parenting classes and were encouraged to attend adult education classes if they needed to further their education; both were available on site in the shelter. Children rode the bus daily to the neighborhood school. Social workers and counselors in the shelter monitored the parents' behaviors and ultimately recommended to the judge whether the children should remain with their parents or live elsewhere. This scenario was not atypical for homeless parents.

The circumstances of physical abuse and/or neglect of children and youth are not uncommon among the homeless (Heflin & Rudy, 1991; Newman, 1999). As a result, these children and youth manifest inappropriate behavioral patterns in school. Therefore, teachers must recognize these behaviors as products of such experiences and must apply salient early intervention techniques that reduce the likelihood that problem behaviors will escalate in the school context (Kauffman, 2000; Stronge, 1995). See Case 12 below:

Case 12

Julie was a chubby pixie about 5 years old living with her parents and siblings in the family homeless shelter located in an old red-brick, vine-covered former nunnery next to a matching Catholic Church downtown in a Midwest city of about 100,000 people. Families in the shelter had their separate bedrooms but shared a community kitchen and living space. One sweltering summer afternoon, Julie's mother was working in the community living space in the basement of the shelter on the workbooks she had to complete to prepare to take the General Education Development (GED) exam. Julie, playing in the hall nearby, was not feeling well and soon vomited down the front of her pink shorts set. Sadly, her mother was unaware. This was a good thing because she would have been beaten mercilessly had the mother been aware.

As it appears, Julie needs special assistance and support from the teacher. Other service providers might also be involved in Julie's program. In addition to the difficulties associated with transience and physical abuse and/or neglect, homeless children exhibit numerous psychosocial characteristics as a result of their homelessness that necessitate special treatment by school personnel.

Adolescent homeless students are infrequently enrolled in school and rarely attend (see Powers & Jaklitsch); 40% have repeated a grade, 25% are in special education, and half are doing below average work or failing (Basuk & Rubin, 1987; Hausman & Hammen, 1993). Unaccompanied minors count for 7% of the homeless population (Mayors' Sixteenth Annual Report, *Hunger and Homelessness in America's Cities,* 2000); these students may have run from physical or sexual abuse or from the law, have addictions, be working as prostitutes, or be teen parents (Rothman, 1991; U. S. Department of Health and Human Services, 1997). Adolescent homeless students are sometimes hard to find and then hard to reach because they tend to distrust adults (Powers & Jaklitsch, 1992). However, outcomes for homeless adolescents are not always bleak; some homeless adolescents are remarkably resilient and thrive despite their circumstances. Case 13 describes such an adolescent.

Case 13

Jeff's mother worked as a prostitute. Her several children lived with her and her own mother in a drafty and dilapidated Victorian home in the inner city of a Midwestern town. Jeff, a quiet young man, had attended and dropped out of the 9th grade four times. He said the principal didn't want him there. At Halloween, he bought a pumpkin for his younger siblings to carve. Someone left the jack-o-lantern burning through the night; it ignited the back porch and engulfed the house. The family continued to live in parts of the burned out residence with no heat and no hot water. Feeling "driven out" of high school, Jeff worked part time and attended GED classes faithfully until he turned 19 and could take the high school equivalency exam, which he easily passed. His GED teacher recognized his artistic talent as he often gave her gifts of sketches depicting his life. She helped him get a Pell Grant to attend a 2-year college where he studied commercial advertising.

HOMELESS STUDENTS: EDUCATIONAL CHALLENGES AND SOLUTIONS

Homeless children and adolescents face the problem of repeated moves and all the challenges associated with not having a permanent home, such as where to sleep, how to get food, how to wash, where to get clean clothes, where to put their meager possessions so they are not stolen, and who to talk to since parents may be preoccupied with their own problems. They are daunted by where to go to school, how to enroll, where to get supplies and funds for fees, how to get to school, who will tease them, how they will adjust to new expectations, and how to complete their homework after school without supplies, a computer, a library card, or transportation anywhere. School phobia is not an unusual phenomenon for homeless students (Tower & White, 1989). Going "home" can also cause emotional turmoil since homeless adolescents and children may sleep in the cold or in crowded and not very private living quarters or may bear physical or sexual abuse. Constant moving, frequent change of schools, congested living conditions, and lack of access to basic resources (i.e., clothing, cooking facilities, and transportation) constitute serious educational challenges (Linehan, 1992).

Factors resulting in academic challenges for homeless students include high rates of developmental delay, about 50% compared to 16% for housed children (Bassuk & Rosenberg, 1988); language disabilities (Winzer & Mazurek, 1998); poor physical health (Institute of Medicine, 1988); frequent depression and anxiety; and behavior problems—3 to 4 times as many as expected in the general population (Bassuk & Rubin, 1987); and mental illness (Leshner, 1992). They have poor rates of school enrollment and attendance and high rates of school failure rates (Hausman & Hammen, 1993). Another challenge facing homeless children and adolescents is poor relationships with peers. Because peers with homes tend to harass them, homeless students want to hide their homelessness and resist trusting peers as friends.

These feelings of being different lead to feelings of inadequacy and isolation if not addressed by sensitive teachers, and emotional turmoil may be expressed in aggression or withdrawal (Grossman, 1991; Tower & White, 1989). As a consequence, teachers should be careful to understand the function of these behaviors and not allow their anger, impatience, or impulse to overreact to further isolate the homeless student (Beck & Malley, 1998).

To deal with problems associated with homelessness requires extreme personal resilience on the part of these students. Sagor (1996) defined resilience as "the set of attributes that provides people with the strength and fortitude to confront the overwhelming obstacles they are bound to face in life" (p. 38). Resilient characteristics include high intrinsic motivation, self-reliance, the ability to seek help for problems, and the ability to continue learning despite them (Westfall & Pisapia, 1994; Richardson & Nixon, 1997). Students need to feel competent at something, feel useful to someone, feel that they belong to an important group, feel that they are potent or have power as a group member, and feel optimistic about the future (see Sagor). School personnel can and must help foster these resilient traits for homeless children.

There is little that younger homeless children can do to improve their environment. A young homeless student's best friend is a caring adult, whether that person is a parent, guardian, social service worker, administrator, and teacher–these individuals have the power to make some changes. Responsible adults must see that a child's basic needs for food, clothing, shelter, and emotional security are met. Medical, dental and health needs must be attended to. Adults must also arrange appropriate schooling and educational support services for the child and engage schools in preventing school failure (Finn & Rock, 1997). In addition, these adults should be involved in helping peers to understand and accept the homeless child without teasing or harassing (Guetzloe, 1997). Learning appropriate social skills improves resiliency for children (Gordon, 1995) and improves the way they are treated by peers. School personnel should assume the role of responsible, caring adults with the power to make things better.

The homeless adolescent student's needs are both similar to and different from those of younger homeless students. In common, they need support when they are harassed by peers, or even by school administrators, if they are to remain in school. Students frequently need adult understanding and adult emotional and academic support (Wilder, 2001). Teachers can create opportunities for small success experiences that build students' confidence and provide outlets for fear and frustration (e.g., drama, drawing, music, athletics, and counseling) (Tower & White, 1989). One way that unaccompanied homeless adolescents' needs may be different from those of younger homeless students is that they will most likely have immediate and pervasive needs for long-term counseling. Some reasons these youth leave home include poor social adjustment; a reaction to a crisis; parental rejection or expulsion; insufficient family resources; parental substance abuse, divorce, incarceration; sexual or physical abuse; and the perception that they are unloved (Rothman, 1991). Patterns of early stressors in their lives have a direct relationship to their quality of adaptation later in life (Werner & Smith, 1992). Both risk factors that add to the probability that youth will fail in school and protective factors that may prevent school failure have to be identified (Hawkins, Catalano, & Miller, 1992). Adolescent homeless youth need vocational counseling and job exploration opportunities.

It is important that teachers help homeless youth to recognize risk factors that lead to school failure, such as aggression, teen pregnancy and substance abuse, and provide productive outlets for students, such as cross-age tutoring opportunities, club membership, athletic activities, and service learning opportunities to channel energies in a positive manner (Pisapia & Westfall, 1994; Westfall & Pisapia, 1994). Students should be taught to recognize protective factors, such as educational engagement; counseling; religiosity (Payne, Bergin, Bielema, & Jenkins, 1991); extra curricular activities; vocational, social skills, and life skills training; and recognize the positive traits that they have developed as a result of their experiences (Finn & Rock, 1997; Westfall & Pisapia, 1994). The more protective factors they can nurture, the more resilient they can become. Since homeless students' lives tend to be tumultuous, teachers should provide a stable school environment with predictable expectations and temporal structure. This stability promotes feelings of safety, security, and consistency, as well as the sense that someone cares. A friend who grew up on a ranch once said that whenever the family bought a new cow or bull, the animal would rub against the fence, and make a trip all the way around the borders of its restricted space. Students want to know where their limits are, whether someone will enforce those limits for their safety, and whether someone cares enough to notice whether they are inside or outside of the fence. Consistent rules, with reinforcement and consequences, regular routines, and reliable adults create a secure environment (Levin & Nolan, 1996; Obiakor, Mehring, & Schwenn, 1997; Wilder & Gunsalus, 2001). Part of a teacher's responsibility in creating this secure environment for homeless students is to stop others from harassing them whenever it occurs and to teach housed and homeless students to treat others with respect.

As it appears, teachers can provide space for homeless students' personal belongings in the school including clothes and personal items, find a place for students to shower, or link them to social service agencies that will help meet their basic physical needs, health care needs, and dental needs. Teachers should inform their administrators if students are homeless, so that other school personnel, such as social workers or special teams that address problems that decrease student effectiveness at school, can be enlisted (Tower & White, 1989). Administrators who are aware of the extent of a student's problems sometimes arrange outreach enrollment, tutoring, or even instructional services in shelters (Johnson, 1992; Rountree, 1996). One more protective factor that may improve outcomes for homeless students is their involvement in organized religion. Although the research is unclear, there is some evidence to support the assertion that religious engagement increases students' prosocial behaviors through the socialization that takes place among members of a particular faith (Johnson, Jang, Larson, & De Li, 2001). Religiosity has been positively correlated with student well-being and self-esteem, family satisfaction, and with the inhibition of premarital sexual behavior, alcohol and drug abuse, and suicide (Payne et al.,). Implementing even a few of the suggestions in this section could improve educational outcomes for homeless children and youth.

HOMELESS FAMILIES: EDUCATIONAL CHALLENGES AND SOLUTIONS

The fastest growing group among the homeless is homeless families with school-aged children (Anderson & Koblinsky, 1995). Families now account for 37 percent of homeless individuals (Mayors' Sixteenth Annual Status Report, 2000). A number of difficult problems exist for parents of homeless children. The existence of personal problems should in no way suggest to school personnel that homeless parents love their children any more or any less than other parents do or should be bypassed when schools attempt to solve problems of homeless students. Parents should be consulted and included as much as possible.

Substance abuse is often a major problem for homeless adults. Although figures vary, alcohol and drug abuse have been found to be present in about 30 to 38 percent of homeless adults. In addition, physical health problems are common among the homeless. About the same percentage of adults who report substance abuse problems report health problems; most adults reporting poor health say their poor health has prohibited them from working during the past year (Committee on Health Care for Homeless People, Institute of Medicine, 1988; Stronge, 1992). Homeless parents may have mental health problems. The deinstitutionalization of America has caused some of the mentally ill to live on the streets (Hausman & Hammen, 1993); 22 percent of homeless individuals are mentally ill (see the Mayors' Sixteenth Annual Report, 2000). Further, homeless parents sometimes abuse or neglect their children (Rountree, 1996); the stress from conditions of poverty is likely overwhelming. Significant others may abuse their usually female partners who, when running from the abuse, become heads of homeless families (Lively & Kleine, 1996; Stronge). Homeless adults frequently have low levels of educational achievement and are unemployed. Although 1/3 of homeless adults do have jobs (Gorder, 1988), income from their employment may not be enough to support the family in a home, as low-income housing does not exist in quantities sufficient for the families in need.

The emotional burdens of homeless adults, especially those responsible for the care of children, are very real. Both children and adults have safety and security needs (Johnson, 1992). Since the school is the only unfragmented institution in the lives of many homeless students, teachers and other school personnel have the responsibility to reach out to homeless parents as partners in providing the safety and security in both the educational and living environments that homeless students need (Reed & Sautter, 1990). Consider Case 14 below.

Case 14

> James was huge, probably 6′ 5″ and 300 pounds. The personnel at the family homeless shelter where the judge had mandated that he and his family live for 6 months requested that he complete an educational assessment to determine his academic skill level. James had recently been released from prison. During the testing, James threw his test to the floor, spouted expletives at the teacher, and stomped out of the room causing people to be afraid. Later that afternoon, James returned to the testing room where the teacher was grading tests and shut the door behind them. He sat near her and began to cry, confessing he could not read. His large frame shook!

Parental problems that have been discussed above have devastating effects on all but the most resilient of homeless students. Best practices for school personnel in working with parents of homeless children include many of the elements of effective human interactions. There is a power in particular action. First, there is power in positive word choices. Emphasizing students' strengths to parents, assisting with educational solutions, and demonstrating to parents that educational difficulties can be addressed and improved, all help build positive and trusting relationships with parents that are beneficial to the child (Anderson & Koblinsky, 1995; Guetzloe, 1997). Teachers must learn to be aware of their own prejudices and look beyond them (Obiakor, 1994). In order to do this, they must be willing to listen to homeless parents, learn from them, and change their behavior if needed to develop the power of influence that comes with treating all parents with respect. The most salient belief a teacher can transmit to homeless parents is that the school environment matters in the lives of their children and that someone in the school environment truly cares for their children/youth.

SHIFTING SCHOOLING PARADIGMS

For homeless children, the culture of the home will most definitely clash with the culture of the school. Obiakor (2001) illustrates the tragic effects of unnecessary struggles between adults on children with this old Nigerian proverb, "When two elephants fight, the grass underneath suffers." Teaching is more than just pouring academic knowledge into the brains of students. It has social and emotional dimensions as well (Lively & Kleine, 1996). In this grandly diverse world of public schools, it is unethical for teachers to ignore the social and emotional dimensions of teaching. When responsible adults are not concerned about the troubles so real to children and adolescents, results include gang membership, drug addiction, violence, prostitution, suicide, and a host of other ills. Teachers must honor individual characteristics each student brings into the classroom and work to involve parents, even homeless students' parents, in the child's education.

Slavin, Madden, Dolan, and Wasik (1996) believed every child can learn and that every school can ensure the success of every child. For homeless children, just getting to school may pose a difficulty, although access to education for homeless students has improved greatly since the advent of The McKinney Act (National Coalition for the Homeless, 1999). According to the most recent U.S. Department of Education Report to Congress, 88 % of homeless children now attend school (Varner, 2000). Optimism that neighborhood schools can meet the needs of homeless students has caused Congress to consider closing all special schools for the homeless on the grounds that segregation is unequal treatment under the Constitution (Olian, 2001; Varner).

Regardless of where schools serve homeless students, which they must do according to law regardless of whether records can be located, transience and attendance should become concerns for schools. Since homeless shelters usually limit the amount of time individuals stay at one shelter, families move from one to another or go from the street to a shelter; interestingly, the average person waits 5 months to get into an emergency shelter (Mayors' Sixteenth Annual Report, 2000). Sometimes families split so they can survive, the father going to men's shelter, the mother to women's shelter and the children to various foster homes or youth facilities (Anderson & Koblinsky, 1995). Homeless children/ youth attend school sporadically. Transience and inconsistent attendance affect a child's opportunities for stability, structure, and continuity of education and makes the cost of locating and transporting that child to school high (Linehan, 1992). It is known that homeless students feel uncomfortable and like outcasts in schools. Their clothing and personal grooming seem inadequate to their peers, who tease them. Curriculum rarely depicts children like them because their performance at academics may be poor. They need help with homework and lack access to technology. Some need special education, but the identification and placement processes may not be completed before they move again. Many suffer from serious emotional distress expressed as depression and anxiety (Lively & Kleine, 1996).

Enrollment

The McKinney Act declares that each state education agency is responsible to guarantee that each homeless child or youth has access to a free, appropriate education. This education must be commensurate with an education that would be provided to the children of a resident of the state, and the child's attendance must be consistent with the state school attendance laws. Douvanis & Douvanis (1995) suggested the following compliance strategies for schools:

1. If parents with a questionable place of residence present themselves to enroll their child in school, school administrative personnel should ascertain whether the students' residential status qualifies as homeless under section 103(a)1, 2 of the McKinney Act. If the student is so qualified, then decide whether the best interests of the student will be served by continued enrollment in the school attended prior to homelessness or, taking into account needed educational services, special programs, transportation, the student would be best served in the school district where the student is presently residing.
2. Enroll the student and determine free meal, vocational, English for Speakers of other languages, educational, and transportation needs. Use the shelter or a social agency as the student's mailbox.
3. If the student does not have appropriate birth, schools, medical/health records, contact the prior school to request the student's records and discuss immunization information and arrange for temporary appropriate placement. If no information is available, it will be necessary to create a new file for the student.
4. If no immunization information exists, the school must make arrangements with the local health department to ensure that the student has been immunized.
5. If the student comes to enroll at the school without a parent or guardian, enroll the student and take immediate steps to contact the

parent(s) or guardian(s). Document all attempts to communicate with the parents.
6. Homeless children often cannot or will not provide information about parents. In the event that no parent or guardian can be located, contact the appropriate social service agency to report the situation and be prepared to go to court to have a guardian appointed. This may be the case particularly when child abuse is suspected or is an issue. School social workers can serve as guardians with parental permission.
7. Work with social agencies and shelters to help enroll students. Provide them with clear guidelines dealing with residency and enrollment. In shelters with large numbers of homeless children, the ultimate solution may be to provide educational services in the shelters. Grants from the federal government are available to provide such services.
8. School systems must make an honest effort to locate and identify homeless students within their boundaries. Ignoring the existence of homeless children is a violation of both the letter and the spirit of the McKinney Act. (pp. 145–146)

Transportation

An important component of school attendance is getting the homeless child or youth to school. The McKinney Act affords homeless students the right to stay in their original neighborhood school for an entire year, regardless of where and how often students move. The district may provide the transportation or provide bus tickets for public transportation (Rountree, 1996). Transportation is a problematic issue for school districts serving homeless students (Linehan, 1992).

Special Schools

Some districts attempt to solve the transportation problem by opening special schools for homeless students either on site in shelters or in a central location in a district. Special schools may resolve issues of transportation, social service integration, consistency, and sense of belonging, but their legality is being challenged by a bill introduced to Congress during February 2001 that would eliminate separate schools (Olian, 2001). The argument raised by Walter Varner (2000), President of the National Association for the Education of Homeless Children and Youth, is that special schools segregate students and offer them inferior educational opportunities, since a full range of educational options is not available at one special school. Nonetheless, special schools provide necessary educational options.

In-service Training

"The most important thing teachers can do for their homeless students is to become educated on the subject of homelessness" (Tower & White, 1989, p. 34). The Department of Health and Human Services (1997) reported that the school is the one institution that has the power to moderate the effects of prejudice on homeless students. Linehan (1992) recommended inservice training that brings together school personnel, shelter staff, social service agency personnel, and formerly homeless parents to help school personnel understand the needs of homeless children. Skills for school personnel working with homeless students should include commitment to persist in problem solving, collaboration with social service agencies, competence in multiculturalism, attention to learning styles differences, and facilitation of social skills competence in students (Peterson, 1992).

Health Services

Homeless students may need physical examinations, immunizations, and medical attention for chronic diseases and other illnesses. Homeless children and adolescents have upper respiratory infections, ear infections, anemia, and serious skin disorders at twice the rate of those who are not homeless (Johnson, 1992). They are reported to have gastrointestinal problems, asthma, and diarrhea. They need dental care and some need medical attention for conditions related to sexual activity and substance abuse. It is important that a school nurse does a thorough health assessment when the homeless student enrolls. The student's vision, hearing, and dental status should be evaluated. The student should be referred to medical professionals for further needed assessment or treatment, and the school nurse should arrange transportation. The nurse will also locate the student's immunization and health records or assists in creating them. Another important role of the school nurse is to teach personal hygiene and nutrition, and to give information related to sexual activity (see Johnson).

Clothing Services

Homeless children are likely to need several changes of clothes that are fashionable and easy to keep clean and thus do not cause them to be unduly noticed by their peers. Clothing banks are sometimes maintained by shelters or by social service agencies or donation facilities. Some schools even provide clothing for children in need, particularly if the school is a special school for homeless children and youth. Chapter 1 funds are available for the purpose of providing clothing to inappropriately clothed children, and businesses are usually eager to donate for this cause (Johnson, 1992).

Meal Programs

Homeless children and youth rarely have access to fresh fruits, vegetables, meat, grains, and dairy products; therefore, they often do not eat regular or nutritionally balanced meals. Schools can provide much needed nutritious meals, both in the morning and at noon, and they may even offer after-school snacks (Johnson, 1992). The paperwork that must be completed to enroll in these programs should be advanced quickly for homeless students. Further, health professionals in schools can inform students about health and nutrition.

Mentoring

"If schools are to be viewed in the context of community, then the principal's and teacher's professional knowledge base must include an understanding of daily neighborhood life" (Quint, 1994, p. 122). Harris and Associates (1994) and Obiakor et al. (1997) found that caring teachers are a powerful source of school-to-postsecondary success for students. Adult mentors have been demonstrated to be a vital link to success for students for whom the dominant social structure is an unfamiliar territory (Wilder, Jackson, & Smith, 2001). If teachers cannot spend the time it takes to be effective mentors for homeless students, they can certainly arrange for mentors from the outside community.

Academic Support Services

Schools can provide before and after school programs, homebound or on-site shelter services, mentor programs, evaluation and counseling, funds for fees, school supplies, daycare for teen parents, tutoring, expedited special education testing and placement, confidential handing of records (especially for victims of abuse to ensure their safety), as well as a warm, safe and secure environment that invites students to feel welcome. These services, which can be funded by federal grants, or by community and business funds, are necessary for the survival of homeless students in the educational environment. As Stronge and Tenhouse (1990) pointed out, "While providing appropriate educational opportunities to these students may not result in the disappearance of homelessness, ignoring education for the homeless will most certainly perpetuate it" (p. 31).

COMMUNITIES AT WORK FOR THE HOMELESS

Members of many communities have feared and sometimes treated the poor and the homeless as outcasts. The ranks of homeless families with children and homeless youth, however, are so numerous that no community could free itself of all homeless students. The most humane thing communities can do is to assist with feeding, clothing, furnishing, housing, and providing educational opportunities and emotional support for homeless individuals who then can make informed choices about their behavior. In a related fashion, ignorance about and fear toward minority groups, individuals with extremely low socioeconomic status, individuals who speak different languages, and individuals with disabilities has improved but still needs attention by communities (Winzer & Mazurek, 1994).

The lack of affordable housing is one of several causes of homelessness. In recent years, a healthy economy has inflated the price of housing to a level that the working poor cannot afford; 26% of homeless individuals have jobs (see the Mayors' Sixteenth Annual Status Report, 2000). One reason that housing is unaffordable for the working poor is that an adult making minimum wage cannot pay for rent, electricity, phone, food, transportation, childcare, and other expenses necessary for independent living on those wages. Stacey Bess, a teacher in a Salt Lake City homeless shelter, remarked, "One of the hardest things about working with these people is not that they are difficult to love or to understand. It is watching them do the best they can when their best still isn't good enough" (Bess, 1994, p. 158). Caring communities cannot turn a blind eye to human problems of affordable housing, substance abuse, violence, domestic violence, crime, gangs, mental illness, low paying jobs, changes in public assistance, racism, and prejudice against the poor that cause or add to the burdens of homelessness (Newman, 1999; Obiakor et al., 1997).

People in caring communities can, first, inform fellow citizens of the difficulties of others through public service announcements on the television and radio, statements on billboards, and speakers to community groups. Citizens can undertake more equitable distribution of resources, and those who have time can volunteer in mentoring programs. Individuals and communities with money can give financial support for basic needs, adequate shelter space, and support services. Those who can teach can tutor, and those with health knowledge can assist with personal hygiene. In addition, those with mathematical skills can teach budgeting, and those with parenting skills can instruct in parenting or childcare. Simply, those with advocacy skills can advocate and, anyone with listening skills can provide an ear. All of these ventures can help to socialize homeless individuals into the culture of the larger community (U. S. Department of Health and Human Services, 1997). Part of the job of effective community leaders is to match community needs with community resources, without judging why someone might have a need and without conforming to the attitude that homeless individuals deserve their troubles. Some communities are coordinating and streamlining services to poor families by locating psychological, social, and health services in schools (Reed & Sautter, 1990). In collaboration with schools, community centers, YMCA and YWCA, churches, colleges, and philanthropic and neighborhood organizations can work together with the homeless to solve the challenges of homelessness (Quint, 1994; Rothman, 1991). Solutions chosen by community leaders who are unfamiliar with the situation and needs of the homeless will not work.

Prevention of homelessness is, of course, the most effective strategy for communities (Rothman, 1991). This approach includes providing support services for the working poor who are trying to make ends meet. Forms of support might include money for books, childcare for students on Pell Grants, pro-family economic and employment policies, inexpensive transportation, vocational exploration (Wilder, in press), and community mental health services. More affordable low-income housing would certainly improve conditions for a myriad of individuals including children and youth that are currently homeless. Two men who have worked toward this solution are Millard Fuller who founded Habitat for Humanity, and Curtis Cluff who founded Partners in Action (Gorder, 1988). Kozol (1999), a man who has passionately championed the needs of the poor for many years and whose writings have supported the need for comprehensive educational approaches as prescribed by Obiakor (2001), reacts to what appears to be a societal lack of concern in his call for action. As Kozol noted:

> Children, whatever the color of their skin or the condition of their birth, bless us by their mere existence on this earth. The great, unanswered question of our age is whether our societies plan to bless them in return. The answer to this question calls for courage of a kind that we can win only by sharing our unique strengths with each other. . . . A call to action, therefore, needs to be a call to solidarity in the old-fashioned sense. If we are to serve our children well, it will take a lot more than "a village." It will take the full, collective force of an inspired society. (p. 2)

GOVERNMENT'S ROLE IN HELPING THE HOMELESS

The role of government in aiding the homeless, as in the aiding the disabled, the poor, minorities, and students for whom English is a second language, is to design laws that protect and support these individuals because prejudice is so effusive and affects them in real ways (Newman, 1999; U. S.

Department of Health and Human Services, 1997). These laws must carry adequate sanctions, meaning the refusal to follow them should have consequences, grave enough that they will be respected and implemented. Two such laws affect homeless students. The first is the Runaway Youth Act of 1974, revised as the Runaway and Homeless Youth Act of 1977. During the past decade, family dysfunction has been the major cause of homeless youth. This Act seeks to minimize the problems of homeless youth, and to reunite them with their families when feasible, as well as create counseling, stable living, and future-oriented opportunities such as vocational training (Rothman, 1991). Funds from this act maintain the National Runaway Switchboard, which works as a clearinghouse for referral and provides crisis intervention services by telephone. The second law affecting homeless children and youth is the Stewart B. McKinney Act of 1987 (P.L. 100-77), Education Act of Homeless Children and Youth (EHCY), with its 1990 amendments (P. L. 100-645). It was enacted because fewer than 50% of homeless children and youth were attending school regularly. In brief, the original Act provides grants to states for the purpose of reviewing and rewriting laws, policies, and practices relative to homeless students that may be barriers to their enrolling in, attending, and succeeding in school. The amendment allows states to provide funding to districts for direct services to homeless students (NCH Fact Sheet #10, 1999). These services might include expedited enrollment, special education assessment and services, school psychologist services, meals, funds for fees and school supplies, special transportation, academic support services such as tutoring and after-school or on-site shelter educational programs, electronic tracking systems, and health services (Rountree, 1996).

A major criticism of programs funded by the Runaway and Homeless Youth Act is that, at best estimates, only about a fifth of homeless youth are receiving services. A second criticism is that youths returning home after staying in a shelter seldom receive badly needed long-term counseling assistance. (Rothman, 1991). The Act has yet to receive full funding (NCH Fact Sheet #10, 1999). Despite many improvements since the McKinney Act, a 1995 evaluation found that guardianship, immunization records, transportation, and fees remained barriers to school enrollment. Poor health and transience, as well as inadequate food, clothing, and school supplies remain barriers to school success (NCH Fact Sheet #10, 1999). Basically, the role of the federal government in aiding the homeless is to legally mandate equitable policies that can be implemented practically for the good of the people. Federal laws are enacted to help groups that do not currently hold the power to make positive changes for themselves without assistance. Government solutions for the homeless comprise a heightened commitment to affordable housing along with full funding of and better compliance strategies for current laws (Douvanis & Douvanis, 1995; Mayors' Sixteenth Annual Status Report, 2000).

Some argue that legislation that disallows segregated schools would improve conditions for homeless students (Varner, 2000), although others disagree (Olian, 2001). Promoting systems' integration, providing better outreach and access to existing programs, and generating and disseminating information are ways in which government agencies can contribute to solving some of the problems of the homeless (Leshner, 1992).

CONCLUSION

Although professionals in the fields of education and psychology take great pains to write about homelessness with the distance that most scholarly writing requires, there surfaces in the literature a great deal of righteous indignation about our disinterest in homeless individuals from the few scholars who address this topic. Some of the solutions to the problems of homeless students are clear and can be accomplished. As with many of the problems of other at risk students, such as students with emotional and behavioral disorders, we know what works. My fear is that we do not have the resolve to accomplish what must be done. My agony is that these "invisible" students truly are not cared about. The good news is that even the skeptics understand that homeless people are people too. As a result, we must educate all learners, including those who are homeless if we are serious about maximizing the fullest potential of **all** students.

REFERENCES

Anderson, E. A., & Koblinsky, S. A. (1992). Homeless policy: The need to speak to families. *Family Relations, 44* (1), 13–19.

Bassuk, E., & Rubin, L. (1987). Homeless children: A neglected population. *American Journal of Orthopsychiatry, 57* (2), 279–286.

Bassuk, E. L., & Rosenberg, L. (1988). Why does family homelessness occur? A case-control study. *American Journal of Public Health, 78,* 783–788.

Beck, M., & Malley, J. (1998). A pedagogy of belonging. *Reclaiming Children and Youth, 7,* 133–141.

Bess, S. (1994). *Nobody don't love nobody.* Carson City, NV: Gold Leaf Press.

Douvanis, G., & Douvanis, C. (1995). When the student has no mailbox. *Journal for a Just and Caring Education, 1* (2), 142–150.

Finn, J. D., & Rock, D. A. (1997). Academic success among students at risk for school failure. *Journal of Applied Psychology, 82,* 221–234.

Gordon, K. A. (1995). Self-concept and motivational patterns of resilient African American high school students. *Journal of Black Psychology, 21,* 239–256.

Grossman, H. (1991). Special education in a diverse society: Improving services for minority and working class students. *Preventing School Failure, 36* (1), 19–27.

Guetzloe, E. (1997). The power of positive relationships: Mentoring programs in the school and community. *Preventing School Failure, 41* (3), 100–105.

Harris & Associates (1994). *Pilot survey of young African American males in four cities.* New York: Commonwealth Fund.

Hausman, B., & Hammen, C. (1993). Parenting in homeless families: The double crisis. *American Journal of Orthopsychiatry, 63,* 358–368.

Hawkins, J. D., Catalano, R. F., & Miller, J. Y. (1992). Risk and protective factors for alcohol and other drug problems in adolescence and early adulthood: Implications for substance abuse prevention. *Psychological Bulletin, 112* (1), 64–105.

Heflin, L. J., & Rudy, K. (1991). *Homeless in need of special education: Exceptional children at risk.* Reston, VA: ERIC Clearinghouse on Handicapped and Gifted Children. (ERIC Document Reproduction Service No. ED 399 167)

Institute of Medicine. (1988). *Homelessness, health, and human needs.* Washington, DC: National Academy Press.

Johnson, J. F. (1992). Educational support services for homeless children and youth. In J. H. Stronge (Ed.), *Educating homeless children and adolescents: Evaluating policy and practice* (pp. 153–178). Newbury Park, CA: Sage.

Kauffman, J. M. (2000). *Characteristics of emotional and behavioral disorders of children and youth* (7th ed.). Upper Saddle River, NJ: Merrill.

Kozol, J. (1988). *Rachel and her children: Homeless families in America.* New York: Crown Publishers.

Kozol, J. (2001). A call to action. *Reaching today's youth: The community circle of caring journal.* [On-line]. Available: www.nesonline.com/rty.call.html

Leshner, A. I. (1992). *Outcasts on main street: Report of the Federal Task Force on Homelessness and Severe Mental Illness.* Washington, DC: National Institute of Mental Health.

Levin, J., & Nolan, J. F. (1996). *Principles of classroom management* (2nd ed.). Needham Heights: Allyn & Bacon.

Linehan, M. F. (1992, September). Children who are homeless: Educational strategies for school personnel. *Phi Delta Kappan.* Bloomington, IN: Phi Delta Kappan.

Lively, K. L., & Kleine, P. F. (1996). *The school as a tool for survival for homeless children.* New York: Garland.

Mayors' Sixteenth Annual Status Report (2000), *Hunger and homelessness in America's cities.* [On-line] Available: www.usmayors.org/uscm/news/press_release/documents/hunger_release.html

National Coalition for the Homeless (1999, June). *Education of homeless children and youth: NCH fact sheet #10.* [On-line]. Available: www.nch.ari.net/edchild.html

Newman, R. (1999). *Educating homeless children: Witness to a cataclysm.* New York: Garland.

Obiakor, F. E. (1994). *The eight step multicultural approach: Learning and teaching with a smile.* Dubuque, IA: Kendall/Hunt.

Obiakor, F. E. (2001, March). *Redefining "goodness" of schools: By their fruits we shall know them*. Paper presented as a Visiting Scholar at Brigham Young University, Provo, UT.

Obiakor, F.E., Mehring, T. A., & Schwenn, J. O. (1997). *Disruption, disaster, and death: Helping students deal with crises*. Reston, VA: The Council for Exceptional Children.

Olian, C. (Producer). (2001, February 4). *CBS 60 Minutes*. New York: CBS Worldwide.

Payne, I. R., Bergin, A. E., Bielema, K. A., & Jenkins, P. H. (1991). Review of religion and mental health: Prevention and the enhancement of psychosocial functioning. *Prevention in Human Services, 9,* 11–40.

Peterson, R. (1992). *Life in a crowded place: Making a learning community*. Portsmouth, NH: Heinemann.

Pisapia, J., & Westfall, A. (1994). *Developing resilient schools and resilient students. Research Brief #19*. Richmond, VA: Metropolitan Educational Research Consortium.

Powers, J. L., & Jaklitsch, B. (1992). Adolescence and homelessness: The unique challenge for secondary educators. In J. H. Stronge (Ed.) *Educating homeless children and adolescents: Evaluating policy and practice*. (pp. 115–132). Newbury Park, CA: Sage.

Quint, S. (1994). *Schooling homeless children: A working model for America's public schools*. New York: Teachers College Press.

Reed, S., & Sautter, R. C. (1990, June). *Children of poverty: The status of 12 million young Americans. Phi Delta Kappan Special Report*. Bloomington, IN: Phi Delta Kappan.

Richardson, G. E., & Nixon, C. J. (1997, November). A curriculum for resiliency. *Principal,* pp. 26–28.

Rothman, J. (1991). *Runaway and homeless youth: strengthening services to families and youth*. White Plains, NY: Longman.

Rountree, M. (1996). Opening school doors to the homeless. *Thrust for Educational Leadership, 26* (1), 10–13.

Sagor, R. (1996, September). Building resiliency in students. *Educational Leadership,* pp. 38–43.

Stronge, J. H. (1992). The background: History and problems of the homeless. In J. H. Stronge (Ed.), *Educating homeless children and adolescents: Evaluating policy and practice*. (pp. 3–25). Newbury Park, CA: Sage.

Stronge, J. H. (1995). Educating homeless students. *Journal for a Just and Caring Education, 1* (2), 128–142.

Stronge, J. H., & Tenhouse, C. (1990). *Educating homeless children: Issues and answers*. Bloomington, IN: Phi Delta Kappa Educational Foundation.

Slavin, R. E., Madden, N. A., Dolan, L. J., & Wasik, B. A. (1996). *Every child, every school: Success for all*. Thousand Oaks, CA: Corwin Press.

U. S. Department of Health and Human Services (1997). *Understanding youth development: Promoting positive pathways of growth*. (CSR Publication No. 105-95-1735). Washington, DC: Author.

Varner, W. (2000, September). Educating homeless children. *FDCH Congressional Testimony*. (pp. 1–4).

Westfall, A., & Pisapia, J. (1994). *At risk students: Who are they and what helps them succeed?* Richmond, VA: Metropolitan Research Consortium.

Wilder, L. K. (2001, May). Success in college for students with disabilities. *Theories and Practices in Supervision and Curriculum, 12,* 31–34.

Wilder, L. K., & Gunsalus, C. (in press). Managing student behaviors in inclusive settings. *OASCD Journal.*

Wilder, L. K., Jackson, A., & Smith, T. (2001). Multicultural transition of secondary exceptional learners: A Navajo Native American experience. *Preventing School Failure, 45,* (3), 119–124.

Winzer, M. A., & Mazurek, K. (1998). *Special education in multicultural contexts.* Upper Saddle River, NJ: Prentice-Hall.

Chapter 6

PREPARING TEACHERS FOR ALL STUDENTS

Jeffrey P. Bakken, Gregory F. Aloia, and Stephen F. Aloia

The Greeks believed in a well-rounded education focusing on education of the body as much as education of the mind. They also required teachers and students to develop a sound philosophy of life, believing that teachers had to live a life consonant with the education they professed. In I.F. Stone's (1989) classic, *The Trial of Socrates*, he made the point vividly clear that Socrates was brought to trial not for corrupting the minds of youth, but rather for not being a good citizen. In short, Socrates was condemned to death for failing to participate in his society.

It is important that teachers are not just simply knowledgeable, but are also good citizens. The Greeks would find it incompatible to think that you could assume that teaching was disconnected from the life of the teacher. There must be coherence between one's life and that of being a teacher. The connection between the two, one's life and the life of teaching youth, is related to the nature of teaching human beings as contrasted with training animals. To teach is to impart not simply knowledge, but to facilitate the construction of meaning within the mind of a child. This process implies that meaning is contextualized within the rubric of the teaching/learning process. A teacher cannot expect to facilitate learning and the construction of meaning around units of knowledge in the absence of his or her belief system. Students learn far more in the teaching/learning process than simply facts, or systems or theories. The teaching/learning process involves both the spirit of teaching as much as the content of teaching. The spirit of teaching cannot be separated from the knowledge associated with learning any more than the soul can be removed from the body. The Greeks strongly believed in the body-mind-spirit connection. Learning requires the animation of the teacher, which is influenced by his or her aggregate set of beliefs. Hence, as the Greeks believed, a teacher, more than almost any other professional would have the obligation to reflect a philosophy of life consonant with the philosophy of education.

Preparing future teachers is a daunting and complicated task. Not only do institutions of higher learning have to prepare teachers to be knowledgeable and effective, they also have to prepare them to deal with the issues of self, families, schools, communities, and the government. In addition to knowledge and field experiences, it is the obligation of institutions of higher learning to develop critical thinkers, problem-solvers, and reflective practitioners. Curricula must be carefully planned to provide a multitude of opportunities to practice and develop these skills. Through this process, the needs of self, families, schools, communities, and the government must also be addressed. The role of the teacher and the art of teaching are not independent of themselves, they are interwoven with these other significant factors. To be the most effective and successful teacher, one must recognize the importance of one's self, families, schools, communities, and the government. Independently, these entities will function properly, but the education of all students will not be maximized to its greatest potential if they fail to work together. Working in unison and collaboratively, they have the ability to produce knowledgeable, sympathetic, and caring citizens for all of society. Although the teacher is definitely a critical factor in this process of educating all students, he/she cannot do everything alone.

The purpose of this chapter is to focus on the important facets of preparing teachers for all students. As we advance in this new century, we need teachers who have the characteristics and theoretical and practical knowledge to teach all learners. The information we provide will get readers to think about what is important in the preparation of future teachers who will be teaching a more and more diverse group of students and how institutions of higher learning might best meet their needs.

TEACHER KNOWLEDGE AND CHARACTERISTICS

Traditional knowledge-based models for teacher training programs are guided by the goals and objectives of professional societies. For instance, the National Board for Professional Teaching Standards (NBPTS, 2001) agreed that teachers must be trained to be (a) committed to students and their learning, (b) know the subjects they teach and how to teach those subjects to students, (c) be responsible for managing and monitoring student learning, (d) think systematically about their practice and learn from experience, and (e) be members of learning communities. In addition, accreditation agencies, such as the National Council for Accreditation of Teacher Education (NCATE), serve as repositories and disseminators of various models of knowledge. As Christensen (1996) pointed out, however, ". . . knowledge based descriptions fail to support the concept of a single generally accepted knowledge base undergirding teacher education; rather, teaching and learning are extremely complex phenomena that trigger a vast array of knowledge" (p. 42). Some teacher preparation models are oriented toward pedagogical skill development, some toward humanistic enhancement of the teachers-in-training, and some toward developmental psychological awareness. Unfortunately, no one person could possibly master them all in any training program.

A good teacher knows himself/herself, knows about human development, and knows how to run a classroom. Good teachers are defined as those who bring about optimal levels of learning for all students; if they're teaching reading, then children learn to read; if they're teaching arithmetic, then children learn arithmetic; and, if they're teaching morals, then children behave in a morally responsible way. Good teachers teach with results. Like the Greeks, good teachers teach the whole child. They realize that their professional contributions are beneficial to children and society at large, and they are proud of their profession. It is important that teachers know themselves and have a firm understanding of who they are and why they are in education. This requires a reflective and contemplative orientation to self. Cruickshank (1987) noted that reflective teachers are self-critical and constantly engage in a process of reflection and introspection. They question themselves on a daily basis about their teaching, progress, integrity, and professionalism. Critical self-reflection is an ongoing process of improvement.

One way to know oneself is to develop a sound moral philosophy. Strike (1996) noted that there is an association between ethics and good teaching and indicated that "trustworthiness, caring, and integrity are internal to good teaching . . . people learn moral concepts, learn how to attach them to the world, and acquire virtues required to sustain them in practice by being initiated into the practices of such [moral] communities" (p. 882). He further stated that teachers need the moral knowledge to balance the conflicting values in the classroom. In short, teachers need to have a sound philosophical base upon which the elements of good teaching are founded. In the words of Strike:

> Given the argument to this point, the considerations of practices that will facilitate ethical competence among educational professionals needs to address three topics. The first is a discussion of classroom practices for teaching ethics; the second is the characteristics of schools as moral communities;

and the third is the characteristics of an educational profession that sustains moral competence in such institutions. (p. 881)

This mandate implies that teachers develop a sound philosophy of life and of education. It also implies that teachers realize their role as teacher and educator. Teachers are role models and students look up to them for guidance, wisdom, and insights. As Gow (1989) so aptly stated,

> Clearly in our institutions of learning we need to reemphasize the kind of education that cultivates the minds and character, that communicates and affirms ethical normality, and that helps young people develop the moral and intellectual discernment needed to distinguish between true and false, right and wrong, noble and base. (p. 85)

Obviously, teachers must know the difference between good and bad, right from wrong, true from false, and noble from base.

The NBPTS (2001) stressed the importance of proper attitudes in the following statement about teachers:

> Character and competence contribute equally to their educative manner. They exemplify the virtues they seek to impart to students: curiosity and a love of learning; tolerance and open-mindedness; fairness and justice; appreciation for our cultural and intellectual heritages; respect for human diversity and dignity; and such intellectual capacities as careful reasoning, the ability to take multiple perspectives, to question received wisdom, to be creative, to take risks, and to adopt an experimental and problem-solving orientation. (p. 2)

The N1BPTS (2001) noted that morals and ethics are an integral component of effective teaching to such a degree that they should not be neglected in the curriculum of teacher training institutions. This statement captures the importance of character as a mediating variable influencing not only the teacher, but more importantly, the student, the subject matter, and the environment of the classroom as well. The character and morals of the teacher combine to produce a caring and loving environment. It is evident that a positive and enhancing classroom environment cannot be overstated especially since it contributes to overall learning and classroom management (Noddings, 1992). A well grounded philosophical approach to life, dignity, and education will posit a trusting and mutually responsible environment (Shimahara & Sakai, 1995). The skillful teacher assumes the role of a good coach and looks for the strengths of each student and attempts to use these strengths in order to bring about the greatest change and optimal growth of the student. Every year every coach in every sport reassesses his/her team and looks for strengths of individuals and strengths of the team in order to orchestrate a successful season. And, as in coaching, successful teams are built around successful players.

THEORIES, METHODS, AND STRATEGIES FOR FUTURE TEACHERS

The theories of learning can have a direct impact on the way instruction is implemented. Teachers must be prepared to know, explain, and analyze these theories. It is not enough to say, "I am eclectic" as a defense for theoretical ignorance. Teachers need to know what these theories mean and how they affect learning and teaching. The following sub-sections discuss these theories.

Constructivist Learning Theory

The most contemporary model of learning at the turn of this century is the constructivist model, wherein students construct meaning to information in the form of knowledge. A constructivist orientation places the construction of meaning on the student by actively involving him or her in the learning process. The student actively constructs the meaning of information.

Behavioral Learning Theory

Behavioral learning strategies involve the use of reinforcement and forms of extinction in order to shape behaviors and influence learning. Behavioral theories help general and special educators to guide students from external controls over their behaviors toward intrinsic, self-control over behaviors.

Direct Instruction

Direct instruction is usually represented through a set of behaviorally-oriented teaching procedures. The term began as a general description of effective teaching behaviors (e.g., Rosenshine, 1976) and moved to a more comprehensive view that included not only effective instruction but also curriculum design, classroom management, and teacher preparation (Gersten, Woodward, & Darch, 1986). The term then became officially known as direct instruction (DI) (Engelman & Carnine, 1982; Gersten & Keating, 1987) with a prescriptive set of instructional materials for teachers to insure that effective teaching behaviors are incorporated into individual lessons (Kavale & Forness, 1999; White, 1988). Each DI program is structured around six essential features (see Gersten, Carnine, & Woodward, 1987):

1. An explicit step-by-step strategy.
2. Development of mastery at each step.

3. Immediate corrective feedback for student errors.
4. Gradual fading from teacher-led to student independence.
5. Systematic practice with a range of examples to implement.
6. Cumulative review of newly learned concepts.

Mastery Learning

Mastery learning is a process of continued teaching and testing until each child had achieved a specific level of mastery. The teacher using a mastery learning approach would have her students tested frequently and their progress monitored just as frequently. Some of the steps involved in mastery learning are (a) specifying what is to be learned; (b) motivating students; (c) providing materials to foster learning; (d) presenting materials at differential rates depending on student progress; (e) monitoring progress; (f) diagnosing learning difficulties and providing remediation; (g) giving specific praise and encouragement for good performance; (h) giving review and practice; and (i) maintaining a high rate of learning over time.

Attribution Theory

One of the more recent theories of motivation that has a direct influence on the psychology of learning is attribution theory, a construct that accounts for how children internalize success and failure (Weiner, 1979). Through this attributional orientation general and special educators are given insight in terms of how children internalize their successes and failures and more importantly, how these internalizations influence a child's expectancy for success or failure in future activities. Essentially, four attributes to which a child will base the causes of his or her success are *ability, effort, luck,* or *task difficulty*. Failures, hopefully, should be attributed to the lack of effort, strategy use, or effective strategy, while successes should be attributed to positive effort towards the task and effective strategy use. When students attribute failures and/or successes to outside sources, teachers must redirect these thoughts to students themselves.

Seligman (1975) noted that some children have an orientation referred to as learned helplessness, which is a predisposition of belief that it is futile to try under any circumstance since they feel too inadequate to try to accomplish anything. Some children are too predisposed to failure, whether it is situationally specific or a generalized expectancy for failure. As MacMillan (1982) pointed out, children who have experienced an excess of academic failure, such as individuals with mild to moderate mental retardation "tend to use an excess of energy in avoidance behaviors. After repeated failure . . . the child can resort to (1) noninvolvement, (2) token observance of tasks, or (3) reducing the sense of failure by not competing" (p. 402). He noted that each of these behaviors is an impediment to cognitive growth. As teachers, it is important to watch children closely and individually so that avoidance behavior does not end up as patterns of learned helplessness. The critical mandate is to provide a sufficient degree of challenge to each student on an individual basis without running the risk of making the challenge a deterrent to motivation. In fact, the motto should be "out of reach, but not out of sight."

Assistive Technology and Computer Assisted Instruction (CAI)

Generally, CAI has been found advantageous in general education (e.g., Niemic, Samson, Weinstein, & Walberg, 1987), and CAI has also been incorporated into special education programs and classrooms (e.g., Budoff, Thormann, & Gras, 1984; Lewis, 1993). The use of CAI may take a variety of forms including problem solving, games, guided practice, tutorials, simulations, and discovery learning (Malouf, Jamison, Kercher, & Carlucci, 1991). CAI has been useful in reading, writing, math, and critical thinking (e.g., Lieber & Semmel, 1985). Bakken and Whedon (2001) implemented a survey to investigate perceptions of general and special education teachers from two midwestern states to ascertain what they knew about assistive technology. All teachers had a difficult time defining assistive technology and their responses to different kinds of assistive technologies they have heard about and used were limited. Special education teachers, however, were able to list more types of assistive technologies. Most teachers, however, felt uncomfortable teaching a person how to use most of the assistive technologies they listed. Also, many did not know the difference between high and low-tech assistive technologies. In regards to education on assistive technology, 58 percent of special educators and only 14 percent of general educators indicated they had at least one course on assistive technology. All special educators had at least one course where assistive technology was addressed, while 32 percent of general educators never had even one course where it was addressed. Finally, all special educators attended at least one assistive technology workshop while over 80 percent of general educators had never attended a workshop on assistive technology. The findings of this investigation clearly indicate that general and special education teachers need to be more educated on what exactly assistive technology is, become trained in assessing students needs with regard to assistive technology, and trained in implementing those assistive technologies.

FIELD EXPERIENCES IN TEACHER PREPARATION

> Field experiences and clinical practice are integral program components for the initial preparation of teacher candidates and candidates for other school personnel roles. They provide the opportunity for candidates to apply their knowledge, skills, and dispositions in a variety of settings appropriate to the content and level of their program...Student teaching or an internship is the culminating experience for teacher candidates...Field experiences and clinical practice are characterized by collaboration, accountability, and an environment and practices associated with professional learning. (NCATE, 2000, p. 15)

With massive teacher shortages and a high mortality rate of new teachers in their first three to five years in the profession, the importance of high quality field experiences for teacher education candidates has never been more crucial than at this present time. The ability to observe, apply, test, and reflect in a "real world" context on the theories and concepts previously learned is essential if entering teachers are to have a sound grasp of realities and demands of not only the classroom and the teaching process but also expectations encompassed in the culture of the school (McIntyre, Byrd, & Foxx, 1996). Preservice teachers need quality field experiences throughout their training. Quality field experiences are designed to synthesize, enrich, and extend the knowledge and methods received by preservice education majors in their formal courses and seminars. There is a clear consensus among researchers, educational leaders, teacher unions, and national accrediting bodies on the importance of quality field experiences for preservice teachers (Goodlad, 1990b; Knowles & Cole, 1996; Feldman, 2000; Riley, 2000; NCATE).

Although reform efforts and national accreditation agencies have emphasized the importance of field experiences for preservice teachers (e.g., NCATE, 2000), there is no consensus on how and what constitutes an effective field experience. There is no guarantee that merely increasing the frequency and/or duration of the field experience will increase the quality, effectiveness, or competencies of the teacher education candidates. The U.S. Department of Education echoed this concern in a report entitled, *Teacher Quality Initiative*. The report delineated a series of major issues needed to be addressed if public schools are to have quality-trained teachers (Riley, 2000). The need for quality field experiences for preservice majors was specifically addressed under the heading of "Inadequate and Poorly Structured Curriculum." As Riley explained, "Inadequate field experiences that come too late in a teacher education program, are too short to provide adequate teaching practice, and are not focused on preparing teachers to teach where they are needed most" (p.12). Compounding Riley's concern about the field experience is the lack of "high-quality supervising teachers" needed to provide the guidance, support, and example as mentors necessary for the full development of the preservice teacher. Interestingly, Riley's apprehensions were previously articulated by Knowles and Cole (1996), when they stated, ". . . field experience, though commonly touted as the most meaningful part of preservice teacher preparation, is not without its flaws and does not escape criticism" (p. 648). They added that most field experiences are ". . . too short, too structured, too focused on the immediacy of classroom action, and too detached from the personal; consequently, they often provide little more than superficial, 'rites of passage' experiences" (p. 655).

Elements of a Quality Field Experience

There are many perspectives on what constitutes a quality field experience (Knowles & Cole, 1996). A quality field experience examines (a) the organizational relationship between program and the participating school, (b) the characteristics of the cooperating teacher, (c) the attributes of the university supervisor, and (d) the personal "legacy" of each preservice teacher candidate. It is evident that an active collaborative relationship between the participating schools and the college of education is essential to insure that the preservice teacher receives a quality experience. According to NCATE:

> The school and unit (i.e., college of education) share and integrate resources and expertise to support candidates' learning in field experiences and clinical practice. Both unit and school-based faculty are involved in designing, implementing, and evaluating the unit's conceptual framework(s) and the school program; they each participate in the unit's and school partners' professional development activities and instructional programs for candidates and for children. The unit and its school partners jointly determine the specific placements of student teachers and interns for other professional roles to maximize the learning experience for candidates and P-12 students. (p.13)

There should be a successful marriage between the theories expounded in the "Ivory Tower" and the realities experienced in the classroom. As a consequence, cooperating teachers should be actively involved in the development of the training program's goals. Riley (2000), in his report, emphasized that cooperating teachers are an effective part of the preservice experience and stressed that they should be compensated for their extra responsibilities as mentors.

Concerns have been present for many years about the role university/college supervisors and their relationships with preservice students (Boydell, 1991; Diamonti, 1977; Madsen & Kaiser, 1999). Although there are many attributes that an effective university supervisor requires (e.g., interpersonal skills, knowledge of pedagogy, understanding of the curriculum, knowledge of the schools, and basic counseling techniques), the relationship between the preservice student and the supervisor must be developed to the point where the two individuals can comfortably address the two persistent concerns that most student teachers experience. The first is the student's fear of being inadequately prepared in the discipline, and the second, the fear of failing as a teacher. Addressing these concerns will be the cornerstone of an effective relationship between supervisor and student.

Supervisors must understand the extent in which past experiences shape preservice teachers perceptions, expectations, and awareness of the entire educational environment (e.g., pedagogical approaches, expectations of students, the role of teachers, and purpose of schools). According to Knowles and Cole (1996), "students entering formal preservice preparation programs bring with them beliefs, attitudes, ideals, influences, and expectations developed over years of life experience and exposure to a wide variety of teaching and learning situations and contexts" (p. 564). They expressed a concern that most teacher education programs have a very narrow view of the student's field experiences. Instead of focusing almost exclusively on the dynamics found within the classroom walls, they argue that the "contextual realities" and the "complexity of the teaching" (p. 457) should be emphasized. As they described it ". . . most preservice preparation programs concentrate too almost entirely on teaching preservice teachers to teach; relatively little attention is placed on helping them become teachers . . ." (p. 457). Their concerns were reaffirmed by Potthoff, Dinsmore, Eifler, Stirtz, Walsh, and Ziebarth (2000) who found that providing students with broader experiences (e.g., involvement in community-based human service programs) increased their knowledge of democracy and diversity. Interestingly, the university faculty in the Potthoff et al. study (2000) were not as positive about the experience as their preservice students were. Paralleling these findings was the work of Sconzert, Iazzetto, and Purkey (2000) who reported that when preservice teachers from rural liberal arts institutions were actively in contact with each other, shared common living arrangements, were involved in professional development and culturally diverse activities, they had very successful experiences in urban schools during their student teaching assignments. Increasing the diversity and complexities of the field experiences enriches the development of the student. In the same dimension, Riley (2000) addressed the need for early field experiences in a variety of K-12 classrooms, with at least one field experience in an urban or high-poverty school before student teaching. When student teaching begins, it needs to be extended in duration "to provide a meaningful learning experience" (p. 12).

Innovative Programs for Integrating Field Experiences

There are many innovation programs attempting to address complexities of the classroom in the twenty-first century by insuring that preservice majors experience fuller and more enriched field experiences. Riley (2000) provided an example of a partnership that addresses many inherent problems currently faced by teacher training programs. He recognized the University of Cincinnati, Cincinnati Public Schools, and the Cincinnati Federation of Teachers for their efforts to provide a training program to preservice teachers that extends for five-year duration and includes a year-long paid internship as the culminating experience. Another example of a program that incorporates many of the key attributes of effective field experiences is the "Genesis" program at Florida Atlantic University (Messmore, 1994; Miller, 2001). As Miller explained, it is an inservice professional development model that facilitates the collaborative partnership between the College of Education, the university lab school, and the local school districts in surrounding counties. The partnership with the participating schools is designed to enhance professional development centers that implement actions and promote high-quality student learning that supports exemplary teaching practices. Four primary goals of the "Genesis" project include (a) mentoring and modeling exemplary teaching practices, (b) research-based school restructuring, (c) extended internships, and (d) sharing and collaboration between school and university faculty. To date, the program has received high praise for its efforts to integrate many of the key elements of an effective training program with rich, diverse, and multiple field experiences. See Table 1 for a listing of the key characteristics of the Genesis project (see Messmore, 1994).

CONCLUSION

In this chapter, we have highlighted some of the important facets of preparing teachers for all students. As we advance in this new century, we need teachers who have the characteristics and theoretical and practical knowledge to teach all learners. To teach is to impart not simply knowledge, but to facilitate the construction of meaning within the mind of a child. A teacher cannot expect to facilitate learning and the construction of meaning around units of knowledge in the absence of his or her belief system. Students learn far more in the teaching/learning process than simply facts, or systems or theories. The teaching/learning process involves both the spirit of teaching as much as the content of teaching. It is important that teacher training programs are guided by goals and objectives of professional societies and that

Table 1
CHARACTERISTICS OF THE GENESIS TEACHER EDUCATION PROJECT

- *Genesis* is an experimental teacher preparation program in the College of Education at Florida Atlantic University.
- *Genesis* is designed to prepare professional educators and give them a comprehensive elementary-secondary educational perspective.
- *Genesis* provides an effective model for preparing teachers for the inevitable, dynamic changes of the new millennium.
- *Genesis* brings together students and mentoring faculty in field-based experiences to address complex educational problems.
- *Genesis* students will be eligible for certification in elementary education, middle school education, high school education, and endorsement in ESOL education.
- *Genesis* students major in an area of liberal arts or science, *and* in education.
- *Genesis* students are taught by interdisciplinary mentoring faculty teams representing ESOL, elementary education, middle school education, high school education, counselor education, exceptional student education, and technology and research.
- *Genesis* students will become broadly educated, reflective, professional educators.
- *Genesis* students will be able to understand and work with issues in curricular and instructional design. They will also understand the development of children and youth and will be capable of addressing how both school and non-school experiences impact students' educational success.

they incorporate the needs of self, families, schools, communities, and the government into the teaching philosophy and process.

Good teachers must be knowledgeable, reflective, and problem-solvers who understand human growth and development, control their classroom, and teach the entire child. Teachers not only teach and convey knowledge, morals, and ethics, but also are approached by students for guidance, wisdom, and insights. Effective teachers must have a repertoire of skills and strategies to meet the needs of all students. It is important that our future teachers are educated on different learning theories, methods, and strategies so they can best address all aspects of their students. Knowing one method or strategy well is not enough to be effective. An effective teacher must know many methods and strategies to meet the individual needs of all students. They also must be able to critically think and problem-solve what method or strategy is most appropriate and reflect and assess how beneficial it is to the student.

In addition, field experiences are an instrumental variable in teacher education. These experiences are essential in the development of future teachers. A variety of experiences (from observational to actual teaching) throughout students, educational program (freshman through senior years) are needed so they can practice and develop as future teachers for all students. It is imperative that these programs have quality role models (i.e., cooperative teachers and supervisors) and classrooms with a diverse group of students. Finally, it is very important to have a collaborative component that addresses not only dealing with other teachers, but also families, schools, communities, and the government. Teachers must to reach out and establish positive relationships with these other entities to be the most effective teacher and to produce the best overall students. There is no simple solution, but if we all work together at educating our students it will be a more effective, beneficial, and fruitful endeavor.

REFERENCES

Bakken, J. P., & Whedon, C. K. (2001, April). *Teachers' perceptions and knowledge of assistive technologies for students with mild disabilities.* Paper presented at the Council for Exceptional Children's Annual International Convention, Kansas City, MO.

Boydell, D. (1991). Issues in teaching practice supervision research: A review of the literature, In L.G. Katz (Ed.), *Advances in teacher education* (pp. 115–125). Norwood, NJ: Ablex.

Budoff, M., Thormann, M. J., & Gras, A. (1984). *Microcomputers in special education: An introduction to instructional applications.* Cambridge, MA: Brookline.

Christensen, D. (1996). The professional knowledge-research base for teacher education. In J. Sikula, T. Buttery, & E. Guyton (Eds.), *Handbook of research on teacher education* (2nd ed., pp. 38–52). New York: MacMillan.

Cruickshank, D. R. (1987). *Reflective teaching: The preparation of students of teaching.* Reston, VA: Association of Teacher Educators.

Diamonti, M. (1977) Student teacher supervision. *Educational Forum, 41,* 477–486.

Engelmann, S., & Carnine, D. W. (1982). *Theory of instruction: Principles and applications.* New York: Irvington.

Feldman, S. (2000). AFT calls for higher standards for new teachers and teacher education programs. Building a profession. [On-line]. Available: *http://www.aft.org/stand/previous/2000/0600.html.*

Gersten, R., Carnine, D., & Woodward, J. (1987). Direct instruction research: The third decade. *Remedial and Special Education, 8,* 48–56.

Gersten, R., & Keating, T. (1987). Long-term benefits from direct instruction. *Educational Leadership, 44,* 28–31.

Gersten, R., Woodward, J., & Darch, C. (1986). Direct instruction: A research-based approach to curriculum design and teaching. *Exceptional Children, 53,* 17–31.

Goodlad, J. (1990b). Better teachers for our nation's schools. Phi Delta Kappan, 72, 184–194.

Gow, H. B. (1989). The true purpose of education. *Phi Delta Kappan, 70,* 545–546.

Kavale, K. A., & Forness, S. R. (1999). Effective intervention practices and special education. In G. N. Siperstein (Ed.), *Efficacy of special education and related services* (pp. 71–81). Washington, DC: The American Association on Mental Retardation.

Knowles, J. G. & Cole, A.L. (1996) Developing practice through field experiences, In F. Murray (Ed.), *The teacher educator's handbook: Building a knowledge base for the preparation of teachers* (pp. 648–688). San Francisco: Jossey-Bass.

Lewis, R. B. (1993). *Special education technology: Classroom applications.* Pacific Grove, CA: Brookes.

Lieber, J., & Semmel, M. I. (1985). Effectiveness of computer application to instruction with mildly handicapped learners: A review. *Remedial and Special Education, 6,* 5–12.

MacMillan, D.L. (1982). *Mental retardation in school and society* (2nd ed.). Boston: Little, Brown and Company.

Madsen, C., K., & Kaiser, K., (1999) Pre-internship fears of student teaching. *Applications of Research in Music Education, 17,* 27–32.

Malouf, D. B., Jamison, P. J., Kercher, M. H., & Carlucci, C. M. (1991). Integrating computer software into effective instruction. *Teaching Exceptional Children, 23,* 54–56.

McIntyre, J., Byrd, D., & Foxx, S. (1996). Field and laboratory experiences, In J. Sikula, T. Buttery, & E. Guyton (Eds.), *Handbook of research on teacher education* (2nd ed., pp. 171–193). New York: Macmillan.

Messmore, P. (1994) The genesis project. Boca Raton, FL: Florida Atlantic University *http://www.fau.edu/divdept/coe/genesis/intro.htm.*

Miller, C. (2001) Genesis Academy for Teaching Excellence (GATE), Florida Atlantic University *http://www.fau.edu/divdept/coe/gate/what_is.htm.*

National Board for Professional Teaching Standards. (2001, January). Proposition #4: Teachers think systematically about their practice and learn from experience. [On-line]. Available:*http://www.nbpts.org/standards/know_do/prop_4.html.*

NCATE (2000, May) *Unit standards.* Washington, DC: NCATE Accreditation Board.

Niemic, R., Samson, G., Weinstein, T., & Walberg, H. J. (1987). The effects of computer-based instruction in elementary schools: A quantitative synthesis. *Journal of Research on Computing in Education, 20,* 85–103.

Noddings, N. (1992). *The challenge to care in schools: An alternative approach to education.* New York: Teachers College Press.

Potthoff, D., Dinsmore, J., Eifler, K., Stirtz, G., Walsh, T., & Ziebarth, J. (2000) Preparing for democracy and diversity: The impact of a community-based field experience on preservice teachers' knowledge, skills, and attitudes. *Action in Teacher Education, 22*(1) 79–92.

Riley, R. (2000) *Teacher quality initiative.* Washington, DC: U.S. Department of Education.

Rosenshine, B. (1976). Classroom instruction. In N.L. Gage (Ed.), *The psychology of teaching methods: The seventy-fifth yearbook of the national society for the study of education* (pp. 109–143). Chicago: University of Chicago Press.

Seligman, M.E.P. (1975). *Helplessness: On depression, development, and death.* San Francisco: Freeman.

Sconzert, K., Iazzetto, D., & Purkey, S., (2000). Small-town college to big-city school: Preparing urban teachers from liberal arts colleges. *Teaching & Teacher Education, 16,* 465–490.

Shimahara, N.K., & Sakai, A. (1995). *Learning to teach in two cultures.* New York: Garland.

Strike, K.A. (1996). The moral responsibilities of educators. In J. Sikula, T.J. Buttery, & E. Guyton, (Eds.), *Handbook of research on teacher education* (pp 869–892). New York: Simon & Schuster.

Weiner, B. (1979). A theory of motivation for some classroom experiences. *Journal of Educational Psychology, 71,* 3–25.

White, W. A. T. (1988). A meta-analysis of effects of direct instruction in special education. *Education and Treatment of Children, 11,* 364–374.

Chapter 7

COMMUNITY INVOLVEMENT IN EDUCATION

ELIZABETH A. DOOLEY AND CHRISTINE M. TOSCANO-NIXON

Recently, there has been growing concern about the role of communities in building effective schools. The reason is that communities most often influence the quality of schools with their varying degrees of supports. These supports may or may not be consistent over time or they may not be consistent across communities. This chapter presents an overview of a community and problems associated with it. In addition, the power structure of communities is discussed to develop a framework for restructuring communities and building proactive relationships between the community and school.

DEFINING COMMUNITIES

A community is defined as a society of people having common rights and privileges, or common interests, civil, and political, and living under the same laws and regulations. Because of the heterogeneous nature of the society, there are many different types of communities. Communities take on many different forms and often times, social, political, cultural, economic norms, and/or values influence the capacity of the community. Typically, communities are either described as urban, suburban, or rural.

Each of these communities has different characteristics, and although these communities may experience certain challenges, there are some challenges more unique to each area. In addition, when schools are placed in a local context, they are regarded as being located in rural, urban, or suburban areas. These are communities in which children are being educated. Each community poses a different set of circumstances. Therefore, it is important to present those contexts that are commonly associated with schooling and the education of children and youth. As community members begin to engage in restructuring, they need to be acutely aware of challenges facing children and youth in their school. The following section highlights characteristics of different communities.

Urban Communities

An urbanized area includes places and their adjacent densely settled surrounding territory that together has a minimum population of 50,000 (U.S. Department of Commerce, 1992). Problems associated with urban communities range from violence, crime, guns, lack of role models, racism and ethnic prejudice, drugs and drinking, suicide, gangs, and homelessness (Pryor, Sarri, Bomby, & Nikolovska, 1999). There is a presumed loss of a collaborative community in urban areas, people seem isolated in their own worlds, and there appears to be little to no communication among community members. One very important point to make is the fact that youth living in urban areas recognize the problems associated with their communities. In a study on urban youths' views of violence in their communities, 350 students representing ethnic and different socioeconomic groups were asked to share their perceptions of their communities and they identified violence as the main problem (see Pryor et al.).

Suburban Communities

Suburban communities have been described as residential areas outlying a city. While parent involvement is high in this area (National Center for Education Statistics, 1994), there were problems associated with suburban communities. These problems are primarily moral, such as value differences, lack of political involvement, egotism, materialism, gossip, and the lack of unity. Another problem is the lack of community centers and/or establishments for youth to socialize.

Rural Communities

Rural communities have been defined as areas that are not urban, they are places with less than 2,500 people (US Census Bureau, 1994). According to the National Center for Education Statistics (1994), 43% of most districts are rural, 47% are nonrural and 10% include both rural and nonrural schools.

Rural schools exist in communities outside of a standard metropolitan statistical area, distant/remote from a large city, and in counties where the population density is low (Jacob-Timm, 1995). Most problems in rural areas are said to be due to inequalities. While inequalities persist, poverty continues to be a major concern and challenge for children living in poor rural communities (U.S. Department of Education, 1997). Many rural counties are referred to as the 535 rural persistent poverty (RPP) counties, and are defined as those counties below the poverty level in each of the census years 1960, 1970, 1980, and 1990 (U.S. Department of Agriculture, 1997). Problems associated with impoverished areas include deep social stratification and often times a dual educational system. Expectations of students in these areas are usually low. Jobs are scarce, so children do not see a direct benefit of their schooling. Rural schools are not supported financially and have fewer educational programs (Alexander, 1990). Another problem associated with rural communities is high staff turnover schools, lack of specialized services in the school and community, heavy caseload for school psychologists, and low salaries.

COMMUNITY INTERESTS AND POWERS IN EDUCATING ALL LEARNERS

The community plays an important role in educating all learners. As a result, the development, and implementation of a strategic plan to restructure communities are necessary. Three questions appear critical in this regard. How do communities play a role in the educational process? Who in the community is charged with the responsibility for initiating and continuing change? How do communities determine change is needed and then make those changes? Communities hold a vested interest in schools. Likewise, school systems contribute to the community through developing students who are productive citizens and give back to their community. Preparation of students is a shared process between the school, home, and community. In fact, preparing students for the challenges of tomorrow is a common goal among parents, teachers, and community members/organizations (Springate & Stegelin, 1999). The learning environment created in the community can influence how students perform in school and grow. The values, mores, and beliefs held by community members are often imprinted into the school environment. The belief system held in a community is unique to that particular community. While the positive influences within a community can promote school achievement among students, the negative influences could interfere or hinder progress. When negative influences persist and very few community supports exist, all members, citizens, regardless of parental status must play a role in helping to define positive educational and social outcomes of children and youth within those communities.

Role of Community

Communities are vital to the comprehensive development of students. They play a supportive role in educational systems. This supportive role positively affects the growth and development of students both academically and social-emotionally. Frequently, students have little or no control over environmental influences that are critical to their success. The ecological systems theory developed by Bronfenbrenner (1979) defines the role that the community plays in educating all students. Based on the ecological systems theory, each student's development is embedded in a series interrelated environmental systems including the macrosystem (i.e., historical events and broader cultures), exosystem (i.e., parent's workplace, social networks, and local government), mesosystem (i.e., day care centers, school, and peer systems), and microsystem (i.e., home, child, mother, and father) (Springate & Stegelin, 1999).

The successful performance of students can be attributed to the overall contributions of environmental systems in the community. For example, a student's school performance, health, and development of self-concept can be influenced by interactions and relationships of the four levels of environmental systems. The levels within the ecological systems model are hierarchical. The microsystem, lowest level, contains individuals and events that have a direct influence on the student. Family members, school, and church are examples of relationships within the microsystems level. The mesosystem consists of environments in which the people actively participate in (such as, for a child, the relations between home, school, and neighborhood peer groups) (Bronfenbrenner in Peck, Odom, & Bricker, 1993). As part of the mesosystem, the community can play an integral role in shaping and protecting students by creating supportive programs and activities, building a bridge with educational systems, and fostering an environment which is free of negative peer influences. The exosystem is the third level of ecological systems. It is characterized as environments that do not involve people as active participants, but in which events occur that affect, or are affected by, what happens in the environment containing the child (Bronfenbrenner, 1979 in Peck, et al). Events in the exosystem that are community-based include legislation, town meetings, community initiatives, and employment opportunities. Finally, the macrosystem encompasses all lower levels of ecological systems. The macrosystem contains broader cultural contexts that exist among the microsystem, mesosystem, and the exosystem. The macrosystem level is an important level for lasting change. Organizational structures, professional practices, and cultural beliefs are issues often targeted for change in the macrosystem. For example, a change in the professional dress code of educators may change the way the community perceives the school's commitment to their professional standards and practice. In turn, the community may be more willing to support levies and bonds that could provide additional programs and supplies for students.

It is important to note that the ecological systems theory demonstrates that students can be directly and indirectly affected by events or actions in the environment. These events or actions can create short-term and long-term changes that positively or negatively influence students. Communities should accept their moral obligation to students by making the choice to be actively involved in them and helping them grow. Communities focusing on the education of children will identify those events and actions that lead to lasting and substantial change.

Context of Communities

In order to protect children of respective communities, community members must work together to promote positive change and community reform. Morrison and Howard (1997) indicated that "many urban neighborhoods are in trouble, as are the youths and families who reside in them" (p. 527). A closer look at problems that students are having in communities sheds light into problems they are having in schools. Upon entering school, children and youth do not leave their problems at the school doorstep. Likewise, problems are not simply dropped off in their lockers with the rest of their baggage. This is a difficult task even for most sophisticated and professional adults. The statement made by Morrison and Howard also suggested that schools are in trouble, and in order to strengthen them, neighborhoods must be strengthened. Communities are often characterized by the outcome of their reform efforts. There are many methods that have been attempted to strengthen the community. Following are discussions on variety of categories:

Dysfunctional and Struggling Communities

In dysfunctional communities, often the problem can be traced back to either the role that community members are playing or the direction that community members are following. In order to meet demands in today's society, individuals may fail to accept their responsibility to a community. In these communities, there is little participation in the change process. Figure 1 illustrates an example of a community power structure where the school

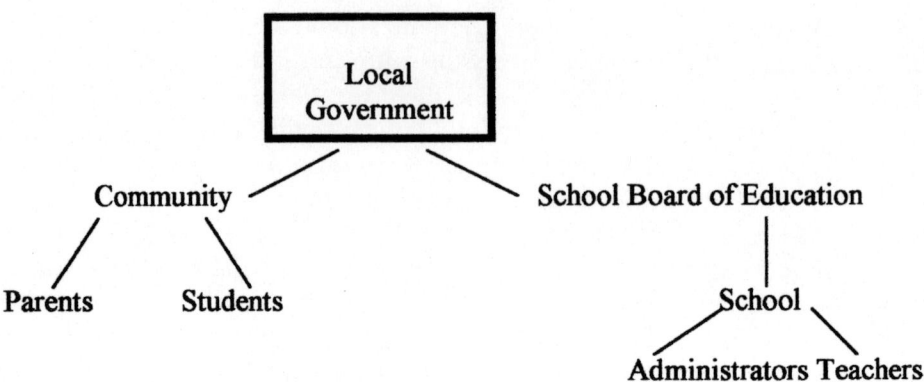

Figure 1. Dysfunctional Community Model

board of education and the local government operate as separate entities. In dysfunctional communities, the local government and school board are disconnected which leads to a lack of accountability by the school board. According to Bjork and Lindle (2001), the community is defined as inert and the school board is seen as sanctioning. As a result, the school board members become independent decision-makers. In this particular community power structure, the local government assumes little, if any, financial responsibility of the school system.

Borderline Communities

In these communities, there is minimal community participation and the citizens rely heavily on the government to impose changes. See Figure 2 below. In borderline communities, the local government maintains fiscal responsibility. In this power structure, the local government is described as dominant and the school board is described as dominant. The superintendent serves as a functionary to the community. Although this power structure yields some result, it does not support community-based collaboration. While community members play a role in the education of students, they may lack direction, initiative, and a common goal. Therefore, little change is observed from their efforts. Educationally-based decisions are controlled by the availability of funding through the local government; education may or may not be a priority for local officials.

It is important to note that the role of community leaders is to initiate and maintain change. In situations in which parents or other community members lack skills or the political savvy to invoke change, it is up to elected officials to assume greater political responsibility and assume ownership of failing

Figure 2. Borderline Community Model

communities. Typically, local officials are responsible for carrying out the restructuring of communities for educational benefit. Portz (2000) agreed that mayors are becoming the "saviors" of urban education. Many are beginning to recognize the importance of elected officials playing a major role in the renewal of many communities in the midst of grave hardships. Portz also stated that "mayoral leadership is needed to bring full engagement of the communities to public education and ensure accountability of the school system" (p. 397). These leadership changes have been identified in Chicago, Illinois, Boston, Cleveland, and Detroit (Wong & Jain, 1999; Ziebarth, 1999). Many of these cases cited that elected board members were replaced with an appointed school board having managerial and fiscal responsibility over the public school. This type of change where the public school is run by politicians has not been easy, and in some cases, change has occurred slowly, but the end result has been extremely positive because what has emerged is a unified system for educating all children. The mayor, superintendent, and school administrator all have a commitment to improving public education. In Boston, the mayor for example has made education a priority, and as a result, funding for education has increased by 34% between fiscal years 1994–1999. In fact, Portz pointed out that:

> Boston's mayoral path to school reform has resulted in a number of important accomplishments. Central to this success has been institutional alignment and strong leadership. The new alignment between the school system and city hall has clarified political and fiscal accountability. Accountability was fragmented under the elected school committee; school committee members were elected to guide the system, but they lacked overall fiscal authority. With mayoral appointment of the school committee, the mayor has assumed both political and fiscal responsibility. In turn, the mayor's leadership has rallied support for the schools system and directed resources to sustain reform efforts. (pp. 405–406)

While there is merit in Figure 2, especially in securing financial support, there is still the need for parents to be devoted to having input in their child's education. As Delpit (1988) so eloquently stated, "Appropriate education for poor children and children of color can only be devised in consultation with adults who share their culture. Black parents, teachers of color, and members of poor communities must be allowed to participate fully in the discussion of what kind of instruction is in their children's best interest" (p. 296). This is not only true for poor and children of color, all children can benefit from parental and teacher involvement.

RESTRUCTURING COMMUNITIES TO BENEFIT ALL LEARNERS

To restructure communities, all stakeholders have invaluable roles to play. The purpose of the restructuring process must be to increase community involvement and the role that communities play in better educating all children. Community restructuring is a complex and gradual process. Community restructuring has been defined in a broad range of terms that include "community capacity building" (Chaskin, 2001), "community development" (Glickman & Servon, 1997), and "community planning" (Gittell, Newman, & Ortega, 1995; Goodman et al., 1998). Typically, the definitions of community restructuring are narrow in scope and range and tend to emphasize only certain aspects of community restructuring. Community restructuring is a multifaceted process, whereby all members of the community endeavor to be conscientious and more cognizant of their role in initiating proactive changes within the community. This conscientious approach to community reform fosters goal-oriented networks, creates supportive community membership of all stakeholders, buttresses collaborative-based models, and leads members within the community to redefine funding structures.

Conscientious Communities

A conscientious community is one in which all members assume their social and moral responsibility to contribute to their community's social and economic growth and sustainability. As a result, schools within those communities are held in high regard and community members, school personnel, and others work together to maximize student success. In addition, family participation is encouraged. Members of the conscientious community recognize the relevance and importance of community-based collaboration between multi-agencies. See Figure 3 below. In community based collaborative models, Arllen, Cheney & Warger (1997) identified the following factors as essential:

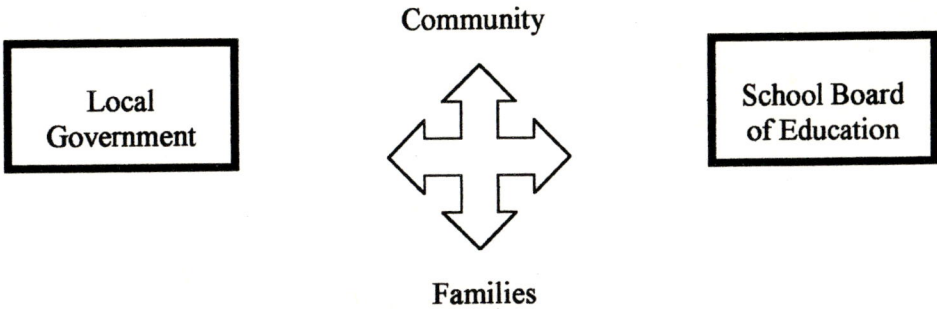

Figure 3. Conscientious Communities

1. The strengths and needs of the child and family must drive all services.
2. Services must be comprehensive and cohesive.
3. All participants must value cultural backgrounds and norms.
4. Stable funding and other resources must be attached to community-based efforts.
5. Quality evaluation of services and program is essential.

In a conscientious community, all individuals and organizations holding membership are responsible for the education of students. When youth are directly involved with proactive social organizations such as schools, churches, agencies, and clubs, they tend to avoid antisocial behaviors (Chavkin, 2000). Community membership is comprised of students, parents, non-parents, social organizations, and businesses. Individuals within a community may hold membership both as community members, as parents, employees, and employers within the community. For example, a teacher may be a parent as well as work within a community's school. Therefore, their responsibility to the community may be even greater in reaching out to give back to those in the community. There are also individuals who live within different communities than the community in which they work, this is a common pattern in today's society as suburban areas increase in population. Unfortunately, for many communities, this situation presents a growing problem. Although individuals take from the community in which they work, they give little back to the future development. In preparing students for tomorrow, communities must be dependent upon all individuals whether their membership is short-term or long-term.

In a conscientious community, social organizations within the community play a role in working with students and families. Primarily, social organizations contribute to the nurturing of communities by developing community networks. These networks should be comprised of all human service professionals who are trained to collaborate with one another. However, when communities relate to schools, several key players are involved (e.g., those who make specific contributions to the community including local governments such as mayors, local board of education, and the superintendent of the local school system). In order for restructuring to take place, the specific needs of any community must be met. Obviously, the needs vary based upon demographics and variables of any one community. Given the variability across and within communities, it is difficult to prescribe a single formula for building community capacity. Because of the complex nature of communities, each community must assess its strengths and weaknesses and then begin to build bridges between organizations and community groups and the local schools. Neighborhoods must be strengthened by developing community networks, these networks should be comprised of all human service professionals. Additionally, to develop nurturing communities, there must be a bridge between the community and the school—such a bridge will crease parental involvement necessary in the education of children and youth. As organizations begin to collaborate, parents need to be integrated into the network as stakeholders. Epstein (1992) described the synergistic relationship between parents, schools, agencies, businesses, cultural organizations, and other groups in the education of children. In most cases, these relationships help create access to services and supports.

In a conscientious community, the larger society serves as the economical base. If schools are suffering because of the lack of adequate financial support, then it makes sense to seriously rethink how neighborhood schools are being funded. When addressing issues of funding, it is necessary to look at current funding structures; assess whether the current structure provides equitable resources across schools; and determine best reform efforts. Most reforms concerning school funding are directed at changing the ways in which schools are funded. For example, financing schools through the local property tax is viewed as ineffective because there are disparities in property value (Gittell & McKenna, 1999). Because schools in predominantly urban and rural areas are not funded at the same level as schools in suburban America or those areas with a substantially higher tax base, fewer resources are available for establishing and maintaining quality educational programs in urban communities. As conditions worsen, members of various constituent groups within the community begin to question the commitment towards educational outcomes for children and youth.

Gittell and McKenna (1999) conducted a nine-state study on politics and education between 1995 and 1997. In their study, they interviewed individuals such as city council members, city and state superintendents, gubernatorial staff, legislative members and their staff, union representatives, business executives, education advocates, university faculty, directors of professional associations, and mayoral staff. They reported that most individuals mentioned the need for additional state funding to address issues of high dropout rates, student failure to pass basic competency tests, and poor quality teachers. It was clear from this particular study that funding is unlikely without community advocacy and gubernatorial and legislative supports. When funding is unlikely or minimum funding is available, other reform efforts must occur. Communities within the larger society must begin to position themselves within the larger framework to begin coalition and capacity building–this can be done through the development of community networks and the creation of an agenda that specially addresses the needs of individual communities. While there are varying degrees of income, a community can only be conscientious when its members accept their social and moral responsibilities.

BUILDING PROACTIVE COMMUNITY/SCHOOL LINKAGES

According to Chaskin (2001), community capacity is based on four fundamental characteristics: sense of community, level of commitment among community members, ability to solve problems, and access to resources. Proactive community linkages entail the involvement of community members in the school and the ability of the community to unite with the school to play a role in educating students. To implement proactive restructuring techniques that actively evaluate community needs and make changes based on needs, efforts must be made to evaluate the current infrastructure in place and local needs, and gain the attention of all members of the community. As community members begin the restructuring process, the following are recommended.

1. Building community capacity for change–this includes:
    a. Developing human capital (i.e., skills and knowledge) by providing educational and employment opportunities.
    b. Developing social capital such as relationship building that includes opportunities for information flow, social norms, expectations, obligations, sanctions, and trust within the community (Colman & Hoffer, 1987).
    c. Developing educational opportunities.
    d. Developing an evaluation plan.
2. Evaluate current capacity–this includes:
    a. Assessing the number and type of community supports currently in place.
    b. Assessing the nature of community school partnerships.
    c. Assessing the level of funding for community support organizations.

d. Identifying funding sources.
   e. Assessing employment opportunities.
   f. Determining business school partnerships.
3. Gain the attention of all members of the community—this includes:
   a. Forming equal partnerships with representatives of government, education (including higher education), economic development agencies, extension, churches/heritage institutions, civic groups, foundation, public/private entities, local media, and families.
   b. Creating new opportunities and infrastructures for young people to stay in and assist in the development of their own communities (Carter, 1999).

CONCLUSION

In this chapter, we have demonstrated that community is a very complex concept and at times appears to be abstract because any given community is defined by citizens who reside in them. Often times, the citizens are influenced and/ or controlled by factors in which they have limited or no control. It is also evident that without a clear focus and without a designated leader or organization, there is no clear infrastructure upon which the communities can function. Without an infrastructure in place, it is difficult for communities to effectively interface with schools. We believe communities need to have standards, expectations, and a structures in place to support children and youth. While it makes sense for communities to have high standards, they must have support. Parents within communities must feel as if they have a sense of control over the outcome of their children's lives. We cannot restructure communities without the family, and we cannot bridge the gap between the community and the school without parental involvement. With a Comprehensive Support Model (CSM) as devised in Chapter 1, conscientious communities can be developed to allow all entities within the community not only to play major roles but also to educate all children. We must begin to recognize schools as places to provide direct educational services to our youth that cannot operate sufficiently without the support of parents and community members. In the end, we must understand that schools make communities, and communities make schools.

REFERENCES

Alexander, K. (1990). Rural education: Institutionalization of disadvantage. *Journal of Education Finance, 16* (2), 121.

Arllen, N., Cheney, D., & Warger, C. (1997). Recapturing the promise of a future Imperiled: Ways to make community-based collaboration work. In L. Bullock & R. Gable (Eds.), *Making collaboration work for children, youth, families, schools, and communities* (pp. 39–43). Reston, VA: Council for Exceptional Children.

Bickel, R., & Lange, L (1995). Opportunities, costs, and high school completion in an Appalachian state: A near-replication of Florida research. *Journal of Educational Research, 88* (6), 363–370.

Bjork, L., & Lindle, J. C. (2001). Superintendents and interests groups. *Educational Policy, 15* (1), 76–91.

Bronfenbrenner, U. (1979). *The ecology of human development.* Cambridge, MA: Harvard University Press.

Carter, C. S. (1999). Education and development in poor rural communities: An interdisciplinary research agenda. [On-line]. Available: http://www.ed.giv/database/ERIC_Digests/ed438154.html

Chaskin, R. J. (2001). Building community capacity. *Urban Affairs Review, 36,* 291–324.

Chavkin, N. (2000). Family and community involvement policies: Teachers can lead the way. *Clearing House, 73,* 287–290.

Colman, J. (1988). Social capital in the creation of human capital. *American Journal of Sociology, 94,* S95–S120.

Coleman, J.S., & Hoffer, T. (1987) *Public and private high schools: The impact of community.* New York: Basic Books.

Delpit, L. D. (1988). The silenced dialogue: Power and pedagogy in educating other people's children. *Harvard Educational Review, 58,* 280–298.

Epstein, J. (1992). School and family partnerships. In M. Alkin (Ed.), *Encyclopedia of educational research* (pp. 1139–11510). New York: Macmillan.

Gittell, M., & McKenna, (1999). Redefining education regimes and reform the political role of governors. *Urban Education, 34,* 268–291.

Gittell, M., Newman, K., & Ortega, I. (1995, May). *Building civic capacity: Best CDC practices.* Paper presented at the annual Urban Affairs Conference, Portland, OR.

Glickman, N., & Servon, L. (1997). *More than bricks and sticks: What is community development capacity?* New Brunswick, NJ: Center for Urban Policy Research.

Goodman, R. M., Speers, L., McLeroy, K., Fawcett, S., Kegler, M., Parker, E., Smith, S.R., Sterling, T.D., & Wallerstein, N. (1998). Identifying and defining the dimensions of community capacity to provide a basis for measurement. *Health Education and Behavior, 25,* 258–278.

Eddowes, A. (1993). Education of younger homeless children in urban settings. *Education & Urban Society, 25,* 381.

Ianni, F.A. (1989). *The search for structure: A report on American youth today.* New York: Free Press.

Jacob-Timm, S. (1995). Best practices in facilitating services in rural settings. In A. Thomas & J. Grimes (Eds.), *Best practices in school psychology-III* (pp. 301–309). Washington, DC: The National Association of School Psychologists.

Morrison, J., & Horward, J. (1997). Strengthening neighborhoods by developing community networks. *Social Work,* pp. 527–534.

National Center for Educational Statistics. (1994). *Parent involvement in education.* Washington, DC: Office of Educational Research and Improvement.

Peck, C. A., Odom, S. L., & Bricker, D. D. (1993). *Integrating young children with disabilities into community programs.* Baltimore, MD: Paul H. Brookes.

Portz, J. (2000). Supporting education reform mayoral and corporate paths. *Urban Education, 35,* 396–417.

Pryor, C.B., Sarri, R. C., Bombyk, M., & Nikolovska, L. (1999). Urban youths' views of violence in their communities: Implications for schools. *Social Work in Education, 21,* 72–88.

Springate, K. W., & Stegelin, D. A. (1999). *Building school and community partnerships through parent involvement.* Columbus, OH: Merrill/Prentice Hall.

U.S. Bureau of the Census. (1994). *Census of the population: County and city data book.* Washington, DC: U.S. Government Printing Office.

U.S. Department of Agriculture, Economic Research Service. (1997). County types: Persistent poverty counties in understanding rural America. [On-line]. Available: http://www.econ.ag.gov/epubs/htmldoc/aib710/aib710.htm

U.S Department of Education, Office of Educational research and Improvement. (1997). National Institute on the Education of At-Risk Students. [On-line]. Available: http://www.ed.gov/offices/OERI/At0Risk

Wong, K., & Jain, P. (1999). *Mayors and schools: Integrated governance and educational accountability.* Paper presented at the annual meeting of the American Political Science Association, Atlanta, GA.

Ziebarth, T. (1999). *State takeovers and reconstitutions policy brief.* Denver, CO: Education Commission of States.

Chapter 8

PROFESSIONAL DEVELOPMENT: AN ESSENTIAL COMPONENT FOR EDUCATING TEACHERS AS LIFELONG LEARNERS

Cheryl A. Utley, Festus E. Obiakor, and Bridgie Alexis Ford

In the twenty-first century, schools must rethink the nature and purpose of professional development activities in relation to their school's mission, examine their current structure and organization, and identify concerns of their teaching staff. Professional development programs must be viewed as a potentially vital source of scaling up the use of effective teaching practices and improving student outcomes. There is little evidence to support the continued use of a "traditional one-shot in-service training" workshop as a teacher training format. The lessons learned from professional and staff development research conducted in the 1970s and 1980s suggest that even though significant advances have been made in understanding effective teaching practices, there is a continued need for lifelong professional development for teachers.

Most professional development programs provide teachers with little or no training in appropriate assessment strategies to use in the classroom and allocate little time during the day for teachers to collaborate, discuss their problems, or share information about what they do know about assessment (Hargreaves, 1997; Wilson & Daviss, 1994). Unfortunately, most school districts lack experience with professional development activities that have a demonstrated record of fostering positive change. This chapter (a) addresses the professional development concerns of teachers; (b) describes key features of effective professional development programs (e.g., teachers' beliefs, teacher thinking, and school context variables), (c) identifies key features of professional development programs, and (d) describes components of a multicultural professional development training program in the comprehensive support model (CSM).

DEMOGRAPHIC CHALLENGES FACING U.S. SCHOOLS: RATIONALE FOR PROFESSIONAL DEVELOPMENT

The growing number of culturally diverse students in the society and schools constitutes a demographic imperative that educator and Schools of Education must respond to. In 1980, culturally diverse teachers in our nation's schools made up 12.5% of the teaching force (Banks, 1997). In fact, culturally diverse teachers of color are deplorably underrepresented in schools: of the 2.3 million teachers in the United States, about 10% are described as minority and this number has decreased recently and is expected to decline even further (U.S. Bureau of the Census, 1993). The percentage of culturally diverse students in the nation's schools is rapidly increasing as the percentage of culturally diverse teachers is declining precipitously. Succinctly stated, the majority of educators appear to be Anglo American, monolingual speakers of English and the composition of the teaching force does not reflect the changing ethnic and language composition of children to be served (Obiakor & Schwenn, 1995; Utley & Obiakor, 2001 Zeichner, 1993). Because of the changing demographics of society and student population, a large percentage of teachers work with students who differ from them racially, culturally, linguistically, and in social-class status. In addition, there is increasing evidence that urban schools tend to be negatively impacted by many variables such as limited financial and material resources, teacher burnout, overpopulated classes, and violence in the communities. Even with the glaring nature of these problems, school districts consistently fail to provide culturally relevant professional development training for their teachers, therefore, increasing the dangerous potential for misidentification, misassessment, misplacement, and misinstruction of culturally diverse students (Obiakor, 1994; 1999).

PROFESSIONAL DEVELOPMENT CHALLENGES

The hiring of underprepared teachers and unequal distribution of well-qualified teachers in the nation's schools is a major obstacle to providing an equitable education for all children. The National Commission on Teaching and America's Future (1996) reported that (a) nearly 23% of all secondary teachers have less than a minor in their main teaching field; (b) among teachers who teach a second subject area, 36% are unlicensed in their field and

50% lack a minor in their field; and (c) 56% of high school students taking physical science, 27% of students taking mathematics, and 21% of students taking English are taught by out-of-field teachers with the highest proportion of teachers in high-poverty schools and lower-track classes. Many Schools of Education and school districts offer traditional professional development programs. Darling-Hammond (1997) reported that:

> ... until recently many teacher education and ongoing professional development programs separated theory and application almost completely. People were taught to teach in lecture halls, from textbooks, and teachers who frequently had not themselves ever practiced what they were teaching. Their courses on subject matter topics were disconnected from their courses in teaching methods, which were in turn disconnected from their courses on foundations and psychology. They completed this coursework before they began student teaching, which was a brief taste of practice typically appended to the end of their program with few connections to what had come before.... In-service training programs were less transformative. Large groups of teachers amassed in auditoriums after school had brief encounters with packaged prescriptions offered by outside consultants. Divorced from the daily concerns and practice, these hit-and-run events were generally forgotten when the next day's press of events set in. Difficult problems of teaching and learning (How can I explain quadratic equations? What's keeping Ellen from being able to explain what she reads?) were never raised in these training contexts, much less explored and discussed. (p. 320)

In addition, school administrators adhere to the philosophy that professional development is an individual teacher's responsibility that is undertaken throughout their teaching career. These school districts do not believe it is their responsibility to support professional development activities of teachers; therefore, they place the responsibility of implementing professional development activities with school principals and do not encourage an integrated, connected set of activities that foster opportunities for teachers.

Within the last few years many Schools of Education and school districts have been a part of programs offered by the Holmes Group of Education Deans and the National Network for Educational Renewal to:

> ... create professional development schools where novices' clinical preparation can be more purposefully structured ... these schools are sites for state-of-the-art practice and are also organized to support the training of new professionals, extend the professional development of veteran teachers, and sponsor collaborative research and inquiry. Programs are jointly planned and taught by university and school-based faculty. Cohorts of beginning teachers get a richer and more coherent learning experience when they are organized in teams to study and practice with these faculty and with one another. Senior teachers report that they deepen their knowledge by serving as mentors, adjunct faculty, co-researchers, and teacher leaders. Thus, these

> schools help create the rub between theory and practice that teachers need in order to learn, and at the same time they create more professional roles for teachers and build teachers' knowledge in ways that improve both practice and ongoing theory building. (p. 321)

The need for greater teacher knowledge is imperative! According to Hollins (1996), to ensure that "all students have adequate opportunities to learn requires enhancing the capacity of all teachers–their knowledge of students and subjects, and their ability to use that knowledge–by professionalizing teaching. This means that teacher education policies must ensure that all teachers have a stronger understanding of how children learn and develop, how assessment can be used to evaluate what they know and how they learn, how a variety of curricular and instructional strategies can address their needs, and how changes in school and classroom organization can support their growth and achievement"(p. 258). No doubt, an effective professional development program must focus on the knowledge, skills, beliefs, and attitudes needed to work effectively with students from diverse, racial, ethnic, linguistic, and social class groups. This type of program is especially important because many teachers will remain in the classroom as their student population changes racially, ethnically, linguistically, and in social class status. Without a strong professional development program, these teachers are likely to develop negative attitudes and lower expectations as the characteristics of students in their classrooms change. In addition, professional development must focus on the conditions of schools, intrinsic rewards for teachers, and teachers' commitment to and engagement in their work (Louis, 1995).

FEATURES OF EFFECTIVE PROFESSIONAL DEVELOPMENT PROGRAMS

The research on school effectiveness indicates that the quality of classroom instruction is critically important in determining student achievement, however, the nature of classroom instruction is shaped decisively, for instance, by the extent to which teachers collaborate, trust each other, and believe they are encouraged to innovate (Sebring, Bryk, Roderick, & Camburn, 1996; Soltman & Moore, 2000). The following sub-sections discuss necessary features of effective professional development programs.

Teacher Beliefs about Students and Classroom Practices

According to Placier and Hamilton (1994), "teachers' beliefs are not construed in isolation, but in contexts such as the family, community, classroom (both as student and teacher), and teachers' lounge. American teachers share certain beliefs as a result of their socialization in teacher education programs, membership in a common profession, and central role in the culture of the American school" (p. 136). Thus, teaching is concerned with the formation of teachers' beliefs and expectations about their work, which in turn, have a strong effect on the equity of students' achievement in schools (Fenstermacher, 1978; Lee & Smith, 1994). Despite the evidence that all children can learn, many teachers (a) hold on to the belief that some students can not learn (Louis, 1995); (b) view diversity of student backgrounds as a problem rather than as a resource that enriches teaching and learning (Zeichner, 1995); and (c) use a watered down and fragmented curriculum for poor ethnically diverse students rather than a challenging, innovative, and intellectually rigorous curriculum (Nieto, 1996).

More recently, researchers have attempted to understand the relationship between teachers' beliefs, learning, and the curriculum in relation to the use of classroom practices (e.g., reading instruction). Richardson (1994) conducted a qualitative study using extensive belief interviews with 39 grade 4, 5, and 6 teachers in five schools. Teachers were asked about their notions about reading comprehension and how students learn to read, in general. She found that belief interviews predicted classroom practices very successfully and that teachers' beliefs follow changes in practice as based upon seeing positive results of different behaviors in terms of student learning. Her experiences suggested that staff developers "should become knowledgeable about the beliefs that the participants hold, and their current practices. The process should involve discussing teacher-held beliefs and practices, and relating them to the practices and underlying theories that staff developers are discussing" (p. 101). For substantial changes in classroom practices to occur, professional development activities must go beyond a discussion on theory or only on student problematic behaviors. Teachers' beliefs, ways of thinking, and classroom practices are interconnected in the teacher change process.

Teacher Thinking

Advances in the study of teachers' beliefs and knowledge should be viewed as precursors of the research on teacher thinking. Artiles (1996) and Rueda and Kim (2001) proposed a research agenda on teacher thinking in urban schools that incorporates a constructivist or sociocultural viewpoint of teacher thinking as a mediating variable in the study of urban school processes and outcomes. This approach is based upon the assumption that "individuals' cognitive processes are understood in the sociocultural context in which they occur" (Artiles, p. 41). Key elements of a sociocultural approach include (a) social interactions with peers, (b) the influence of culturally based knowledge, practices, and technologies, (c) understanding the mediating role of symbols, (d) using our cultural tools, and (e) viewing teacher thinking as inseparable from social and cultural activities.

Chandler (1992) and Artiles (1996) suggested that teacher thinking must be understood as an integral part of sociocultural contexts and applied to teacher-student social interactions in classrooms. As Artiles pointed out, the infrastructure of urban schools, as based upon a sociocultural approach, is predicated upon the following assumptions.

- Classrooms are communicative environments.
- Contexts are constructed during interactions.
- Meaning is context specific.
- Inferencing is required for conversational comprehension.
- Teachers orchestrate different participation levels.
- Students have an active role in knowledge construction. (pp. 41–42)

To further understand urban school contexts, it is important to acknowledge that teachers' beliefs, knowledge, thinking, and cognitive processes about at-risk students are intricately connected and intertwined with complex institutional constraints and practices. Decision-making processes of teachers are linked to inherent characteristics, opportunities, rules in the classroom, the classroom culture, resources, and constraints of urban schools.

Understanding of School Contexts in Professional Development

Little (1981) affirmed that "the political and cultural characteristics of schools are essential components of professional development. . . . School organization is not merely the context of staff development but the heart of the matter"(p. 4). The working conditions encountered by teachers, particularly in urban school districts, are highly related to lower teacher expectations for their own performance, teacher engagement, and student achievement. According to Placier and Hamilton (1995), the conditions for successful professional development activities must include a host of factors that include: (a) stressful working conditions that can inhibit teachers' motivation to participate in professional development activities; (b) teachers' sense of autonomy to change classroom practices; (c) the school culture (i.e., collaboration and collegiality, positive principal -teacher relationships) that supports innovation; and (d) teachers' views of themselves as a community.

Teacher Engagement

A different perspective related to understanding working conditions of the school, especially urban schools, to professional development is presented by Louis (1995). She stated that "unless teachers engage in teaching and feel that they are effective, students are less likely to make rapid progress in learning.... From the student's vantage, teacher engagement is a prerequisite for student engagement; and from the teacher's vantage, student engagement is the most important predictor of teacher's interest and effort" (p. 84). To further understand the concept of teacher engagement, Louis connected teacher engagement and the organizational conditions of the school to student success. She described teacher engagement as follows:

Human Relationships in the School

- **Engagement with the school as a social unit.** This form of engagement reflects a sense of community and personal caring among adults within the school and promotes integration between personal life and work life. We see this form of engagement among teachers who "wouldn't want to work at any other school." These teachers refer to peers and students as friends and family, and attend after hours school events as often as they can. They are quick to rally together if faced with a troubling event.
- **Engagement with students as unique whole individuals** rather than as "empty vessels to be filled." Teachers demonstrate this type of engagement when they listen to students' ideas, get involved in students' personal as well as school lives, and make themselves available to students who need support or assistance. Other examples of teacher engagement with students are formal and informal coaching, sponsoring, mentoring, and counseling activities.

Teaching and Learning

- **Engagement with academic achievement.** Teachers can engage in students' achievement in many ways. They can participate in curriculum writing and development, share ideas, and experiences about the craft of teaching with other teachers, make good and creative use of class time, express high expectations for performance, provide useful feedback to students, and actively consider student assessment.
- **Engagement with a body of knowledge** needed to carry out effective teaching. Particularly, in secondary schools, teachers need to keep current in their content fields and incorporate new subject matter into instruction. Expressing one's personal passion for a subject, seeking ways to connect the subject to students' lives, participating in professional organizations, and pursuing advanced degrees exemplify this form of engagement. (p. 85)

Elements of Professional Development Activities

More recently, Allington and Cunningham (1996) highlighted and described key characteristics of schools implementing professional development activities as:

- **Resource adequate** instead of resource deprived. Teachers had a least the minimum curriculum materials and classroom resources needed to accomplish their goals.
- **Integrated** rather than segmented. Integrated schools had a unity of purpose shared goals, and a shared sense of responsibility. Segmented schools, in contrast, had clear divisions within the faculty, an us versus them attitude about school administration, and little commitment to any common vision of what the school should or could be doing.
- **Collegiality** versus isolation from peers. Multiple collegial interactions created a school where colleagues were seen as a constant source of support and ideas for improving teaching. When teachers felt isolated in their own classrooms, they often failed to go beyond complaining about students and parents.
- **Problem-solving** orientation instead of problem hiding. In a problem-solving environment, teachers assumed a need for continued learning about teaching. They developed a strong sense of group and were likely to reflect routinely upon their own teaching. In problem-hiding schools, on the other hand, teachers kept to themselves and rarely shared concerns or difficulties with their peers.
- **Investment-centered** rather than payoff focused. When schools were investment centered, teachers were seen as resources rather than as problems. Through a variety of methods, investments were made in improving teaching, not just by rewarding the few who were deemed superior teachers. In investment-centered approaches, teachers were encouraged to take risks and to seek out resources for improvement. (p. 150)

Culturally Responsive Components of Professional Development Activities

More recently, Gay (2000) suggested that an infrastructure within schools must be created to support teachers who are implementing culturally responsive teaching. Components include features such as (1) staff development to acquire knowledge about ethnic diversity and culturally responsive teaching; (2) availability of necessary instructional materials; (3) systematic ways in which teachers can receive constructive feedback on their efforts and recognize their accomplishments in implementing culturally responsive teaching; (4) activities in other aspects of the educational enterprise, such as administration, counseling, curriculum design, performance evaluation, and extracurricular activities comparable to culturally responsive teaching; and (5) clearly defined techniques for meeting the opposition that culturally diverse people and programs may encounter in both the school and community.

One example of a teacher-directed professional development program is Project CRISP–Culturally Responsive Instruction for Special Populations (Voltz, Brazil, & Scott, 2000). This program was designed to foster teachers' knowledge and skills related to understanding and addressing culturally influenced learning and behavioral differences. Project CRISP activities include a three-day interactive seminar on culturally responsive pedagogy and issues related to the disability versus cultural difference conundrum. In addition to the traditional lecture format, participants engaged in (a) hands-on-activities and demonstrations, (b) small-group discussion and planning meetings with their school-based team members, and (c) developing professional development plans, activities, products/logs that spanned a period of several months after the seminar(i.e., approximately 15 weeks). Evaluation procedures consisted of (a) pre and post assessment survey instruments to assess teachers' knowledge base, attitudes, and perceptions related to the teacher-directed nature of professional development activities; (b) lesson plan analysis to determine the extent to which they were reflective of culturally responsive pedagogy; and (c) pre and post assessment interviews to assess teachers' knowledge base of related to a multicultural perspective.

MULTICULTURAL-BASED TRAINING MODEL FOR FORGING PARTNERSHIPS

School, family, and community partnership require the support and commitment of all major stakeholders (e.g., school administrators, certified and licensed school personnel, and the targeted significant community resources) and the adequate preparation of school personnel. Ford (1995, 1998) and Ford and Reynolds (2001) outlined a three-phase training model designed to prepare practicing school personnel to productively connect and collaborate with *significant community resources (SCRs)*. The three phases of the multicultural-based training model relative to the preparation of educators and school counselors are discussed below (see Table 2).

Phase One

Phase One activities reshape and redefine personal attitudes and definitions of professional development for practicing teachers about multicultural families and their communities. This *core phase* is a prerequisite that conditions

Table 2
TRAINING EDUCATORS AND SCHOOL PERSONNEL TO CONNECT SCHOOLS WITH SIGNIFICANT MULTICULTURAL FAMILY AND COMMUNITY RESOURCES–A THREE PHASE MODEL

Phase One: Reshaping Attitudes and Personal Redefinition
Phase Two: Development of an Accurate Knowledge Base
    a. Examination of Historic and Present School, Family, and Community Partnerships and Activities
    b. Creation of a Comprehensive and Inclusive Database of *SCRs*
Phase Three: Productive School, Family, and Community Networks
    a. Establishment of Inclusive School and Community Connections
    b. Utilization of *SCRs* to Aid Multicultural Families and Learners with and without Disabilities

the mindset. Practicing educators and other school personnel (e.g., school counselors) are exposed to structured multicultural education classes or in-depth multicultural workshops to obtain a better understanding of themselves and their beliefs about their own and other cultural/ethnic groups. Colleges and universities have an awesome role to play in preparing educators and other school personnel to function effectively in school, family, and community partnerships within *all* communities. Two major concerns surface: (a) the quality of the multicultural professional development training program; and (b) demonstration of competency in this area. Utley (1995) recommended the use of a multicultural perspective as a framework for special education programs. Earlier, Ford (1992) outlined the inclusion of four specific multicultural experiences in education training programs (emphasis on special education):

- Engaging teachers in self-awareness activities to explore their attitudes and perceptions concerning their cultural group and beliefs-as well as the effects of their attitudes on students in terms of self-concept, academic abilities, and educational opportunities.
- Exposing teachers to accurate information about various cultural ethnic groups (e.g., historic and contemporary contributions and lifestyles, value systems, interpersonal-communication patterns, learning styles, and parental attitudes about education and students with and without disabilities).
- Helping educators explore the diversity that exists between, as well as within, cultural ethnic groups.
- Providing educators with opportunities to manifest appropriate application of cultural information to create a healthy learning climate. (p. 108)

During this phase, specific emphasis must be placed on *performance-based assessment of practitioners* regarding the ability of teachers to apply acquired knowledge/skills into actual program planning and implementation with multicultural families and learners. Additionally, many school districts nationwide have Local Professional Development Committees (LPDC) to aid in the continued professional development of certified school personnel. Typically, the LPDC is responsible for recommending professional activities to school personnel and/or approving or disapproving activities submitted by school personnel. To assist school personnel in serving multicultural learners with and without disabilities, some vital questions that must be answered include: Are multicultural activities and topics included on the list of recommended professional development activities? What weight and priority are given to school personnel participating in multicultural education activities? If certified and licensed school personnel do not voluntarily select multicultural professional activities, what are the incentives for them to do so or consequences of not doing?

Clearly, if school districts are serious about improving the competency levels of school personnel to deliver equitable, quality service to multicultural learners with and without disabilities, then mechanisms must be incorporated for them to do so. In recognition of the need for a multicultural framework for professional development programs, one of the primary professional special education organizations, The Council for Exceptional Children (CEC) (1996) included specific multicultural-oriented items in the "CEC Common Core of Knowledge and Skills" essential for all special educators. In addition, school counselors who are enrolled in CACREP accredited counselor education programs are required to have coursework that address an understanding of issues and trends in a multicultural and diverse society. Monitoring activities and/or post-workshop activities should be conducted to aid practicing educators and other school personnel in understanding how to incorporate the acquired knowledge base and skills.

Phase Two

In Phase Two, attention is focused on practicing teachers (a) developing an understanding of past and current local school, family, and community partnerships; and (b) obtaining an accurate knowledge base about the varied local *SCRs*. If educators and other school personnel are to become committed to the identification and inclusion of *SCRs*, meaningful structured school, family, and community activities must become a part of their entire professional development program. Family and community involvement activities must be explicitly emphasized in all professional development activities rather than a brief or isolated assignment. At a minimum, school, family, and community involvement assignments must become essential components of all professional development plans, goals and objectives, and levels of performance. To address Part (a) of Phase Two, practicing teachers could interview local principals, teachers, school counselors, and other school personnel (i.e., school and community liaison) to learn about past and current local school, family, and community involvement practices. As a professional development activity, these practices could be critiqued regarding their inclusiveness (e.g., range of SCRs and productivity, nature and degree of use by school personnel, and potential influence on student outcomes). Next, during Phase Three, practicing teachers could outline ways to refine local school, family, and community involvement policies and practices. As appropriate, these recommendations could be shared with local school personnel.

The compilation of local *SCRs* by participating teachers and direct participation in the local programs are performed during phase two. For example, cooperative groups could create a database of easily accessible human and published resources to help them gather information about local *SCRs*. Written and human resources such as "informational resource" (e.g., Blackbook and Blackpages—a city or regional specific publications that lists Black-owned businesses, civic and social organizations, and churches), directors of community centers, members of fraternities and sororities, and informed parents. Next, practicing teachers would select a community program and interview the program planner or other relevant staff to obtain more information. When learning about the local community and families, the use of a "participation-observation" format is recommended (Garcia, 1991; Harry, Torguson, Katkavich, & Guerrero, 1993). Under this framework, teachers would participate fully in cultural group experiences. To this end, teacher and school counselor trainees, with permission from program directors, perform systematic observations. This observational experience would be designed to allow trainees the opportunity to interact with paid and volunteer community staff. From observations and interviews, trainees obtain answers that aid them to understand the program's offerings. Finally, trainees could construct a user-friendly practical product such as a Thematic Community Resource Calendar (Ford, 1995). Each month would be assigned a theme or topic (e.g., education month, nutrition and health month, self-awareness month, and family month). Community-based resources, extracted from the participating teachers' databases that provide services would be depicted. For instance, the education month would briefly describe programs and resources that offer tutoring or other academic-oriented activities; and self-awareness and family month may include resources providing cultural enrichment programs, and family togetherness activities.

Congruent with the goals of Phase Two, *practicing* teachers would (a) acquire information about past and present partnership efforts within their school building (and local school district), and (b) identify and make contact with *SCRs*. Similar to pre-service trainees, practicing teachers and school counselors can obtain an understanding of the nature of the collaboration activities from building personnel (e.g., principal, school, and community liaison) and possible effectiveness. When critiquing current school and community partnerships, questions to be considered could include the following:

1. Are present linkages and partnerships inclusive? Are *all SCRs* included (e.g., multicultural resources, both formal and informal grassroots)? Who determined who should be included? In the linkages, who initiates cooperative activities?
2. How often are the linkages used? When?
3. Does the partnership help enhance educational outcomes for *all* students (e.g., including multicultural learners with and without disabilities and talents)? In what ways?
4. What modifications in the partnership arrangements need further modification such that student outcome is positively impacted?

As indicated, these same or similar questions can be addressed by both the school and *SCRs* in order to refine school and community relationships. During Phase Two, the examination of current practices could serve as the springboard to discuss ways to expand the use of *SCRs* and/or rationale for the compilation of more comprehensive resources.

To help identify *SCRs*, as an initial activity, practicing teachers could work with the school's community outreach specialist/school-community liaison person to obtain information about local *SCRs* and corresponding contacts. In addition, a [school] survival kit prepared by the Educational Research Service (1997) in cooperation with National Association of Elementary School Principals that outline specific strategies to help schools identify and tap into local community resources could be used. Earlier, Garcia (1991) noted that teachers must study the community of their students. For instance, they can join and develop friends in nonschool-related community groups and survey the community to obtain understanding and appreciation of it. To increase the probability of school personnel capitalizing on the expertise of *SCRs* contacts, a building-level team (BL-Team) approach could be instituted. The special educator and school counselor could lead the formation of the team to help facilitate objectives. During Phase Three, The BL-Team, along with selected *significant* community representatives could comprise the School and Community Team (SCT). The SCT could (a) examine present school and community involvement policies and practices, and (b) restructure ways they could better work together by using each other's strengths to improve educational outcomes for multicultural learners with disabilities. The special educator, school counselor, and building administrator could assume leadership in instituting this process in Phase Three. For instance, they could orchestrate the compilation of the SCT (i.e., BL-Team and community representatives) using processes that ensure representation from traditional community organizations, local businesses, and those previously *untapped SCRs*. The BL-Team could take responsibility for sharing information about the SCT with certified and noncertified personnel throughout the school building. In addition, the BL-Team could encourage the active involvement of certified/licensed school personnel in local community-based programs and illustrate how to connect multicultural youth with services offered by *SCRs*.

Phase Three

Phase three concentrates on the facilitation of school, family, and community collaborative activities to influence student outcomes. As discussed in Phase Two, practitioners from local multicultural community resources are encouraged to institute mechanisms that provide a systematic way to refine as needed current school and community partnerships. Efforts may encompass several formats such as (a) bringing human and published community resources into the school and classrooms; (b) providing professional development activities for school personnel so that they may connect students and their families to needed *SCRs*; and (c) combining school and community resources to combat issues that limit students' opportunities to maximum performance (e.g., deteriorating physical school structure, school violence, and inadequate curriculum materials).

CONCLUSION

In this chapter, we have discussed the rationale for viewing teachers as lifelong learners and initiating professional development activities that are linked to school, family, and community partnerships. It is imperative that school personnel and parents are connected and collaborate with *SCRs*. *SCRs* within multicultural communities have traditionally been devalued and ignored. Recent crises in education, however, demand the authentic inclusion of these valuable assets. *SCRs* have the potential to provide varied services to help schools improve educational attainment for families and their children. We strongly believe special training is needed to help practicing school personnel to work collaboratively with *SCRs* in multicultural communities. Culturally based models can equip school personnel with the needed attitudes, knowledge base, and skills as they interact with community members.

REFERENCES

Allington, R.L., & Cunningham, P.M. (1996). *Schools that work: Where all children read and write.* New York: Harper Collins.

Artiles, A.J. (1996). Teacher thinking in urban schools: The need for a contextualized research agenda. In F.A. Rios (Ed.), *Teacher thinking in cultural contexts* (pp. 23–54). Albany, NY: State University of New York.

Banks, J.A. (1997). *Educating citizens in a multicultural society.* New York: Teachers College Press.

Chandler, S. (1992). Learning for what purpose? Questions when viewing classroom learning from a sociocultural curriculum perspective. In H.H. Marshall (Ed.), *Redefining student learning* (pp. 33–58). Norwood, NJ: Ablex.

Council for Exceptional Children (1996). *What every special educator must know: The international standards for the preparation and certification of special education teachers* (2nd ed.). Reston, VA: Author.

Darling-Hammond, L. (1997). *The right to learn: A blueprint for creating schools that work.* San Francisco: Jossey-Bass.

Fenstermacher, G.D. (1978). A philosophical consideration of recent research on teacher effectiveness. In L. Shulman (Ed.), *Review of research in education,* (No. 6) (pp. 157–185). Itasca, IL: F.E. Peacock.

Educational Research Service (1997). *Getting parents meaningfully involved.* Arlington, VA: Author.

Ford, B.A. (1992). Multicultural education training for special educators working with African American youth. *Exceptional Children, 59*(2), 107–114.

Ford, B.A. (1995). African American community involvement processes and special education: Essential networks for effective education. In B.A. Ford, F.E. Obiakor, & J.M. Patton (Eds.), *Effective education for African American exceptional learners: New perspectives* (pp. 235–272). Austin, TX: Pro-Ed.

Ford, B.A. (1998). Productive school and community partnerships: Essentials to improve educational outcomes for ethnic minority students. In A. Freeman, H. Bessent-Byrd, & C. Morris (Eds.), *Enfranchising urban learners for the twenty-first century* (pp. 91–113). Kearney, NE: Morris.

Ford, B.A., & Reynolds, C. (2001). Connecting with community resources: Optimizing the potential of multicultural learners with mild disabilities. In C.A. Utley & F.E. Obiakor (Eds.), *Special education, multicultural education, and school reform* (pp. 208–227). Springfield, IL: Charles C Thomas.

Garcia, R.L. (1991). *Teaching in a pluralistic society: Concepts, models, strategies.* New York: Harper Collins.

Gay, G. (2000). Culturally responsive teaching: Theory, research, and practice. New York: Teachers College Press.

Hargreaves, A. (1997). *Rethinking educational change with heart and mind.* Alexandria, VA: Association for Supervision and Curriculum Development.

Harry, B., Torguson, C. Katkavich, J., & Guerrero, M. (1993, Fall). Crossing social class and cultural barriers in working with families: Implications for teacher training. *Teaching Exceptional Children,* pp. 48–51.

Hollins, E. R. (1996). *Transforming curriculum for a culturally diverse society.* Mahwah, NJ: Lawrence Erlbaum.

Lee, V., & Smith, J. (1994). *Effects of restructured teacher worklife on gains in achievement and engagement for early secondary school students.* Paper presented at the Annual Meeting of the American Educational Research Association, New Orleans, LA.

Little, J.W. (1981). *Assessing the prospects for teacher leadership.* Paper presented at the Annual Meeting of the American Educational Research Association, Washington, DC.

Louis, K.S. (1995). Teacher engagement and real reform in urban schools. In B.W. (Ed.), *Closing the achievement gap: A vision to guide change in beliefs and practice* (pp. 81–102). Philadelphia, PA: Research for Better Schools.

National Commission on Teaching and America's Future (1996). *What matters most: Teaching and America's future.* New York: Author.

Nieto, S. (1996). *Affirming diversity: The sociopolitical context of multicultural education.* White Plains, NY: Longman.

Obiakor, F.E. (1994). *The eight step multicultural approach: Learning and teaching with a smile.* Dubuque, IA: Kendall/Hunt.

Obiakor, F.E. (1999). Teacher expectations of minority exceptional learners: Impact on "accuracy" of self-concepts. *Exceptional Children, 66,* 39–53.

Obiakor, F.E., & Schwenn, J.O. (1995). Enhancing self-concepts of culturally diverse students: The role of the counselor. In A.F. Rotatori, J.O. Schwenn, & F.W. Litton (Eds.), *Advances in special education: Counseling special populations* (Vol. 9, pp. 191–206). Greenwich, CT: JAI Press.

Placier, P., & Hamilton, M.L. (1994). Schools as contexts: A complex relationship. In V. Richardson (Ed.), *Teacher change and the staff development process: A case in reading instruction* (pp. 135–158). New York: Teachers College.

Richardson, V. (1994). The consideration of teachers' beliefs. In V. Richardson (Ed.), *Teacher change and the staff development process: A case in reading instruction* (pp. 90–108). New York: Teachers College Press.

Rueda, R., & Kim, S. (2001). Cultural and linguistic diversity as a theoretical framework for understanding multicultural learners with mild disabilities. In C.A. Utley & F.E. Obiakor (Eds.), *Special education, multicultural education, and school reform: Components of quality education for learners with mild disabilities* (pp. 74–89). Springfield, IL: Charles C Thomas.

Sebring, P.B., & Bryk, A.S., Roderick, M., & Camburn, E. (1996). *Changing reform in Chicago: The students speak.* Chicago, IL: Consortium on Chicago School Research.

Soltman, S.W., & Moore, D.R.(2000). *Ending illegal segregation of Chicago's students with disabilities: Strategy, implementation, and implications of the Corey H. Lawsuit.* Paper prepared for the Conference on Minority Issues in Special Education, The Civil Rights Project of Harvard University, Cambridge, MA.

U.S. Bureau of the Census (1993). *Monthly News.* Washington, DC: Author.

Utley, C.A. (1995). Culturally and linguistically diverse students with mild disabilities. In C.A. Grant (Ed.), *Educating for diversity: An anthology of multicultural voices* (pp. 301–324). Boston: Allyn & Bacon.

Utley, C.A., & Obiakor, F.E. (2001). Multicultural education and special education: Infusion for better schooling. In C.A. Utley & F.E. Obiakor (Eds.), *Special education, multicultural education, and school reform: Components of quality education for learners with mild disabilities* (pp. 1–29). Springfield, IL: Charles C Thomas.

Voltz, D., Brazil, N., & Scott, R. (2000). *Teacher directed professional development for culturally responsive instruction: A proactive strategy for reducing the overrepresentation of students of color in special education programs.* Paper presented at the Conference on Minority Issues in Special Education, The Civil Rights Project of Harvard University, Cambridge, MA.

Wilson, K.G., & B. Daviss (1994). *Redesigning education.* New York: Teachers College Press.

Zeichner, K. M. (1993). *Educating teachers for cultural diversity.* East Lansing, MI: National Center for Research on Teacher Learning, Michigan State University.

Zeichner, K. M. (1995). Educating teachers to close the achievement gap: Issues of pedagogy, knowledge, and teacher preparation. In B.W. (Ed.), *Closing the achievement gap: A vision to guide change in beliefs and practice* (pp. 39–52). Philadelphia, PA: Research for Better Schools.

Chapter 9

STATE GOVERNMENTS: THE ROLES THEY MUST PLAY

SUNDAY O. OBI

Public education is one of the most vital of all governmental services, and it is primarily the responsibility of state and local governments to administer and finance public schools, colleges, and universities. The importance of this responsibility creates controversy on how public education should be implemented and on what policy directions state and local governments should take (Engel, 1999). Three composite issues have been especially contentious: (1) financing and administering of schools, (2) determining the purpose of public education, and (3) dealing with racial, gender, religious, and ethnic differences. While in the public mind, education and politics are not supposed to mix, the aforementioned issues are embedded in politics. Somehow the schools are supposed to remain above partisan and ideological conflict. In actuality, they cannot and do not. According to Engel, the development of public education has been shaped by politics, and its future direction is a political issue.

The federal government's involvement in education has been continuous and is not likely to be substantially reversed in the future. There appears to be an intriguing traditional battle between those who want education to be controlled locally and those who look to Washington to solve social problems. Part of the drift to "big" government over the last 60 years has been that the federal government has enormous resources; the power to tax has enabled the national government to become a financial giant with billions of dollars at its disposal. Like their counterparts at state government levels, the individual members of this policymaking circle may not view themselves as either having power or holding elite status; they have, nonetheless, a remarkable tenacity, retaining their positions for several years; surviving changes in administrations; and shifting from one office to another within the same substantive domain.

During a period when the federal government was both hobbled by its enormous deficits and distracted by the politics of subtraction, states in essence were compelled to carry out larger public agendas. The summit of 1989 signaled a new era in education policy with the state, through their governors, assuming leadership in education reform. Moreover, as a result of fewer discretionary federal dollars, and partly as a manifestation of a principled stance, a serious effort was made to create the most efficient and effective strategies both to focus and leverage federal investment in education and to eliminate overlapping programs and duplication. The most important and fundamental shift has been in the role taken by the federal government vis-à-vis the states and the locals. Where as in the past the role of the federal government was principally regulatory, federal policy is no longer aimed at categorizing, labeling, and forgetting particular funds at particular groups of children. Rather, the states are at the heart of educational reform through their role in developing plans and working with their own locals. Ninety-five percent of Goals 2000 monies in the second-year flow through the states to local districts by guidelines that states developed (Borman & Cookson, 1996).

A New Era: Who Is In Charge?

The appropriate roles for state in the education of all children continues to be an issue of urgent concern. In other words, the U.S. school system has been for less centralized control than the school systems of most advanced industrial societies. The federal era of the last two decades is giving way to a new phase in which initiatives are more likely to come from states, although a sustained federal role continues to be important in strengthening equality of opportunity for access, supporting center of excellence, and balancing out regional and inter-state disparities in general support for educators. The United States Constitution does not grant authority over education to the federal government. The states have constitutional sovereignty over education, and furthermore, they allow local districts great power over the day-to-day functioning of the schools (Campbell, Cunningham, & Nystrand, 1980; Wirt & Kirst, 1982). This decentralization of authority is enhanced by the fact that U.S. schools receive most of their funds not from the national government but from state and local sources. The U.S. entered the field of education mainly through the power of the Congress to provide resources and authorize expenditures for education, and in so doing, regulate behaviors indirectly by setting conditions for the eligibility or receipt of aid. An increased federal role also has emerged based on the "equal protection" clauses of the Fourteenth Amendment (Burn, 1977).

In recent years, schools are firmly opposed to having their fate in the hands of federal authorities. Most school districts tend to favor decision making at the state level, in part from the conviction that federal coordination entails excessive regulation, interference, bureaucratization, and needless delays. Schools find themselves in difficult position of serving two masters because of the division of responsibilities between the state and federal governments, with the federal government calling for the balanced development of schools and providing the funds on the basis of approved courses, and the state government calling for the Local Education Agency to meet state needs (Burn 1977). The centralization of educational policy in the 1960s and 1970s was designed to address equity issues and to overcome problems that the local schools were unwilling or unable to solve, such as the segregation of minority students. Wise (1982) argued that these equity problems of access to resources and programs should not be decentralized to the local level because "community control and citizen participation tend to serve the dominant political interests within the community" (p. 203). He further pointed out the unlikelihood that minority student interests will be served in a system of decentralized governance.

As it stands, efforts to hold all schools accountable based on standards and student outcomes are being cast onto an uneven playing field in which some schools are less able to provide students with the opportunities to learn content reflected on the state tests (Darling-Hammond, 1992). This means the degree of local community and school "empowerment" that will result from a decentralized governance structure will be unequally distributed across poor and wealthy communities. Concern regarding the inequalities between local school communities—and thus the differentiated degrees of school empowerment under a more decentralized governance structure—were partly addressed by policy makers who expanded the Goals 2000 legislation to include voluntary opportunity-to-learn standards or strategies to assess student access to educational resources and high-quality instruction or practices. States that develop improvement plans and receive a portion of the federal funding for Goals 2000 must include opportunity-to-learn strategies that are comparable to the voluntary national opportunity-to-learn standards (Lewis, 1994; U.S. Department of Education, 1994).

THE STATE GOVERNMENT: EDUCATIONAL FUNCTIONS AND POLICIES

Each state has an educational agency whose organization parallels that at the local level. At the top is a chief officer or superintendent, a state board of education, and an executive branch or agency that carries out the activities of the department. State regulation specifies the scope of state support, establish curricular content and minimum time for each subject, sets minimum standards for the promotion and graduation, describes the rights and competencies of teachers, defines the characteristics of administrative structure, and creates rules for the physical safety of school inhabitants (Benson, 1982; Wirt & Kirst, 1974). So, state departments of education adopt curricular guidelines which teachers must follow, and many states approve a specific set of textbooks. With concern for educational standards and accountability, there has been an increased state investment in the day-to-day workings in schools, particularly in regard to standardized testing and curricula. It has become common for states to work with test developers to create proficiency examinations that are administered statewide to students, at designated grade levels. These proficiency tests have a tremendous impact on the way teachers handle the curriculum.

The passage in 1965 of Title V of the Elementary and Secondary Education Act, which provided federal funds to bolster their professional staff of state education agencies, greatly increased state level educational activity. It led, for example, to increased research, media, and consulting services to local school districts, and administration of federal funds for compensatory education. State monitoring of local graduation standards and instructional quality is essential and reinforced by regional accrediting agencies. During the nineteenth century, secondary school courses were so diverse that universities had no way of knowing what and how much their incoming students knew. They therefore established the practices of certifying the curricula of given schools and then accepting their students without entrance examinations. Eventually, these certification practices were institutionalized, and the resulting agencies visited high schools to approve their curricula, certify their students, and "accredit" their programs. These agencies have made secondary school course offerings more uniform, at least for college-preparatory programs; and they have created an external watchdog function, which reduces the autonomy of schools and districts (Bennette deMorrais & LeCompte, 1995).

In most states the board is elected, and the chief state school officer (CSSO) is either elected or appointed by the governor. Usually, as is the case on the local level, the CSSO is expected to assume policy leadership with the cooperation and under the supervision of the board. The administrative details are attended to by the staff of the State Department of Education (Engel, 1999). State officials must guarantee that local officials operate within the limits of state law. In matters such as teacher certification, school accreditation, and special and vocational education, most states exercise a great deal of control. Indeed, state mandates have become especially significant in the education of special needs students. In other concerns, such as curriculum, teacher employment, and school construction, there is considerable variation. For example, most southern states apply statewide courses of study and limit textbook selection, whereas in the Northeast and Midwest these issues are in good measure local options (see Engel).

Engel (1999) noted that the school reforms of the last 15 years have strengthened the trend toward centralization, especially in curriculum and course requirements, as this would guarantee uniform high standards, as well as a certain degree of educational equality. Advocates of the educational rights of minorities, including students with exceptionalities, see state intervention as the means of achieving their goals. In the area of finance, state governments must surpass local governments as the prime source of revenue for the nation's public schools. In 1996, however, states paid 45 percent of the cost, local governments paid 48 percent and the federal government a mere 7 percent (U.S. Department of Education, 1996). State governments must make efforts to equalize the burden through aid to school districts because certain states depend less on local taxes than do others. As of 1996, the school systems of some states were mostly funded with state aid, and some school systems were heavily dependent on local funding. According to the US Department of Commerce (1997), Hawaii's system is almost entirely state funded, whereas 90 percent of New Hampshire's school money has up to now come from local taxes.

Over the last 15 years, courts in many states have stepped in to redress the balance. One of the first instances, in 1971, was in California, where the State Supreme Court ruled that the system of school finance inherently violated state and federal constitutional guarantee. The state was thus forced by the ruling, and by the impact of Proposition 13, to increase its share of the budget for public education (Engel, 1999). Since property tax seems to be the mainstay of local funds for public schools, this has meant tremendous disparities in the ability of communities to pay for education. Localities with low property values either have to charge exorbitant property taxes or provide inadequate schooling; and wealthy towns and cities did not exert themselves. Kozol (1991) condemned what he calls "savage inequalities" in school systems, resulting in large part from an inequitable funding system. Describing the appalling conditions of public schools in poor and minority communities such as East Saint Louis, Illinois, he asked:

> Why not spend on children here at least what we could be investing in their education if they lived within a wealthy district? . . . Wouldn't this be natural behavior in an affluent society that seems to value fairness in so many other areas of life? Is fairness less important to Americans today than in some earlier times? Is it viewed as slightly tiresome and incompatible with hard nosed values? What do Americans believe about equality? (p. 41)

There has always been disagreement about the role of public education in promoting social and political equality. From ancient to contemporary societies, schools have been seen as a means of protecting the people from a potentially tyrannical government. In the United States to some extent, the intensity of this conflict at first kept states from taking decisive steps to establish public schools. In 1784, the State of New York University was set up as the control agency for a unified school system. Five years later, Massachusetts passed a law requiring towns to set up public elementary schools. Yet, it took 40 or 50 years until there was any real development of a public education system on the local level in either state (see Engel). The struggle between elitists and democrats in public education has marked its whole history. Advocates of a "tracked" system fought for the separation of vocational and academic schools rather than a common education for everyone. The 1950s saw a greater concern for gifted students, the 1960s for disadvantaged students, and the 1970s for students with disabilities. During the 1980s, and continuing into the 1990s, the banner of "excellence" was raised in the battle for school reform. The question of whether public schools can or should promote greater social and political equality is still at the core of the politics of education. As cited by Engel, the United States is, of course, a heterogeneous society. Inevitably, schools have to confront the issue of how to develop educational programs that serve the needs of a diverse population, and how to resolve the conflicts arising over that issue.

The civil rights movement in the 1960s helped culturally and linguistically individuals (e.g., African Americans) to develop a stronger awareness of their history and culture, which had previously been ignored or suppressed by the white majority. As a result, there has been increasing pressure on schools to revamp educational systems and also eliminate what is seen as sexism and racism from the curriculum. One of the demands has been for a "multicultural" approach to education, which recognizes that American society is a combination of diverse racial and ethnic cultural components, and therefore structures the curriculum in that spirit. This has met with strong resistance from most political conservatives who see schools as a means of establishing a common set of "American" values, and who attack multiculturalism as divisive and academically substandard. Thus, state legislatures must continue to shape public education by introducing policies and monitoring their implementation and by exerting financial control on states that violate these policies. In other words, states must assume more control of public education. Despite controls being concentrated in state government, public schools across the nation are very similar. Uniformity among state school system is fostered by the cooperation among states in organizations such as the National Governors Association (NGA). This group, working in cooperation with the federal government, created national goals for the year 2000. With changes in social and economic systems evident, the rapid pace of events in the world today requires a closer look at the changes occurring in education and the direction it is taking. In this chapter, I examine and adequately explore whether the educational system is fulfilling the responsibilities that the American people have assigned to it. Critical questions remain pertinent. What roles must the state play? Are the roles meeting the requirements of today, and will they meet these requirements in the future? How could schools and classrooms be organized to make it possible for all children to learn at their own pace? Are students' abilities being developed more fully today than yesterday? Are adequate attention and funds being concentrated on improving the quality of educational services? Are educational programs developing technical competence to meet work-force requirements?

INTRICATE EDUCATIONAL PROBLEMS CONFRONTING STATE GOVERNMENTS

A number of factors limit states' capacity to influence districts and schools. Some of these limits are structural, essentially beyond state control; and some are political, and heavily influenced by the willingness of state policy makers to make hard political choices. In addition, some are functional, or deeply embedded in the nature of education. States face a structural multilevel governance problem any time they attempt to influence schools. They exert influence on schools through a variety of channels: primarily through local school districts, sometimes through local municipalities, and increasingly directly through schools, which are more and more likely to have their own representative governance mechanisms. Each of these has its own set of constituencies, which in turn have their own priorities. All multilevel organizations, including large corporations, face a version of this problem: how to get nominally subordinate units to operate in concert with each other in the presence of strong centrifugal pressures (Elmore & Fuhrman, 1995). The problem is complicated by the additional fact that subordinate units usually have better information about how to adapt general policies to their immediate environment. But governments face a particularly difficult version of this problem, especially in federated systems, because local governments have significant formal autonomy and well-organized political constituencies of their own. Local governments are less likely to adapt to higher-level policies; and the most likely result of any policy initiative is extreme variability of local response (McLaughlin, 1987). One level of government cannot so much control another, and efforts are made to influence policies through persuasion and exchange of benefits.

Some observers see the state's lack of control more as a political than a structural issue. Despite the multiple layers of governance, states could exert more authority in education, but what they lack is the political will or skill (Iannaccone, 1967). This argument rests on the fact that school superintendent, local school boards, and teachers are among the most active and influential constituents of state legislators. Beholden to these powerful interests, legislators try to assure a steady stream of state funding to their home districts (Elmore & Fuhrman, 1995); and they resist policies that redistribute resources away from their own and toward poorer districts. As a consequence, school finance equalization has been difficult to achieve without holding wealthier districts harmless from losing any aid, and adding more aid for poorer districts (McDonnell & McLaughlin, 1982). Political pressures mean that policymakers usually use a narrow range of instruments, resorting primarily to mandates and incentives, which promise short-term results or provide inexpensive ways to get new programs underway. More long-term strategies aimed at building the capacity of schools and districts to provide quality instruction are rarer (McDonnell & Elmore, 1987; Obiakor, Harris-Obiakor, Obi, & Eskay, 2000). Furthermore, although strategies are limited, individual policies are voluminous and uncoordinated with one another. States are typically scattershot in nature–responding to immediate political pressures rather than to long-term structural problems. Pressing problems are addressed by separate programs, leading to what some have called a proliferation of "magic bullets" and others have called "projectitis" (see Elmore & Fuhrman). Many factors underlie such fragmentation, including the short-term electoral cycles of politicians; institutional separation of powers among board commissions, legislatures; and the high degree of specialization among lobbying groups (see Elmore & Fuhrman).

In many states, the lack of consolidation of school districts exists. Smaller or rural school districts have difficulties in retaining high-quality teachers, upgrading school facilities, and maintaining an enriched curriculum. At the same time, these districts often require a much higher per pupil cost, thereby imposing a heavier burden on the local property taxpayers (Fuller & Pearson, 1969). More specifically, in recent years services to children in rural areas have improved; however, many problems still exist that inhibit the delivery of these services, such as professional isolationism. Small rural school districts cannot afford the luxury of a variety of professional staff specialists. For children with exceptionalities, often, the special education teacher, guidance counselor, or resource teacher will be the lone representative of their specialty (Obi & Obiakor, 2000; Storer & Crosswait, 1995). They may be responsible for 12 grades and spread over several buildings. Classroom teachers may also have duties that extend from 5 to 12. This means staff development activities can become diluted, in the sense that teachers are expected to gain new knowledge and competencies encompassing more topics for a wider age range of students. It also means that a teacher in small rural schools may be the only teacher of a given subject at a given grade level. Teachers have little opportunity to interact with peers facing the challenges (see Obi & Obiakor; Storer & Crosswait). As Bell, Bull, Barrett, Montgomery, and Hyle (1993) pointed out, 81 percent of rural regular and special education teachers express concern about feelings of professional isolation working in rural areas. This problem negatively affects the recruitment and retention of special education teachers. As a consequence, serious shortages of qualified teachers and related service personnel have become critical barriers to providing high quality services to students with exceptionalities (see Obi & Obiakor).

The most difficult to serve in rural school districts are those Helge (1984a) described as low incidence disabilities (students with moderate or severe mental retardation and those with multiple disabilities, vision or learning impairments, orthopedic disabilities, emotional disturbance, and those requiring related services). Historically, these students either were not served, or they were served out of their local district in residential placements. With the passage of federal legislation mandating educational programs for all students with disabilities, Helge noted that more students with low incidence were remaining in their local rural communities. Rural school district personnel struggle with multiple issues in attempting to meet educational needs of students with low incidence disabilities. Service delivery is complicated by the low numbers and the geographical disbursement of students with complex learning needs (Helge, 1984b). If a district has only one or two students with a given disability, such as deafness, it is difficult to obtain the resources needed to provide for the needs of the student. In rural settings, this dilemma is caused by a small general population. Clustering rural students with low incidence disabilities not only prevents districts from serving students in the least restrictive setting, but it creates unreasonable demands for students and their families because of the long distances students may need to travel to have access to these services. Itinerant service delivery options also are complicated by travel difficulties (Sebastian & McDonnell, 1995). In rural areas where there are problems with recruitment and retention of certified special education personnel, stress-induced burnout among special educators has also become a concern of administrators. This results in special educators serving many different roles due to lack of additional supportive personnel (Obi & Obiakor, 2000).

Like other students, rural students deserve effective instructional programming. To disseminate validated instructional practices to those rural students with exceptionalities, a number of principles must be considered. The diversity of rural contexts and people who live within them must be recognized and respected (Davis, 1989; Helge, 1987; Obi & Obiakor, 2000). As these characteristics vary, so too do cultural values and norms, the ability to secure informal and formal supports, and the role of schools and other social institutions in helping families. Helge (1984b) called for the development of methods to resolve dilemmas in rural special education in which the diversity of rural communities should be brought to bear to assist students with disabilities and their families. According to Helge, willful leadership at local, state, regional, and national levels is needed to assure that schools are able to receive their share of resources necessary for the delivery of high quality special and regular education programming. States must increase their compensatory programs (e.g., Chapter 1, now Title 1) and revenues per target students in the lowest poverty districts. Public education funding programs at state levels must allocate more funds per student and more funds to districts with the highest percentage of needy students. The major responsibility for public education lies with the states.

INNOVATIVE STRATEGIES FOR STATES IN THE NEW MILLENNIUM

It is apparent that enhancing public education programs to benefit all students requires a process of system change, as opposed to isolated programs and invalidated instructional practices often common with programming in some school districts. There is a pressing need to help educators meet the needs of all children. A useful process for improving public education is by reviewing the various concerns of researchers, scholars, and advocates who are calling for changes in the way educators provide services in both rural and urban schools. The call for a change came in earnest with inclusive advocates such as Will (1986) urging public education and administrators to become more responsible for the education of students who have special needs in schools, including those who are economically disadvantaged. Her views have been supported by many scholars and educators in recent years. At a national level, the National Center on Educational Outcomes (NCED, 1997) estimated 40 percent to 50 percent of all students with disabilities were excluded from National Assessment of Educational Progress (NAEP; McGrew, Thurlow, & Spiegel, 1993; Vail, 1997). As McGrew et al. argued, "The treatment of most students with disabilities as outlined in our national data collection programs is a concern from an equity and philosophical perspective" (p. 348). Such exclusion is also seen in state-level assessments where there is a wide variability in the extent of special education students' participation in statewide assessments (Erickson, Thurlow, & Ysseldyke, 1996). Furthermore, even when special education students are included in state assessments, results are often excluded from analysis and subsequent reporting of scores (Elliott, Ysseldyke, Thurlow, & Erickson, 1998; Thurlow, Scott, & Ysseldyke, 1995a, 1995b). Overall, this creates a situation where not much is known about the impact of large-scale, assessment programs on students with disabilities (Coutinho & Malouf, 1993; Vanderwood, McGrew, & Ysseldyke, 1998).

Recent shifts in federal policy address the need to measure the learning of all students. The Individuals with Disabilities Education Act (IDEA) Amendments, passed in June 1997, mandated change in this regard. The reauthorized IDEA requires participation of all students, including those with disabilities, in state and district-wide assessment. In instances where a student's disability precludes participation in an assessment, even with modifications, an alternate assessment must be provided. The IDEA Amendments require that state and local education agencies have alternate assessment systems in place by July 1, 2000 (Yell & Shriner, 1997). Similar stipulations also included in the Educate America Act of 1994 (Goals 2000), specifically, Title II, National Education Reform Leadership, standards, and assessments, an essential part of Goal 2000, calls for the development of state assessment systems that fully include all students. As a result of the reauthorization of IDEA, many states must develop new testing guidelines or revise existing practices. It is notable that a few states have started to develop and field-test alternate assessments for students with severe disabilities (Elliott et al., 1998), but only one has a fully implemented alternate assessment (Kearns, Kleiners, Clayton, Burdge, & Williams, 1998; Kleinert, Haigh, Kearns, & Kennedy, in press). With the passage of the Kentucky Education Reform Act in 1990, Kentucky became the first state to require full inclusion of special education students in large-scale assessments (Kleinert, Kearns, & Kennedy, 1997). Thus, Kentucky is in a unique position to provide data that might help other states attempting to meet alternate assessment requirements (Turner et al., 2000).

It seems clear that fundamental changes will have to take place in all educational programs to address the needs of all students. Knoll and Obi (1996) suggested that (a) practitioners currently working in schools must be provided with resources, training, and time needed to develop effective cooperative and collaborative working relationships; (b) universities, engaged in preservice teacher education, need to break down the barriers between urban schools and rural schools; (c) the State Department of Education must have a restructuring task force for every school that provides an opportunity for all stakeholders to buy into the vision and contribute to the local design of reform; (d) the State Departments of Education, regional special education cooperatives, local districts, and universities should collaborate to design regional support teams to assist individual educational programs in working through the process of restructuring; and (e) professional development activities that allow all teachers to examine basic topics in education of all students must be established.

The organizational structures of education programs for students will vary, but the State Departments of Education must strive to introduce policies that will help school districts provide services in terms of good principles. State governments must enforce best practices, in all school districts, so that professionals will continue to provide high quality educational programs for our children in the new millennium. An example is a project for a statewide system change that was implemented in the state of Utah 10 years ago. This effort has focused on developing coordinated preservice and in-service initiatives in rural areas. It has also been a collaborative effort between the Utah State Office of Education, university program faculty, and rural school district personnel. Teachers and administrators might apply Utah's initiative in developing effective programs for all students. Effective projects must be spearheaded by State Office of Education, for individuals, organizations, and schools that share the vision for school reform to work for implementing recommendations contained in this chapter.

State Departments of Education must play dominant roles in making sure that minimum standard for curriculum, pupil promotion, and graduation, and for specific education programs such as kindergarten, vocational education, and high school. States must have detailed courses of study for specific subjects such as social studies and math, and adopt textbooks that are distributed to local schools. They must have detailed regulations regarding the physical features of school buildings and the size of school libraries. They must also define the length of the school day and year. In addition, they must have regulations that are very detailed with respect to requirements for the certification of teachers, and they must increasingly play a major role in financing local schools. In some states, tax limits are set for local districts and requirements are made for certain local budget breakdowns. States must assume greater shares of education expenses since state courts recognize that existing systems of financial support provide unequal educational opportunities. State Departments of Education's activities must include the actual operation of state schools for students with disabilities, and involvement in the operation of vocational programs and teacher preparation colleges. The regulatory activities of State Departments of Education can extend into areas such as curriculum and teaching standards, school construction, school buses, civil defense and fire drills, and other items specified in the state code or constitution.

State legislatures must have a specific legislative committee that is responsible for proposing legislation pertaining to education, conducting hearings on proposed legislation, and recommending to the legislature the passage or defeat of specific laws affecting education. Another exemplary project operated through the auspices of the State Office of Education in which there is a direct effect on *all* students, is the trend toward greater centralization that occurred in 1990 when the Kentucky State legislature, under pressure from the courts, revamped its educational system. In perhaps no other state in the nation has there been an education renaissance as pervasive and extensive as the one in Kentucky in the decade of the 1990s. Three milestones at the beginning of this decade exemplify and guide this renaissance in a state where people have not always cherished education sufficiently. These milestones are the (a) enactment of the Kentucky Education Reform Act of 1990 (KERA); (b) creation of the nation's first Workforce Development Cabinet; and (c) development of the Strategic Plan for Higher Education in Kentucky (1991–1996).

The above factors taken separately—and all three working together—are causing initiatives and accomplishments that are unprecedented for Kentucky, and perhaps any state, even in times of extreme financial difficulty. With unprecedented public support and guidance from a leadership task force, the General Assembly developed an education system that not only addressed the funding issue but established a new era of instruction and school management practices. The plan, known as the KERA, became law July 13, 1990. Kentucky's reform fundamentally changes what children learn and how they learn it. It establishes high academic expectations and measures students' learning against those expectations. Reform sets high standards for districts and schools and empowers them to meet those standards in their own ways. In Kentucky, education reform is a people's revolution, a drive forward, a vision of equal and world-class education for every child. Kentucky has become a model for national education reform initiatives and America's laboratory for systemic reform. In other words, the State of Kentucky has adopted a bold plan to improve its system of public education. The plan reflects the belief that all students can learn and nearly all at high levels. Additionally, it recognizes that there is a need for high standards to be set at the state level and a need for flexibility at the school level. Boldly, it asserts that partnership between schools and families is critical. These initiatives call for putting together the pieces of the puzzle to support change that meets the unique education needs of all students, all schools, and all communities. Key components of the Kentucky plan are:

1. High educational goals set by Kentuckians to clearly state what we expect graduates to know and be able to do.
2. An assessment process to measure whether the goals are being reached by all students.
3. An accountability system to reward schools improving their success with students and to intervene in schools failing to make progress.

4. School councils made up of educators and parents to make decisions on curriculum, instruction, and school management, to create an environment for student achievement and school success.
5. Increased funding for professional development activities for educators to learn new ways to more effectively achieve success with all students.
6. Early childhood education programs to better prepare children who are at risk of educational failure.
7. Funding for a longer school day, school week, and school year to assist students who need more time to achieve academic success.
8. A major commitment to technology as an instructional and administrative resource.
9. Family resource and youth services centers to assist students and families in need, by providing resources and referrals to service agencies in the community so that students can focus on learning.
10. Changes in the governance structure, to reduce the politics involved in the operation of many of Kentucky's school districts and to improve the leadership capability at state and local levels.
11. A new funding system, to correct financial disparity between wealthier and poorer school districts.
12. A major funding commitment to support the new education initiatives in the state.

As it stands, the state of Kentucky has started a bold new course for education. It has laid out a very ambitious plan, which, if given sufficient support and time, can improve teaching and learning in the state. The goal is a quality education that prepares children for the future, regardless of where they happen to live or the economic status of the family (Alston, Brinly, McGuire-Cockrell, Deaton, Hall, & Robbins, 1994). There are other scholars and educators proposing that more priority be accorded to the precise roles state governments must play. According to Burn (1977), the responsibilities of the states must involve the following areas:

1. Basic institutional support of public institutions.
2. Encouragement of the private sector.
3. The promotion of research, especially in agriculture, education, veterinary medicine, and forestry.
4. Student support mainly through the subsidization of the cost of education (low tuition fees) and also through grants and guaranteed loans.
5. Grants and loans for construction of student housing and academic buildings; more for the public than the private institutions.
6. Contracts with institutions to provide consulting applied research, and other services.

7. Contracts with private institutions to operate professional schools.
8. Encouragement of public services of higher education institutions.
9. Increasing importance of the planning and coordinating of state systems of higher education.
10. State regulations on collective bargaining, affirmative action, and other issues.
11. The chartering of institutions and the licensing of institutions to grant degrees, including not just higher education but other types of postsecondary education institutions.
12. The approval of programs and regulation of degrees.
13. Maintenance by state authorities of law and order in the higher education institution and their communities.

States principally support the capital and recurrent costs of maintaining public (and sometimes private) higher education by funding student expenses, and planning and coordinating initiatives. In order to provide more economical uniform educational services, states must move toward the consolidation of school districts. Smaller school districts were said to have difficulties in retaining high-quality teachers, upgrading school facilities, and maintaining an enriched curriculum. At the same time, these districts often require a much higher per pupil cost, thereby imposing a heavier burden on the local property taxpayers (Fuller & Pearson, 1969). In other words, state legislatures must continue to enact laws to reduce the number of school districts, thereby providing better service coordination and cutting of administrative costs.

Both district consolidation and the diminishing local fiscal role in public education are evidence of a more assertive state role in school matters (Wong, 1991). In his analysis of 36 school-policy areas in the early 1970s, Wirt (1977), proposed the concept of a centralization score in assessing the state government's role in all 50 states. The scale ranges from the lowest level of centralization (high local autonomy) with a score of zero (0.0) to the highest level of state policy control with a score of six (6.0). The average score for all 50 states was 3.56, which suggests that the state government generally exercises more control than local districts over school affairs. This pattern comes as no surprise. From a constitutional perspective, local districts are seen as agencies of the state educational system. The states enjoy almost complete control over personnel, compulsory attendance, accreditation, curriculum, graduation standards, and such housekeeping matters as calendar, records, and accounting procedures. Localities generally maintain more discretion over district organization, guidance and counseling, pupil-teacher ratios, and extracurricular activities. These centralizing tendencies notwithstanding, policy-making in education is subject to numerous sources of accountability which allows for citizen participation, interest group input, and political response.

The educational policy process must continue to provide numerous avenues for interest group participation. For example, in recent years, as in the 1950s and 1960s, state educational affairs are largely dominated by coalitions of major professional and occupational groups with a broad range of policy concerns from wages to curriculum. Among the most prominent are the two sets of teacher unions; the state teachers association (affiliates of the National Education Association, or NEA) and state teachers' federations (affiliates of the American Federation of Teachers, or AFT). Other organized interests include state school board associations, state school administrators' associations, and classified school employees' groups (Wirt & Kirst, 1976).

During the late 1960s and the early 1970s, more vigorous lobbying activities came from special-needs groups. Advocacy organizations for people with disabilities, migrant children, and minorities primarily focused on school policy that affected particular disadvantaged groups and targeted their efforts to bring about reform through new legislation or court action (Rosenthal & Fuhrman, 1981). As a result, state court decisions initiated by advocates of the disadvantaged have brought about more equitable distribution of state school funds, new categorical services for children with special needs, and an expansion of equal opportunity regulations. The increase in state fiscal support for public education must be facilitated by events beyond the control of the state legislative and executive branches. State courts must continue to put pressure on state legislatures to bring about a more equitable distribution of state school funds. Finally, the proliferation of federally funded school programs for the needy must have a stimulative effect in encouraging both matching and supplemental state contributions.

CONCLUSION

In this chapter, I have presented issues surrounding the delivery of educational programs to our children, and described the organization and control of school systems in the United States. State reform policies vary in their domains and specificity. They provide directions for school change, but the nature of the guidance and the responsiveness of schools vary. State policymakers have many tools with which to influence school practices, but the effects of policies tend to be limited rather than diverse (Stevenson & Schiller, 1999). While state policies are an important element of the highly fractured policy environment of schools, other factors may tighten or loosen the linkages of these policies to changes in school practices. For example, state efforts to implement these policies on district office's interpretations and implementation of the policies may influence the effects of state policies. Some recent descriptive studies of district offices suggest that the district's interpretation of state policies can play an important role in shaping school responses to state policy initiatives (Spillane, 1996; Wilson & Gretchen, 1993). As discussed in this chapter, state governments are the major actors in public education in this country. The decade of the 1980s also established state governments as major reformers or innovators in the field. Many states were engaged in some type of education reform effort in that decade. Despite interstate emulation, including themes and goals common to all reform proposals, states have continued to vary in approaches to change and in education spending and program performance (Roeder, 1994).

Overall, it is apparent that many states have been involved in thoughtful and ongoing development of both participation and accommodation policies. It is encouraging to see that even before legal mandates were put in place (e.g., IDEA), several states took the initiative to work toward including all students in their assessment. As we continue to struggle with and address issues of participation of students with disabilities in state and district assessments, as well as how to most appropriately include them, we will continue to strive for holding schools accountable for the education of every student who attends (Thurlow et al., 2000). In the new millennium, state governments must direct their attention on local school districts if the problems they face are to be reduced, thus, enabling districts to meet the needs of all students in the most effective ways. Legislators must realize that public education must strive to improve. This improvement will be solidified when we come to the realization that all students deserve educational opportunities equal to those made available to suburban districts.

REFERENCES

Aston, E., Brinly, B., McGuire-Cochrell, P., Deaton, S., Hall, D., & Robbins, P. (1994). *A citizen handbook: The Kentucky education reform act.* Frankfort, KY: Legislative Research Commission.

Bell, T. L., Bull, K. S., Barrett, J. M., Montgomery, D., & Hyle, A. E. (1993). Future special education teachers perception of rural teaching environments. *Rural Special Education Quarterly, 12,* 31–38.

Bennett, K., & LeCompte, M.D. (1995). *The analysis of education* (2nd ed.). White Plains, NY: Longman.

Benson, C. S. (1982). The deregulation of schools: Views from the federal, state, and local levels. [Editor's introduction]. *Education and Urban Society, 14,* 395–397.

Borman, K. M., & Cookson, Jr. P. W. (1996). Sociology of education and educational policy: When worlds collide or happily ever after? In K. M. Borman, P. W. Cookson, A. R. Sadovnik & J. Z. Spade (eds.), *Implementing educational reform: Sociological perspectives on educational policy*, (pp. 3–20). Norwood, NJ: Ablex.

Burn, B.B. (1977). The changing balance in federal-state responsibilities: Postsecondary education in Australia and the United States. In B. B. Burn & P. Karmel (Eds.), *Federal/State responsibilities for postsecondary education: Australia and the United States* (pp. 1–54). NY: International Council for Education Development.

Campbell, R. F., Cunningham, L. L., Nystrand, R. O., & Usdan, M.D. (1980). *Organization and control of American schools* (4th ed.), Columbus, OH: Merrill.

Coutinho, M., & Malous, D. (1993). Performance assessment and children with disabilities: Issues and possibilities. *Teaching Exceptional Children, 25* (4), 62–67.

Davis, P.C. (1989). Implementing comprehensive parent services in small rural school districts. In *Education and the changing rural community: Anticipating the 21st century: Proceedings of the 1989 ACRES/NRSSC Symposium*. Bellingham, WA: American Council on Rural Special Education.

Darling-Hammond, L. (1992). *Standards of learner-centered schools*. New York: National Center for Restructuring Schools and Teaching.

Elliott, J., Ysseldyke, J., Thurlow, M., & Erickson, E. (1998). What about assessment and accountability? *Teaching Exceptional Children, 31* (1), 20–27.

Elmore, R. F., & Fuhrman, S. H. (1995). Opportunity-to-learn standards and the state role in education. *Teacher College Record, 96*, 1–26.

Engel, M. (1999). *State and local government*. New York: Peter Lang.

Erickson, R.N., Thurlow, M. L., & Ysseldyke, J. E. (1996). *Drifting denominators: Issues in determining participation rates for students with disabilities in statewide assessment programs*. Minneapolis, MN: University of Minnesota, National Center on Educational Outcomes.

Fuller, E., & Pearson, J. M. (1969). *Education in the States*. Washington, DC: National Education Association.

Helge, D. I. (1984a). The state of the art of rural special education. *Exceptional Children, 50*, 294–305.

Helge, D. I. (1984b). Models for serving rural students with low-incidence handicapping conditions. *Exceptional Children, 50*, 313–325.

Helge, D. (1987). *Rural family-community partnership: Resources, strategies, and models*. Bellingham, WA: American Council on Rural Special Education.

Iannaccone, L. (1967). *Politics in education*. New York: Center for Applied Research in Education.

Kearns, J., Kliners, H., Clayton, J., Burdge, M., & Williams, R. (1998). Inclusive educational assessments at the elementary level: Perspectives from Kentucky. *Teaching Exceptional Children, 31*, 16–23.

Kleinert, H., Haigh, J., Kearns, J., & Kennedy, S. (in press). Alternate assessments for students with disabilities and IDEA 97: Lessons learned and roads to be taken. *Journal of Special Education, 34*, 69–76

Kleiners, H., Kearns, J., & Kennedy, S. (1997). Accountability for all students: Kentucky's Alternate portfolio system for students with moderate and severe cognitive disabilities. *Journal of the Association for Persons with Severe Handicaps, 22,* 88–101.

Knoll, J., & Obi, S. (1996). *Analysis of inclusive education in Eastern Kentucky* (ERIC Document Reproduction Service No. ED 414 678).

Kozol, J., (1991). *Savage inequalities.* New York: Crown.

Lewis, A. C. (1994). Winds of change are blowing. *Phi Delta Kappan, 75,* 740–741.

McDonnell, L. M., & Elmore, R. F. (1987). *Alternative Policy Instruments.* Santa Monica, CA: RAND Corporation.

McDonnell, L. M., & McLaughlin, M. W. (1982). *Education policy and the role of the states.* Santa Monica, CA.: RAND Corporation.

McGrew, K. S., Thurlow, M. L., & Spiegel, A.N. (1993). An investigation of the exclusion of students with disabilities in national data collection programs. *Educational Evaluation and Policy Analysis, 15,* 339–352.

McLaughlin, M. W. (1987). Learning from Experience: Lessons from policy Implementation. *Educational Evaluation and Policy Analysis, 9,* 171–178.

National Center on Educational Outcomes. (1997). *State special education outcomes: A report on state activities during educational reform.* Minneapolis, MN: University of Minnesota.

Obi, S. O., & Obiakor, F. E. (2000). Rural students with exceptionalities: Methods that work. In F. E. Obiakor, S. A. Burkhardt, A. F. Rotatori, & T. Wahlberg (Eds.), *Intervention techniques for individuals with exceptionalities in inclusive settings; Advances in special education* (pp. 133–148). Stamford, CT: JAI Press.

Obiakor, F. E., Harris-Obiakor, P., Obi, S. O., & Eskay, M. (2000). Urban learners in general and special education programs: Revisiting assessment and intervention issues. In F. E. Obiakor, S. A. Burkhardt, A. F. Rotatori, & T. Wahlberg (Eds.), *Intervention techniques for individuals with exceptionalities in inclusive settings: Advances in special education* (pp. 115–131). Stamford, CT: JAI Press.

Roeder, P. W. (1994). Public education, families, and values. In M. L. Berbaum (Ed.), *Public opinion and policy leadership in the American states* (pp. 160–181), Lexington, KY: University of Kentucky.

Rosenthal, A., & Fuhrman, S. (1981). *Legislative education leadership in the states.* Washington, DC: Institute for Educational Leadership.

Sebastian, J., & McDonnell, J. (1995). Rural students with low incidence disabilities: Recommended practices for the future. *Rural Special Education Quarterly, 14* (2), 31–37.

Spillane, J. P. (1996). School district matters: Local educational authorities and state instructional policy. *Education Policy, 10,* 63–87.

Stevenson, D. L., & Schiller, K. S. (1999). State education policies and changing school practices: Evidence from the National Longitudinal Study of Schools. *American Journal of Education, 107,* 261–288.

Storer, J. H., & Crosswait, D.J. (1995). Delivering staff development to the small rural schools. *Rural Special Education Quarterly, 14* (3), 23–30

Thurlow, M. L., House, A. L., Scott, D.L. & Ysseldyke, J. E. (2000). Students with disabilities in large-scale assessment: State participation and accommodation policies. *The Journal of Special Education, 34,* 154–163.

Thurlow, M. L., Scott, D. L., & Ysseldyke, J. E. (1995a). *A compilation of states' guidelines for including students with disabilities in assessments.* Minneapolis, MN: University of Minnesota National Center on Educational Outcomes.

Turner, M. D., Baldwin, L., Kleinert, H. L., & Kearns, J. F. (2000). The relation of a statewide alternate assessment for students with severe disabilities to other measures of instructional effectiveness. *The Journal of Special Education, 34,* 69–76.

U.S. Department of Commerce (1997*). Statistical of the United States.* Washington, DC: U.S. Government Printing Office.

U.S. Department of Education (1996). *Statistics in brief.* Washington, DC: U.S. Government Printing Office.

U.S. Department of Education (1994). *The Goals 2000: Educate America Act.* Washington, DC: U.S. Government Printing Office.

Vail, K. (1997). Special pioneers. *The American School Board Journal, 184,* 16–21.

Vanderwood, M., McGrew, K., & Ysseldyke, J. (1998). Why we can't say much about the states of students with disabilities in education reform. *Exceptional Children, 64,* 359–370.

Will, M. (1986). Educating children with learning problems: A shared responsibility. *Exceptional Children, 52,* 411–415.

Wilson, B. L., & Gretchen, B. R. (1993). *Mandating academic excellence: High school responses to state curriculum reform.* New York: Teachers College Press.

Wirt, F., & Kirst, M. (1982). *Schools in Conflict.* Berkeley, CA: McCutchan.

Wirt, F. (1977). School policy culture and state decentralization. In J. D. Scribner (Ed.), *The politics of education* (pp. 164–187), Chicago, IL: University of Chicago Press.

Wirt, F. M., & Kirst, M. W. (1974). State politics of education. In E. L. Useem & M. Useem (Eds.), *The education establishment* (pp. 69–86). Englewood Cliffs, NJ: Prentice Hall.

Wirt, F. M., & Kirst, M. W. (1976). Schools in Conflict. In R. Campbell & T. Mazzoni, (Eds.), *State policy making for the public schools: A comparative analysis* (pp. 232–233). Berkley, CA: McCutchan.

Wise, A. E. (1982). *Legislated learning: The bureaucratization of the American classroom* (2nd ed.). Berkeley, CA: University of California Press.

Wong, K. K. (1991). State and local government institutions and education policy. In C. S. Thomas (Ed.), *Politics and public policy in the contemporary American west* (pp. 355–388), Albuquerque, NM: University of New Mexico Press.

Yell, M., & Shriner, J. (1997). The IDEA amendments of 1997: Implications for special and general education teachers, administrators, and teacher trainers. *Focus on Exceptional Children, 30,* 1–19.

Chapter 10

FEDERAL EDUCATIONAL POLICIES AND INNOVATIONS: IMPACTS ON EDUCATING *ALL* STUDENTS

JOSEPH NWOYE AND PEICHI TUNG

In the United States, federal education policies focus on equal opportunity and equal access of all students to education, with emphases on high expectations and high standards for all. Goals 2000 and the Improving America's Schools Act are two important examples of such legislative efforts to reform education. However, the nationwide effort to provide equal educational opportunity for all students only truly surfaced after *Brown v. Board of Education of Topeka* (1954), which declared that the placement of African American students in segregated schools was inherently unequal. This ruling not only helped to provide better educational opportunities to African American students, but it became the driving philosophy behind legislation that provided equal educational opportunity for other disadvantaged groups, including students with disabilities and limited English proficiency.

Educational policies that act to remedy past discrimination or that provide additional resources to disadvantaged students are important in bolstering academic achievement and, consequently, the achievement of graduates in the labor market and the progression of American national development. However, educational policies do not always translate into practice, and very often, when change does occur, it is slow. Furthermore, laws that intend to provide equitable learning experiences for students sometimes not only fail to extend equal opportunities to all students, but sometimes mask inequalities. In education reform, it is necessary to consider whether the resources that schools have or receive through legislation, from the social capital of the local community to textbooks and to professional development, are sufficient to initiate or sustain change. Educational policies should ideally take these factors into consideration, but the links between the availability of local resources and policies; local needs and policies; and educational research and policies are often not forged (Reimers & McGinn, 1997). Policies targeted toward providing equitable education to all children may fall short because of the inability of stakeholders to carry out the law or because the policies themselves lead to unintended outcomes that act to perpetuate inequality. For instance, it has been nearly 50 years since *Brown,* but schools are now headed toward resegregation and many schools never truly desegregated in the first place (Orfield, 1999). Segregation could happen in other, less noticeable ways, such as the overrepresentation of African American males in segregated special education programs (Artiles & Trent, 1994; Harry, 1994). In this chapter, then, we discuss the impact of federal educational policies and innovations on educating all learners.

IN SUPPORT OF A COMPREHENSIVE SUPPORT MODEL: EQUAL EDUCATIONAL OPPORTUNITY

The United States has undertaken several nationwide efforts to improve the education of all children. An example that would work well with the comprehensive support model (CSM) is the Goals 2000: Educate America Act. Because past educational reforms consisted of fragmented categorical programs targeted toward specific populations, Goals 2000 provided a national framework for excellence and equity and established high standards for student performance for new federal programs and the reauthorization of old ones. The language of this Act was inclusive in terms of its recognition of the ability of all students to learn and of its commitment to helping all students achieve academically and with high expectations. Goals 2000 was driven by the long-term assumption that public schools could help support the United States economy with a knowledgeable and skilled workforce. It was the first federal education initiative whose purpose was to aid States and districts in initiating and improving their reform efforts through grants—many of which are awarded on a competitive basis (U.S. Department of Education, 2000). Goals 2000 emphasized flexibility through its encouragement of state and local innovation and decision-making. For example, parent and community involvement would initiate school reform, which might result in better school organization or the professional development of teachers. Instead of being a solely top-down initiative, Goals 2000 recognized that in order for school reform to be effective, bottom-up reform was necessary as well. In order to achieve academic progress according to set standards, grants could be used for a variety of activities that vary according to local needs. These might include teacher development, improvement of curriculum, development of collaborative networks and parent involvement, conducting research and planning to inform school change, strengthening the use of educational technology, and planning or strengthening assessments and accountability mechanisms. The transformation of schools in Goals 2000 as a comprehensive endeavor would support the learning of all students.

As an undercurrent of this reform, Goals 2000 was to articulate a common vision for student achievement that all stakeholders—including students, teachers, administrators, and the local community—could share and understand. To this end, Goals 2000 had eight national objectives that addresses the ability of all students to learn and achieve, and ways through which schools may be reformed:

1. All children will start school ready to learn.
2. The high school graduation rate will increase to at least 90 percent.
3. All students will leave grades 4, 8, and 12 having demonstrated competency over challenging subject matter in core subjects.
4. The Nation's teaching force will have access to programs for the continued improvement of their professional skills and the opportunity to acquire the knowledge and skills needed to instruct and prepare all American students for the next century.
5. American students will be the first in the world in mathematics and science achievement.
6. All American adults will be literate and will possess the knowledge and skills necessary to compete in a global economy and exercise the rights and responsibilities of citizenship.
7. Every school in the United States will be free of drugs, violence, and the unauthorized presence of firearms and alcohol and will offer a disciplined environment conducive to learning.
8. Every school will promote partnerships that will increase parental involvement and participation in promoting the social, emotional, and academic growth of children. (Goals 2000 Act § 102(1)–(8))

Since Goals 2000 strives for standards-based reform, States would develop accountability systems to ensure students and schools were meeting standards of expected learning and performance. The methods used to measure student progress, especially the use of assessments such as standardized tests, have been subject to criticism that they hurt disadvantaged groups such as minority students (Wraga, 1999). Not only is it necessary to create fair and reliable instruments to assess student achievement that can be used as an appropriate measure of accountability, but the inclusion of limited English proficient students and students with disabilities is also necessary. States have different criteria on the inclusion of these groups in assessment procedures and they allow different accommodations in the testing of these populations. While some States are working to make these tests more accessible and valid for students with special needs, many have continued to exclude the participation of these children in varying extents. Thus, it is necessary to consider the types of supports that disadvantaged groups such as urban minority students need in order to meet set standards. While these are the students most at risk for academic failure, the use of standardized tests as accountability mechanisms have been argued to be more of a subtractive measure than an additive one in the reform process. These tests might be subtractive in nature because teaching might be skewed toward areas that are to be tested and learning stalls at low cognitive levels, which contributes to higher drop-out rates–especially for urban students (Kreitzer, Madaus, & Haney, 1989). One example of a standardized test that has undergone much of this type of criticism is the Texas Assessment of Academic Skills (TASS). Rather than making schooling equitable for all students, many critics have argued that the TASS perpetuates inequalities faced by minority youth because many schools provide a curriculum that presents little beyond what is needed to pass the test (McNeil, 2000). However, the intention of Goals 2000 was to avoid a "watered-down" curriculum through such content standards (Riley, 1994).

The needs of disadvantaged students, especially the poor, limited English proficient students or those with disabilities, must be of central concern when planning assessments and implementing reform. While curricula that are relevant to the diverse experiences of students help increase student achievement, the drive of standards-based reform and testing has lessened the concerns of teachers and administrators in addressing multicultural education (Oliva, 1994). Curriculum that is exclusive rather than inclusive has a detrimental effect on minority children. Children who are not in the dominant group have a difficult time identifying themselves or their communities in books and other instructional materials used in their school (see Oliva). "Cultural mismatch" is a significant contributor to minority student underachievement (Cummins, 1984)–such mismatch occurs because "most schools convey content in a manner that is closely aligned to the specific norms of the majority culture. Children must translate behaviors and values across cultures and then assimilate the school culture, which may be at odds with the home culture. Thus, potentially, schools become highly decontextualized, discontinuous learning experiences ... resulting, at times, in opposition or resistance to learning" (Robinson-Zanartu, 1996, pp. 373–384). Such considerations are important in the era of standards-based reform, where standardized assessments are becoming the rule rather than the exception. The national goal, after all, is to educate all children and to have high expectations of each one. Without giving adequate consideration to how schooling can be made more equitable for disadvantaged groups, marginalized groups may be pushed further to the fringes.

While Goals 2000 makes a good effort in trying to ensure local participation in decision-making, inequalities continue to exist in the education system. Goals 2000, of course, is not meant to be a panacea and is not the only federal legislation that addresses the betterment of education for all children. Goals 2000 and the Improving America's Schools Act (IASA) have as their common base the dedication to improve American education through quality teaching and learning and high standards for both. The IASA may be one way to meet Goals 2000, through financial and technical assistance, by helping the nation reach these eight voluntary goals. The IASA is an example of national legislation that has tried to improve the education of all students, with special attention to the education of poor, limited English proficient, and other minority populations. The IASA encourages equality and access to education for all students, while maintaining local flexibility and accountability through standards-based assessments. Riley (1995) noted that there are five priorities set forth by the IASA namely: (a) higher standards for all children, (b) a focus on learning and teaching, (c) flexibility for local initiatives and responsibility for student progress, (d) community-school linkages, and (e) allocation of resources where they are most needed. Resources are most needed to address the achievement gap between disadvantaged and other children and low-achieving students in high-poverty schools. IASA also helps to realize Goals 2000 by providing vast opportunities for local innovation and the development of school-parent relationships, both of which are important to a CSM. In order to achieve the equal education of all children, general and special educators must first consider the needs of specific populations, especially the poor, those with disabilities, and minorities such as African American children. Without this special attention to these populations, educational equality will be difficult to achieve because teaching and other supports will not target their needs.

Students of High-Poverty Families

For many years now, the main tool for improving academic performance has been through specialized legislative endeavors such as the 1965 Elementary and Secondary Education Act (ESEA). Congress has broadened the Elementary and Secondary Education Act (ESEA) supporting comprehensive school reform program to further support schools that receive Title I to provide academic and learning opportunities for low-income families with school age children (House Res. 2264, 105th Cong., 1st Sess., 1997). Title I, the main program of the ESEA, provides support to schools with a high percentage of high-poverty students and is driven by the strong correlation found between poverty and underachievement. According to the philosophy of Title I, high-poverty students should be subject to the same set of high expectations as other students through stated contents and performance standards. More specifically, the purposes of Title I are to (a) improve the delivery of funds to schools and districts with the highest poverty levels; (b) allow funds to be used for whole-school reform; (c) allow targeted assistance schools to help participating students meet high standards, such as through extended day programs; (d) develop parent-school linkages and parental participation; and (e) ensure that mechanisms for performance-based accountability are in place (Riley, 1994). In addition, Title I provides services to parents with the intent of breaking the cycle of poverty and illiteracy through educational opportunities for high-poverty families.

The ESEA, and Title I in particular, supports the CSM because they integrate local needs and high expectations for all students. Title I reflects a holistic approach with enrichment programs for parental involvement, professional development, and equitable educational opportunities for all students. Under the broadened version, more children can actually benefit from the initiative such as children of immigrant workers, adjudicated youth, limited-English-speaking youth, pregnant minors, children in single parent families, children who live in poverty, children with a record of poor attendance or behavior problems, abused children, and homeless children (Olenich & McCroskey, 1992).

Culturally Diverse Students

Although the United States Constitution does not mention the word "education" education was considered to be a local rather than federal responsibility. As it appears, the Tenth Amendment states a general provision for educational matters (U.S. Constit. Art. I, § 8). Also, the Equal Protection Clause of the Fourteenth Amendment prohibits "unfair discrimination against or classification of, any individual or group of individuals," and provides that "no state shall . . . deny to any person within its jurisdiction the equal protection of the laws." Since each State provides public education for all of its citizens, a State cannot discriminate by withholding this education from students of certain groups, such as those who are disabled. The Due Process Clause of the Fourteenth Amendment provides that no state shall "deprive any person of life, liberty, or property without due process of the law." Public education is a "property" interest of children. Prior notice and an opportunity to a hearing must be given to a student before their "property" of basic education is taken away. The Equal Educational Opportunities Act of 1974 reflected the

Constitutional spirit by its emphasis on how "no state shall deny equal educational opportunity to an individual on account of his or her race, color, sex, or national origin, by the failure of an educational agency to take an appropriate action to overcome language barriers that impede equal participation by its students in its instructional programs" (Section 1703(f)). The Equal Protection and Due Process clauses have been used to argue a number of cases involving educational equality, the most important of which was *Brown v. Board of Education of 1954.*

In the landmark school desegregation case of the Civil Rights era, *Brown v. Board of Education,* the United States Supreme Court decided that separate public education facilities for African Americans and Whites were inherently unequal. Segregation violated the right of African American students to equal protection of the laws under the Fourteenth Amendment. Further, the separation of races was determined to be detrimental to the education of African American children, especially in terms of the social stigma they experienced. As it turns out, the *Brown* decision was important not only for African American children, but also for other disadvantaged groups such as children with disabilities. Chief Justice Warren stated: "In these days, it is doubtful that any child may reasonably be expected to succeed in life if he/she is denied the opportunity of an education. Such an opportunity, where the State has undertaken to provide it, is a right that must be made on all equal terms." This statement has been important for later court cases dealing with the educational opportunities of all children. The Brown decision impacted the education of disadvantaged populations by maintaining that state-sanctioned segregation solely due to their "unalterable characteristic," such as race or a disability, was unconstitutional (Yell, 1998).

African American and other minority students have benefited from *Brown* and from legislation such as Title I and Title V of the ESEA, which address more comprehensive reforms. Title V contains a number of provisions to promote educational equity. The development of quality and access of minority students to magnet schools could dissipate the isolation of minority children in schools. African American students also can benefit from the Individuals with Disabilities Education Act, which aims to ensure the proper diagnosis of children with disabilities. This is especially important in the education of African American males, who often are placed in segregated special education programs. In a CSM, particular attention needs to be paid to students who have formerly been discriminated against, such as African American students and students with disabilities, to ensure that their voices are heard. This will, in turn, help to direct any decision-making processes that will affect their educational opportunities.

Students with Disabilities

Much of the federal law on disadvantaged populations focuses on the education of children with disabilities. The Education for All Handicapped Children Act (PL94-142) ensured a free appropriate public education for all children with disabilities between the ages of three and twenty-one. An important part of this law was the Individualized Education Program (IEP), which details a student's abilities, goals, services provided and time period, and assessment procedures. All the stakeholders involved in the education of the child, such as the parents, teachers, and other key school personnel, should be involved in building the child's IEP. In order to ensure that assessment instruments do not violate students' rights, schools should use assessments that are nondiscriminatory. Tests should be relevant and be administered by trained personnel in the student's native language where appropriate. Further, schools must consider a range of evidence about the child's learning and should not depend on something as simple as an intelligent quotient (IQ) score. A multidisciplinary team should conduct evaluations. However, the reality today is that tests are still racially and culturally discriminatory because they are normed on mainstream populations and because there is a lack of trained personnel fluent in students' ethnic languages. The involvement of multiple stakeholders, the creation of a space for dialogue between different stakeholders, and the recognition of diverse cultural and linguistic needs are important in building a CSM.

Another important principle found in the PL94-142 regulations is that of least restrictive environment. To the extent possible, children with disabilities should be educated with their nondisabled peers. The removal of children from regular education classrooms should occur only when the severity of the disability is such that education in the regular education classroom, with the use of supplementary aids, cannot be achieved in a satisfactory manner. Before PL 94-142, more than a million children were excluded from the education system and many others, whose disabilities were undetected, were not receiving an appropriate education (Ysseldyke & Algozzine, 1995). By educating children in the least restrictive environment possible, such as in the general education classroom when appropriate, this eliminates the same type of social stigma associated with the segregated schooling of African Americans. High expectations for all children and the inclusion of formerly marginalized groups in mainstream classrooms, where possible, are also necessary in building a CSM.

In 1990, Congress reauthorized the Education for All Handicapped Children Act and renamed it the Individuals with Disabilities Education Act (IDEA, PL 101-476). It was the IDEA Amendments of 1997, however, that brought many changes to the law. IDEA 97 (PL 105-17) has greatly improved the educational opportunities of children with disabilities. It places increased emphasis on the participation of students with disabilities in the general education classroom and in the general curriculum, with appropriate aids and services. Important goals include raising expectations for children with disabilities; increasing parental involvement, especially in terms of educational placement and the development of their children's IEP; ensuring that regular education teachers are involved in planning and assessing children's progress; including children with disabilities in State- and district-wide assessments (although inclusion criteria currently differs across states), performance goals, and reports to the public; supporting quality professional development for personnel involved in educating children with disabilities; offering voluntary mediation as a means of resolving parent-school controversies; and providing guidance in student discipline. It is important in a CSM to include disadvantaged students such as students with disabilities in assessments in order to ensure that teachers and schools are held accountable for their academic progress.

Students with Limited English Proficiency

The Bilingual Education Act of 1968, or Title VII of the ESEA, was the first time the United States government endorsed bilingual education to assist linguistically different children to get equality of educational opportunity (Cummins, 1984). In order to establish equal educational opportunity for all children, bilingual education should be used for students who are in need of such instruction. Financial assistance should be granted to local education agencies in order to help support bilingual education, and competency in the English language should be the intended outcome of bilingual education programs. Title VII works well with the framework of a CSM because it addresses and helps to provide support for the cultural and linguistic differences that are faced by many students in the American education system. It does not assume that American students are a homogenous group with similar needs.

Over the years, amendments to this Act such as under IASA have increased the eligibility requirements for bilingual services as well as placed more emphasis on English acquisition. The Bilingual Education Act encourages bilingual education but does not mandate it. Thus, plaintiffs with concerns about the adequacy of schools to provide limited English proficient students with an appropriate education have used the court system to address what they believed were violations of their educational rights. *Lau v. Nichols,* a class action suit filed on the behalf of 1,800 Chinese students, was one such case (Fernandez, 1992). Bilingual programs expanded nationwide after *Lau v. Nichols* (1974). The Supreme Court in *Lau* found that "there was no equality of treatment merely by providing students with the same facilities, textbooks, teachers, and curriculum, for students who do not understand English are effectively foreclosed from any meaningful education" (Baca & Cervantes, 1984). The rights of these students to an equal education opportunity was violated because their English was not sufficient enough to profit from instruction in that language. The Court *encouraged* the use of bilingual education programs as a means of providing language minority students with an equal educational opportunity. Further, each school district needed to conduct a language screening, which may be followed by a language assessment, at the start of each school year for all incoming students to help determine the child's language dominance and proficiency. Although the *Lau* decision did not mandate bilingual education, it legitimized the movement for equal educational opportunities for students who were not English proficient (Baca & Cervantes, 1984). In coming to this decision, the court relied on Title VI of the Civil Rights Act of 1964. While the Court in *Lau* left it up to educators to use English or the students' native language as the medium of instruction, it did state that the students' academic achievement shall not be compromised if instruction in English results in less academic progress than these students' English-speaking peers. This philosophy falls in line with the high achievement of all students in American schools as specified through Goals 2000 as well as through a CSM.

Apparently, there are many instances in both federal and state laws in American educational history that minority and other disadvantaged students have been excluded from fully participating in the education system. *Plessy v. Ferguson* (1896), which stated that African American students can be educated in separate but equal schools, is one sad example of exclusion. The trend of federal legislation now is largely in the direction of including all populations and finding ways to address their needs, especially in special education legislation. However, legislation still exists that attempt to exclude students from equal educational opportunity. One example is Proposition 227, which aims to eliminate bilingual education in California despite the fact that the state has the largest population of limited English proficient youth in the country (Office of Bilingual Education and Minority Affairs, 2000).

THE CSM IN THE CONTEXT OF FEDERAL LEGISLATION: BEYOND RHETORIC

Although legislative efforts seem to be substantial and consistent with educational innovations based on the CSM, the real question lies on implementation and evaluation. Are they achieving intended objectives? In order to achieve the goal of meeting the needs of all children and carve out a sustainable comprehensive model, one must first strive for a better understanding of the comprehensive model and how it works. We refer readers to the first chapter of this book, which indicated that the multidimensional nature of the problems that confront American children and youth calls for an integrative approach that combines collaborative strategies with multifaceted interventions. In support of this assertion, we also believe students should not be singled out for blame, and neither should parents, schools, communities, and governments be viewed as sole contributors to this problem. The proposed CSM for all learners is based on system theories that emphasize high-quality interaction between the school and the community. This position is consistent with the African proverb, "It takes a village to raise a child." Our strong belief in this awesome phrase compels us to recommend a collaborative effort by students, parents, and community to ensure success. Many schools are now attempting to reflect America's diverse cultures and their respective contributions within the school curriculum and pedagogical behavior. Many of these schools, however, still lack an adequate support system for implementing the ideals and goals of multicultural education (Banks, 1994; Cornbleth & Waugh, 1995).

The CSM shows the impact of physical, psychological, curricular, professional development, and pedagogical support needed by teachers to promote an educational movement that aims at changing the balance of power and making our schools and ultimately, our society more equitable. Unfortunately, it is difficult to claim that all schools are implementing a CSM that provides adequate treatment for minorities and students with special needs! Not long ago, the first author of this chapter visited two schools with principals who worked hard to develop a systematic approach to incorporate a comprehensive model in their views. The principals showed strong commitment in ensuring that all teachers understood the crucial need for a comprehensive model by providing opportunities for professional development in the area of multiculturalism. In one of the schools, although the principal was convinced of his leadership in ensuring quality education through multicultural-based curriculum and instructional practices (i.e., comprehensive model), there was no evidence that teachers practiced multicultural education in either their curriculum or instructional practices. In fact, in a personal interview with one of the teachers in this school, the teacher showed evidence of her disinterest when asked, "Do you have a policy either from the school or school district on a comprehensive model that incorporates multicultural education?" She responded, "I'm not sure if there are any policies for bilingual classes or multicultural education," and when further pressed, she stated, "My view is essentially based on Eurocentric perspectives.... We don't get into it." Yet, this is the school where the principal has distinguished himself as a strong advocate of multicultural education. Conversely, in the second school where the principal equally was convinced of his leadership in ensuring quality education through multicultural-based curriculum and instructional practices, there was strong evidence that teachers practiced multicultural education in their curriculum and instructional practices. In one of the interviews similar to the one in the first school, which aimed at determining teacher and administrator experiences in relation to multiculturalism, it was found that every member of the school was aware of the policy existence and the need for it. Teachers and administrators in schools where multicultural activities exist consistently attributed their interest in multiculturalism to their personal experiences of cultural difference and to a school policy that helps to keep them focused. In the school, the principal had numerous cultural experiences that helped to sharpen the teachers' beliefs and commitment to multicultural education as evident in their practices. The existence of a school district policy, a supportive principal committed to multicultural education, diverse student and staff populations committed to diverse parental involvement and professional development activities can be powerful. Teachers in the second school were clearly up to date in the area of professional development, which were evident in the practices unlike the first school. For instance, participants were engaged in some form of professional development such as workshops and conferences on the importance of parental involvement and the need for the teacher to be aware of where their students were coming from culturally. We are concerned that teachers' awareness of research on issues of multiculturalism contributed to their level of consciousness and commitment to multicultural education.

Teaching practices are frequently reflective of an individual's experience and commitment to multicultural education. Teachers who are instructed to transform their curriculum to include books written by African Americans, Asian Americans, and Native Americans are motivated to deal with those ethnic groups. For instance, in the second school, multicultural materials, especially materials focusing on women and special education, were incorporated into the curriculum in school and classroom activities. As part of their classroom decoration, two of the teachers created a multicultural quilt that represented the diversity of their students. Parents and members of the community were invited to discuss their cultural background with students and teachers. Teachers also disseminated a multicultural literary magazine written by students with the help of people from different cultural backgrounds. These practices reflected their consciousness of and commitment to multicultural education. We believe merely having a policy statement on multicultural education is the first step, the next step is to have a built-in evaluation mechanism and consequences for anyone whose practices are not in sync with the policy.

Policy statements on multicultural education must put into practice. Policy statements must be designed with the support of all constituents if there is to be a consistent level of commitment from teachers who must implement a multicultural education program. Such programs should be consistent with the CSM where all stakeholders contribute to making our schools suitable for all students regardless of any difference they may have. All children, parents, teachers, schools and communities are negatively affected by lack of multicultural policy statements and practices as evidenced in the aforementioned first school and particularly with the teacher's interview. School officials, and others in leadership positions, must understand the implications to both minority and majority students. Research is clear that children from minority groups are less likely to be academically successful when they fail to see themselves positively in the curriculum. Children from "majority group" populations are less likely to be adequately prepared to deal with the real world diversity. As such, teachers, instructional leaders, parents, government agencies need a great understanding of the issues and therefore be provided with the necessary training to build and sustain a curriculum and instructional practices that will benefit all children. To put more practical perspectives on policies, the following recommendations are important:

1. Administrators and other support groups need to work with teachers to ensure that there are policy statements on multicultural education with specific goals and methods to enable them to reach those goals. Policy development must include input from parents and community members. Before developing a multicultural policy statement, educators and parents need to be informed of what multicultural education is to reduce fear and ignorance.
2. Schools should hire experts in multicultural education to assist in designing the curriculum of the school. This should include making an evaluation mechanism to ensure that practices are consistent with school or district policies.
3. Effective and consistent multicultural training is recommended to enable teachers to use strategies that will lead to a more comprehensive approach. It is imperative that parents, teachers, school administrators, and governments at various levels embrace the CSM, and thus provide future generation of leaders the cross cultural competencies they need to succeed.

CONCLUSION

The proposal we advance in this chapter reflects a comprehensive strategy, a strategy that is grounded on system theories and emphasizes high quality interaction among stake holders whose contributions will lead to achievement of success in both our educational system in schools and in the society at large. We believe with integrated efforts the federal government will advance educational policies such as the Elementary and Secondary Education Act (ESEA), or any other initiative that will be significant in determining success for all children. We therefore propose that the CSM, where all stakeholders can contribute various talents and abilities with the aim of providing needed services, would ensure success for every one, including students, parents, and of course, the community.

The CSM with a synergistic approach presents opportunities to tap into the various strengths whether its from parents, teachers, school administrators, and local, state, or federal governments. This will ensure the achievement of the main goal which is equal educational opportunity for all. Its holistic approach through alignment and leveraging resources will be the key to success. For instance, federal government through the Title I Act aims at providing equal academic and learning opportunities for low-income families with school age children; The Education for All Handicapped Children Act (PL94-142) advocates for free appropriate public education for all children with disabilities; Goals 2000 and the Improving America's Schools Act aligning with local initiatives by schools and parents provide better educational opportunities to disadvantaged students. This approach equally would do the same at local levels where collaborative efforts of the principals, parents, and teachers are taking place. The proposed CSM for all learners is based on system theories that emphasize high quality interaction and would certainly benefit everyone (i.e., students, parents, teachers, school, the community, and government). It is therefore, imperative that school administrators set the tone by examining their policies, practices, and values to reflect synergistic strengths of the collaborators in a manner that is consistent with system theories (Bush, 1995).

REFERENCES

Artiles, A.J., & Trent, S.C. (1994). Overrepresentation of minority students in special education: A continuing debate. *The Journal of Special Education, 27* (4), 410–437.

Baca, L., & Almanza, E. (1991). *Language minority students with disabilities.* Reston, VA: Council for Exceptional Children.

Baca, L., & Cervantes H. (1984). *The bilingual special education interface.* St. Louis: Time Mirror/Mosby.

Blazer, B. (1999). Developing 504 classroom accommodation plans: A collaborative, systemic parent-student-teacher approach. *Teaching Exceptional Children, 32* (2), 28–33.

Board of Education of Hendrick Hudson Central School District v. Rowley (1982). 458 U.S.176.

Brown v. Board of Education of Topeka (1954). 347 U.S. 483, 74 S.Ct. 686, 98 L.Ed. 873.

Cecelski, D.S. (1994). *Along freedom road: Hyde County, North Carolina and the fate of black schools in the South.* Chapel Hill, NC: University of North Carolina Press.

Cummins, J. (1984). *Bilingualism and special education: Issues in assessment and pedagogy.* San Diego, CA: College-Hill Press.

Equal Educational Opportunities Act of 1974, 20 U.S.C. Section 1703(f) et seq.

Fernandez, A. (1992). Legal support for bilingual education and language-appropriate related services for limited English proficient students with disabilities. *Bilingual Research Journal, 16* (3), 117–140.

Fuchs, D., & Fuchs, L. (1994). Inclusive schools movement and the radicalization of special education reform. *Exceptional Children, 60,* 294–309.

Garcia, S., & Malkin, D. (1993). Toward defining programs and services for culturally and linguistically diverse learners in special education. *Teaching Exceptional Children, 26* (1), 52–58.

Gersten, R., Brengelman, S., & Jiminez, R. (1994). Effective instruction for culturally and linguistically diverse students: A reconceptualization. *Focus on Exceptional Children, 27* (1), 1–16.

Gersten, R., & Woodward, J. (1994). The language-minority student and special education: Issues, trends, and paradoxes. *Exceptional Children, 60,* 310–322.

Goals 2000: Educate America Act, PL103-227 (1994).

Gonzalez, V., Brusca-Vega, R., & Yawkey, T. (1997). *Assessment and instruction of culturally and linguistically diverse students with or at-risk of learning problems.* Boston: Allyn and Bacon.

Hardman, M., McDonnell, J., & Welch, M. (1997). Perspectives on the future of IDEA. *The Journal of the Association for Persons with Severe Disabilities, 22,* 86–97.

Harris, K.C. (1996). Collaboration within a multicultural society: Issues for consideration. *Remedial and Special Education, 17,* 355–362.

Harry, B., & Anderson, M. (1994). The disproportionate placement of African American males in special education programs: A critique of the process. *Journal of Negro Education, 63* (4), 602–619.

Hehir, T., & Latus, T. (Eds.) (1992). *Special education at the century's end: Evolution of theory and practice since 1970.* Cambridge, MA: Harvard Educational Review.

Heubert, J.P. (Ed.) (1999). *Law and school reform.* New Haven, CT: Yale University Press.

Individuals with Disabilities Education Act, PL101-476, 20 U.S.C., Chapter 33 (1990).

Kavale, K., & Forness, S. (2000). History, rhetoric, and reality: Analysis of the inclusion debate. *Remedial and Special Education, 21* (5), 279–296.

Kreitzer, A.E., Madaus, G.F., & Haney, W. (1989). Competency and drop-outs. In C. Weis & H.G. Petrie (Eds.), *Dropouts from school: Issues, dilemmas, and solutions.* (pp. 129–152). Buffalo, NY: State University of New York Press.

Lau v. Nichols 414 U.S. 563, 94 S.Ct. 786, 39 L. Ed.2d 1 (1974).

McNeil, L. (2000). Creating new inequalities. *Phi Delta Kappan, 81,* 728–734.

Nwoye, J., & Rose, S. (1999). The value of urban seminar in rural teacher training programs. *Journal of Philosophy and History of Education, 50,* 153–156

Olenick, M., & McCroskey, J. (1992). *Social and health services in Los Angeles County Schools: Countywide data on availability, need and funding.* Los Angeles, CA: Los Angeles Roundtable for Children & Los Angeles County Office of Education.

Office of Bilingual Education and Minority Affairs, U.S. Department of Education (2000). *Survey of states' limited English proficient students and available educational programs and services: 1997–1998.* Washington, DC: Author.

Oliva, P. (1994). *Developing the curriculum.* New York: Harper Collins.

Osborne, A. (1999). Students with disabilities. *The Yearbook of education law 1999,* (pp. 139–179) Topeka, KS: National Organization on Legal Problems of Education.

Plessy v. Ferguson, 163 U.S. 537 (1896).

Reimers, F. & McGinn, N. (1997). *Informed Dialogue: Using research to shape education policy around the world.* Westport, CT: Praeger.

Riley, R. (1994). Redefining the federal role in education: Toward a framework for higher standards, improved schools, broader opportunities and new responsibilities for all. *Journal of Law and Education, 23* (3), 298–361.

Riley, R. (1995). The Improving America's Schools Act and elementary and secondary education reform. *Journal of Law and Education, 24* (4), 513–566.

Robinson-Zanartu, C. (1996). Serving Native American children and families: Considering cultural Variables. *Language, speech, and hearing services in schools, 27* (4), 373–384.

Thomas, S., & Rapport, M. (1998). Least restrictive environment: Understanding the direction of the courts. *The Journal of Special Education, 32* (2), 66–78.

Title VI of the Civil Rights Act of 1964, 42 U.S.C. Section 2000d, et seq., 34 C.F.R. Section 100.1, et seq.

Title VII of the Elementary and Secondary Schools Education Act of 1968, 20 U.S.C. §§3221 et seq. Also the Bilingual Education Act.

U.S. Department of Education. (2000). *Digest of education statistics.* Washington, DC: Author.

Wraga, W.G. (1999). The educational and political implications of curriculum alignment and standards-based reform. *Journal of Curriculum and Supervision, 15* (1), 4–25.

Yell, M., Rogers, D., & Rogers, E. (1998). The legal history of special education. *Remedial and Special Education, 19* (4), 219–228.

Ysseldyke, J., & Algozzine, B. (1995). *Special education: A practical approach for teachers.* Boston: Houghton Mifflin.

Chapter 11

THE ROLE OF TECHNOLOGY IN THE EDUCATION OF ALL CHILDREN

Stephen C. Enwefa and Regina L. Enwefa

Technology has influenced every facet of our lives, including communication, education, business, medicine, and transportation. Although technology has impacted our educational system, today's digital age has had an enormous potential for a profound influence in educating all learners in spite of their abilities or disabilities. In this chapter, we agree that technology has been used in the classroom for assistive and instructional purposes. Assistive technology is any item, piece of equipment, mechanical, electrical, electronic, electro-mechanical, computer powered tool or product system whether acquired commercially, off the shelf, modified, or customized that is used to increase, maintain, or improve the functional capabilities of individuals with disabilities (King, 1999; Lloyd, Fuller, & Arvidson, 1997). This broad definition of assistive technology includes the use of hearing aids, wheel chairs, adapted computers, eyeglasses, enlarged handles on kitchen utensils, aided augmentative and alternative devices, Braille codes on elevator buttons, switches, close-captioned televisions, and grab bars on bathroom walls (Glennen & DeCoste, 1997). By contrast, the use of computers and related technologies for the design, plan, delivery, and support of educational programs is called instructional technology. As it appears, instructional technology can be used by all ages, irrespective of disability.

Assistive technology, a powerful educational tool focuses on the special needs of all ages who may have a variety of special sensory, motoric, cognitive and/or linguistic needs (King, 1999). It enables all students to become equal partners in the educational process. It not only maximizes students success in the classroom, but also creates opportunities for increased expectation, independence, and inclusion in all school activities. Many regular students have used assistive technology to increase their achievement in the classroom, and many with disabilities have traced majority of their successes to the use of assistive technology (see King). For instance, positioning devices have enhanced the active participation of students with physical disabilities in school work and allowed them to join classmates at tables, on the floor, or in a standing position. In addition, auditory trainers, including frequency modulation (FM) systems have provided students with hearing impairments with opportunities to receive the same lessons and enjoy the company of other students in the school playgrounds. Even students with visual impairments have accessed text information independently from library and other sources by using literacy assistive technology equipments such as portable Kurtzweil reading devices, refreshable Braille computer output, tactile graphic display systems, Braille translation software and Braille printer (Anderson & Speck, 2001). Assistive technology can be either high-tech or low-tech. The high-tech assistive technologies include sensory devices but are not limited to memo mate, alternative keyboards, key board emulators, speech recognition systems, voice output systems, computer screen readers, sensory devices for the hearing impaired, Braille printers for the visually impaired, sending fax or e-mail, an electric stair lift, and robotic devices for students who are severely and physically challenged (see King; Lloyd et al.,). Low-tech devices include tape loops, modified knobs on faucets, elevated or adjustable counter tops, calculators, alarm clock, head pointers, adaptive eating utensils, velcro, handwriting with pen or pencil, picture or symbol communication boards, and key guards for standard computer keyboards (see King; Lloyd et al.).

Instructional technology can be classified in several different ways. Means, Blando, Olson, Middleton, Morocco, Remz, and Zorfass (1993) identified four broad categories: tutorial, exploratory, application, and communication. Tutorial instructional technology, traditionally has represented a transmission view of learning where the information to be learned resides in the computer software and is transmitted to the student. Also, tutorial instructional technology includes drill-and-practice software and other explicit instructional applications–these tutorial applications have consistently and continuously emerged as the technology of choice for students with exceptionalities. Exploratory instructional technology evolved with the development of multimedia applications and software. The exploratory application provides students with the opportunity to roam through the application in search of information. Students are able to navigate through the program and control the learning that goes on. Exploratory applications are instructional learning programs that include electronic versions of encyclopedias or multimedia databases. Application is an instructional technology tool used to facilitate tasks such as writing or the classification, and storage of data. Technology applications are database, spreadsheet, and word processor. Communication technologies include Internet, Intranet, e-mail, chat rooms, NetMeeting, netshow, and many others. Communication technology provides students with opportunities to send and receive information in the information super highway.

BARRIERS AFFECTING TECHNOLOGY USE FOR ALL LEARNERS

Although both assistive and instructional technologies provide access and maximize learning opportunities for students across the board, in this chapter, our view is that some barriers to effective use of technology still exist. First, there is the misguided view of the needs of students who use technology in the classrooms. Second, there is a systematic failure to help educators develop relevant understanding of how technology can and should be used with students, irrespective of mental and physical abilities.

The general consensus among educators evidenced in recent research on learning infers that the "transmission" view of knowledge practiced in our nation's classrooms is no longer adequate and justifiable (Bransford, Goldman, & Vye, 1991; Brown, Collins, & Duguid, 1989; Cognition and Technology Group at Vanderbilt, 1990, 1991; Resnick, 1987; Resnick, & Klopfer, 1989). The thrust of traditional pedagogical methodology is to provide well-structured environment for the presentation of learning stimulus through lecture, demonstration, and recitation. The contemporary approach configures new learning in terms of prior knowledge by an active learner in social context asserting that knowledge is best acquired in functional contexts with similarities to situations for future transfer.

ESSENTIAL ELEMENTS OF SCHOOL-BASED TECHNOLOGY SUPPORT SYSTEM

Educators in America's schools are aware of the enormous potential of technology in our educational process. An active school-based support system is required for technology to deliver on its potential. With an active support system in place, educators are given the opportunity to become genuine technology users. The essential elements of a school-based technology support system are administrative supports, consumer education, technology for poets, intimacy with machines, design consultants, and financial issues (Brunner, 1990). Educators need administrators who understand the complexity of integrating technology into the school curricula. The administrative support may mean a change in the physical set up of classrooms, new security problems, and a new relationship to the county/district office and the custodial staff. Also, it may mean educators collaborating in different ways and groups of students working on projects at the same time, and the chaos that could lead to educators asking administrators to write grant proposals for new equipment. All these activities require administrators who are willing to encourage experimentation and collaboration among educators.

It is apparent that educators must not be afraid to risk disruption including short-term failure in the interest of innovation and reform. They must possess an overview of the world of educational technology that helps them become educated consumers. Such overview in a course format must adequately whet their appetite by providing ideas and examples of the uses of technology so they can make informed decisions about hardware or software applications. In addition, educators must enroll in courses designed to help them develop curricula that integrate technology. Practically, this may mean courses in which educators collaborate in creating curricula that are not technology driven but make use of technology. In fact, educators must become user friendly with technology as a tool for teaching and learning. Learning to use technology in the classroom demands patience, time, and instruction, and to a large extent requires access to computers for practice, experimentation, and exploration. Educators need technology design consultants as resource persons in schools and new kinds of specialists to create individualized tools made possible by new technologies. New specialists are those who are trained in educational design, and who can help educators put their ideas into practice by creating software applications for them or by customizing existing technologies.

Adequate financial resources are always an issue when dealing with technology in the classroom. A considerable amount of money is used to purchase hardware, software, and accessories for set up and continuous maintenance. Procuring new technologies and customizing existing ones require financial resources in addition to the technical know-how.

EQUALIZING EDUCATION THROUGH TECHNOLOGY

The present technological advancement has forced educators to redefine literacy in technology classroom as a social process dependent on cultural and electronic contexts (Flood & Kapp, 1995; Leu, 1997; Gallego & Hollingsworth, 1992; Reinking, 1995). The basis for this argument is the assumption that students continue to expand both their reading and writing activities beyond traditional prints to include electronic contexts that involve print and nonprint forms of communication. This implies that literacy now involves the ability to make sense of and navigate through several forms of information including images, sounds, animation, music, and ongoing discussion (El-Hindi, 1998). For instance, students are Internet users, and they respond to e-mail messages, engage in online conversations, chat rooms, Net-Meeting, and navigate through vast amount of information in a combination of print and nonprint formats (Ryder & Graves, 1996–1997). As students continue to interact with electronic contexts through reading and writing, they have the opportunity to increase their success in school. This type of electronic communication by students is accurately described as a new literacy that forces educators to rethink what and how literacy should be thought (Reinking, 1992, 1994, 1995). Through this medium of communication, students are now able to use a variety of technological and informational resources including electronic libraries, databases, computer networks, and videos to gather and synthesize information in addition to being able to create and communicate knowledge.

Education of At-Risk Students

During the education process, many students are faced with variety of problems ranging from academic to personal, and social. A great majority of students at risk never reach their intellectual potential. Socioeconomic problems, and cultural differences, language barriers, belief systems, as well as physical and mental disabilities work against the success of students in schools across the country. Perhaps, almost all of the students from low income families, and minority students are constantly subjected to inequities, stereotypes, and discrimination which put them at risk of failure. To overcome these problems, schools must in effect undergo a paradigm shift and embrace promising new methods of education quite different from the traditional model. To shift paradigms and powers, schools must use technology to zero in on the individual learning problems of students through counseling, tutoring, and motivating them to learn to have high expectations. Technology has the potential and can provide help in ways different from past educational approaches to aid all categories of students learn in school, and become critical thinkers and problem solvers. Studies (e.g., Braun, 1992) have shown that students learn more and better by using and accessing technology in an intelligent and structured environment. As indicated, there are many factors that classify students into at-risk groups. For sure, these students are at risk of dropping out of school and in danger of failing to complete their education with an adequate level of skill (Slavin & Madden, 1989).

The direct consequence of cultural diversity of today's students is the existence of language barriers that put students in at-risk positions. The Black English vernacular or Ebonics spoken at many African American homes differ in many ways from the standard American English at school and therefore causes confusion among students from this ethnic group as to which of the two English-speaking systems is correct. Also, Spanish-speaking immigrants from Latin and South America encounter marked difficulty when they are mainstreamed in all-English classrooms. The placement of these students in effective bilingual classrooms at an early age makes them become successful participants in schools.

Braun (1992) and Uroff and Greene (1991) noted that traditional methods of educating at-risk learners are woefully inadequate to meet their diverse needs. Several different programs have been designed and implemented to meet the needs of such students. Hamilton (1986) reported 17 different successful vocational education programs that effectively increased students' achievement, reduced absenteeism, and decreased drop out rates. The programs among other things were characterized by low educator/student ratios, high time on task, practical real-life applications, and different opportunities to relate learning with out-of-school experiences. Another significant aspect of the programs is the utilization of Mann's (1986) four Cs of a successful education program for at-risk students. The four Cs stands for cash, care, computers, and coalitions.

Cash refers to the opportunity offered to students to make money while utilizing concepts learned in the classroom. This activity is a work experience that enables students to relate subject matter learned in school with the demands in a productive environment.

Care refers to the nurturing environment that results when individualized attention is provided to students in a low teacher/student ratio situations, when high expectations are held for students, and when students are immediately held accountable for learning.

Computers refer to tools that enable educators of at-risk students to efficiently document and track student progress, individualize instruction, motivate, and challenge students in a non-threatening environment as well as provide feedback.

Coalitions refer to bringing together parents, communities, and businesses into a more active and positive participation in the education of youths. Rogers and Widenhaus (1991) suggested differentiating the curricula and mode of teaching of at-risk students from typical regular education programs to atypical programs that emphasize individualized instruction, clear objectives, prompt feedback, and an active role for students in the educational process. Additionally, their observation showed that students respond to programs that are demanding and programs that involve group interaction and decision making.

One of the major advantages of the implementation of technology in the classroom is individualized instruction. Individualization of instructional objectives has been the focus of technology applications in education, allowing all categories of students to work at their own pace with immediate feedback. The continued success of average students in the classroom results from the use of technology and the ability of students to have access to technology in their education programs. Technology can be a great equalizer for at-risk students who face academic, cultural, personal, and social challenges in their education process. It can be an equalizer for racial and ethnic minorities who do not fare well in schools as the majority students. It is nonjudgmental and can provide an instructional sequence that is tailored to the needs of individual students. In addition, technology provides students who are embarrassed by low level work with a sense of academic privacy, and thus gives them a sense of empowerment. It allows students to control their learning, gives them a sense of responsibility, and often improves their self-esteem. The use of integrated software programs motivates at-risk students to learn through simulations, video, and sound. Technology provides the medium for students to relate mental images to ideas and phrases through its various sensory components. The evolving technology-based educational programs have the potential to enable culturally and linguistically diverse students to interact with technology in their native language, while at the same time increasing their productivity. As a result, at-risk students feel less intimidated with technology since it seems to have infinite patience. The use of technology as information sources via bulletin boards or electronic mail system provides students with learning experiences that might not be otherwise possible. Since at-risk students need extra time to prosper educationally, technology can expand the focus of their education beyond basic skills and thus boost their self-image. Technology provides these students with the medium to communicate their ideas effectively in cyberspace, thus giving them a sense of global connection and better perspective on their individual lives (Enwefa, Enwefa, & Banks, in press).

USING TECHNOLOGY TO EDUCATE ALL LEARNERS

Issues in the education of all learners have often centered on teaching strategies that are innovative and successful. Other issues have ranged from individualization of instruction, use of special educators with smaller classes, classroom learning environment, and parental involvement. Therefore, it is no surprise that all learners have similar needs with regard to relevant education. The question then becomes if individualized instruction, classroom learning environment, and parental involvement are effective strategies, what role can technology play to assist educators in facilitating these strategies?

The traditional computer-assisted instruction (CAI) is one excellent example of how technology facilitates the implementation of individualized instruction in the classroom. The use of exploratory tools such as electronic encyclopedias are ideal for a student to individually investigate a problem discussed in class. A typical multimedia platform that is useful for individual instruction is the electronic book *Grandma and Me*–this book encourages creativity, exploration, and can be read in either English, Spanish, or Japanese. This is another example of educational programs that provide opportunities for students to interact with technology in their native language. In addition, CAI programs allow for assessment, drill and practice, instruction, stimulation, or creative productions (Siegel, Good, & More, 1996). Special needs' students can be helped by CAI because these programs are often self paced and individualized for each student's needs. Studies have shown that CAI motivates, teaches, and empowers special needs students as well as helping to improve their communication skills (Bitter, 1993; Cockran & Bull, 1993; Holzberg, 1994). Students categorized as nonverbal have used computers as major components of communication devices (Bigge, 1991). Computers are known to create instructional context that can provide audio and visual stimuli and interactions for educators and students (Giordano, Leeper, & Siegel, 1996). Many schools now use video disks, compact disks, and often software applications that include interaction with audio and video; and educators are now able to program questions or directions into the video to create customized interactive activities for their students and curricula (Brosnan, 1995).

Integrated learning systems provide educators with daily assessments of students' progress and effectively prescribe instructional activities specifically designed for students. Some technologies lend themselves well to collaborative learning activities including computer-based simulations, computer conferencing, NetMeeting, and database access. The use of telecommunication technology means that cooperative learning no longer has to be limited to students in the same classroom or campus, but rather the ability to link students statewide, regionally, nationally, and globally. The mainstreaming of students suggests that cooperative learning environments can be made possible for students to capitalize on their strengths and demonstrate them to others in ways that would be impossible if they were required to compete for rewards with others. Cooperative learning is beneficial to all learners because of the learning that occurs due to interaction.

Technology instruction focuses on basic problem-solving and coping skills appropriate for all students. There are many software packages to assist educators in basic skill instruction, and several of these programs are targeted toward the improvement of problem solving skills. Technology can be an appropriate tool for cross- disciplinary education. In many schools, writing laboratories at all grade levels encourage writing across disciplines in an effort to connect several different subject areas. Computer simulations offer integration approaches for learning, and thus provide opportunity for the incorporation of topics in mathematics, sciences, and language arts. into school instructional lessons. Additionally, technology can be a facilitating tool for parental involvement in the education of students. The most readily available technology in our society is the telephone, and telephone answering machines can provide voice data output to parents calling in for homework assignments and materials covered during the day or week. Telephones are an integral aspect of telecommunication technology and its application from home computers hooked up to databases at school could make electronic encyclopedias available for home use, which will be helpful to both student and parent. Telephone lines can equally be used to provide access to software for home use.

It is important to note that technology provides excellent opportunity for peer tutoring, and students can direct and help others to navigate through a new software package. To a large measure, this frees the educator to manage other learning activities in the classroom. Most of the available subject-specific software packages provide a management component, whereby a tutor and tutee work as a team on lessons and the software provides the educator with a measure of their success. Another technology that is frequently underutilized in the home is the instructional video because most homes own televisions and video players. Video products that can improve student study skills and encourage student-parent interaction are now commercially available to the public. School systems can purchase these video products and encourage their students to take them home–this will provide opportunities for parental involvement in the learning process. In addition to video products, there are hand held calculators and instructional software for home computers that can be effectively used with parents. Apparently, integrated learning systems provide not only excellent reports for educators but automated reports that may be sent home to parents. Several of the available software packages interface nicely with a word processor–these can facilitate easy provision of weekly, quarterly, and annual progress reports.

CONCLUSION

This chapter has addressed the role of technology in the education of all children. Clearly, there are factors including social, financial, cultural, personal, systemic, and demographic problems that make technology less effective in the educational process. However, available and developing technologies offer potential solutions to majority of the problems we are faced with in the education of all children. Technology must be used in new ways that make teaching and learning more effective. If we want to use technology successfully in this millennium and beyond, we must learn from our past experiences. The new ways must include systemic approach to help educators understand the important relationship between technology and learning. Also, we must help educators understand the evils and inadequacy of the traditional transmission approach to teaching. The traditional techniques that were used in the past have proven not to maximize student learning experiences, so the employment of innovative approaches is imperative. An effective way to educate all children must be characterized by stimulating instructional programs and the use of all available resources, including technology.

General and special educators must revisit their philosophies of teaching with an intent to incorporate new and exciting technology-based instructional approaches. Technology can potentially provide the mechanism for reaching students while simultaneously empowering both the student and educator. In the end, schools must be supported as they actively provide powerful technology directly to general and special educators. Also, we must provide them with ongoing educational and staff development opportunities on how technology can be effectively used in the classroom. The system must engage in continuous research activities with respect to understanding the relationship between technology and the achievement of students. Since we believe technology can facilitate the interaction between parents, educators, and students, educators must change their philosophies to recognize when and where the incorporation of technology into instructional techniques can best be implemented.

REFERENCES

Anderson, R. S., & Speck, B. W. (2001) *Using technology in k-8 literacy classrooms.* Upper Saddle River: NJ: Prentice Hall.

Anderson, J., & Lee, A. (1995). Literacy teachers learning a new literacy: A study of the use of electronic mail in a reading education class. *Reading Research and Instruction, 34,* 222–238.

Bigge, J. L. (1991). *Teaching individuals with physical and multiple disabilities* (3rd ed.). New York: Macmillan.

Bitter, G. G. (1993). *Using a microcomputer in the classroom* (3rd ed.). Needham Heights, MA: Allyn & Bacon.

Bransford, J. D., Goldman, S. R., & Vye, N. J. (1991). Making a difference in peoples' abilities to think: Reflections on a decade of work and some hopes for the future. In L. Okagaki & R. J. Sternberg (Eds.), *Directors of development: Influences on children* (pp. 147–180). Hillsdale, NJ: Lawrence Erlbaum.

Braun, L. (1992). The worth of a child. *Momentum, 23*(1), 10–13.

Brosnan, P. A. (1995). *Learning about tasks computers can perform.* (ERIC Document Reproduction Service No. ED 380 280)

Brown, J. S., Collins, A., & Duguid, P. (1989). Situated cognition and the culture of learning. *Educational Researcher, 18,* 32–41.

Brunner, C. (1990). What it really means to integrate technology. *Technology and Learning, 11,* 13–14.

Buggey, T. (1999) Assistive technology for learners with special needs. In G. R. Morrison, D. Lowther, & L. Demeulle (Eds.), *Integrating computer technology in the classroom.* Upper Saddle River, NJ: Prentice Hall.

Cochran, P. S., & Bull, G. L., (1993). Computers and individuals with speech and language disorders. In J. D. Lindsey (Ed.), *Computers and exceptional individuals* (pp. 143–158). Austin, TX: Pro-Ed.

Cognition and Technology Group at Vanderbilt. (1990). Anchored instruction and its relationship to situated cognition, *Educational Researcher, 19* (6), 2–10.

Cognition and Technology Group at Vanderbilt. (1991). Technology and the design of generative learning environments. *Educational Technology, 31*(5), 34–40.

Craver, J. M., & Burton-Radzely, L. (Eds.). (1998). *Technology links to literacy: A casebook of special educators' use of technology to promote literacy.* Calverton, MD: Macro International.

Dunkel, P. (Ed.) (1991). *Computer-assisted language learning and testing: research issues and practice.* New York: Newbury House.

El-Hindi, A. (1998). *The having of wonderful ideas.* New York: Teachers College Press

El-Hindi, A. (1998). Beyond classroom boundaries: Constructivist teaching with the Internet. In D. J. Leu (Ed.), Exploring literacy on the Internet. *The Reading Teacher, 51*(8), 694–700.

Enwefa, S. C., Enwefa, R. L., & Banks, I. W. (in press) Building technologically oriented learning communities: Some early thoughts on teaching and learning in cyberspace. *The Researcher.*

Epstein, J. L. (1987). Parent involvement: What research says to administrators. *Education and Urban Society, 19*(2), 119–136.

Flood, J., & Lapp, D. (1995). Broadening the lens: Toward an expanded conceptualization of literacy. In K. A. Hinchman, D. J. Leu, & C. K. Kinzer (Eds.), *Perspectives on literacy research and practice* (pp. 1–16). Chicago: National Reading Conference.

Gallego, M., & Hollingsworth, S. (1992). Multiple literacies: Teachers evolving perceptions. *Language Arts, 69,* 206–213.

Giordano, G., Leeper, L., & Siegel. (1996). Computer assisted literacy programs. In G. Giordano (Ed.), *Literacy: Programs for adults with developmental disabilities.* San Diego, CA: Singular.

Glennen, S. L., & Decoste, D. C. (1997). *A handbook of augmentative and alternative communication.* San Diego, CA: Singular.

Grosse, C. U., & Leto, L. J. (1999). Virtual communications and networking in distance learning. *TESOL Journal, 9* (1), 1–7.

Hamilton, S. F. (1986, Spring). Raising standards and reducing drop-out rates. *Teachers College Record,* pp. 413–416.

Holzberg, C. S. (1994). Technology in special education. *Technology and Learning, 14* (7), 18–21.

Irvine, D. J. (1979). *Parent involvement affects children's cognitive growth.* Albany, NY: University of the State of New York.

King, T. W. (1999). *Assistive technology: Essential human factors.* Boston: Allyn and Bacon.

Leu, D. (1997). Caity's question: Literacy as deixis on the Internet. *The Reading Teacher, 51*(1), 62–67.

Lloyd, L. L., Fuller, D. R., & Arvidson, H. H. (1997). *Augmentative and alternative communication: A handbook of principles and practices.* Boston: Allyn and Bacon.

Mann, D. (1986). Thinking about the undoable: Dropout programs. In P. Penn (Ed.). *Children at risk: An urban education network conference proceedings* (pp. 1–11). Charleston, WV: Appalachia Educational Library.

Means, B. (Ed.). (1994). *Technology and education reform: The reality behind the promise.* San Francisco, CA: Jossey-Bass.

Means, B., Blando, J., Olson, K., Middleton, T., Morocco, C., Remz, A., & Zorfass, J. (1993). *Using technology to support education reform.* Washington, DC: U.S. Department of Education.

Morrison, G. R., Lowther, D. L., & Demeulle, L. (1999). *Integrating computer technology into the classroom.* Upper Saddle River, NJ: Prentice Hall.

Nardini, M. L., & Antes, R (1991). What strategies are effective with at-risk students? *NASSP-Bulletin, 75,* 67–72.

Nickerson, R. S. (1988). Technology in education in 2020: Thinking about the not-distant future. In R. Nickerson & P. Zodhiates (Eds.), *Technology in education: Looking toward 2020* (pp. 1–10). Hillsdale, NJ: Lawrence Erlbaum.

Reinking, D. (1992). Differences between electronic and printed texts: An agenda for research. *Journal of Educational Multimedia and Hypermedia, 1*(1), 11–24.

Reinking, D. (1994). *Electronic literacy perspective in reading research No. 4.* Athens, GA: National Reading Research Center, Universities of Georgia and Maryland.

Reinking, D. (1995). Reading and writing with computers: Literacy research in a post-typographic world. In K. A. Hinchman, D. J. Leu, & C. K. Kinzer (Eds.), *Perspectives on literacy research and practice, 45th yearbook of the National Reading Conference* (pp. 17–33). Chicago, IL: National Reading Conference.

Resnick, L. (1987). *Education and learning to think.* Washington, DC: National Academy Press.

Resnick, L. B., & Klopfer, L. E. (Eds.). (1989). *Toward the thinking curriculum: Current cognitive research.* Alexandria, VA: Association for Supervision and Curriculum Development.

Rich, D. (1988). Bridging the parent gap in education reform. *Education Horizons, 66*(2), 90–92.

Rogus, J. F., & Widenhaus, C. (1991). Programming for at-risk learners: A preventative approach. *NASSP Bulletin, 75*, 1–7.

Ryder, R., & Graves, M. (1996–1997, December – January). Using the Internet to enhance students' reading, writing, and information gathering skills. *Journal of Adolescent & Adult Literacy, 40*, 244–254.

Siegel, J. (1999). Utilizing technology for the inclusion of individuals with mental retardation. In P. Retish & S. Reiter (Eds.), *Adults with disabilities: International perspectives in the community*. Mahwah, NJ: Lawrence Erlbaum.

Siegel, J., Good, K., & Moore, J. (1996). Integrating technology into educating preservice education teachers. *Action in Teacher Education, 17*(4), 53–63.

Slavin, R., & Madden, N. A. (1989). What works for students at-risk: A research synthesis. *Educational Leadership, 46*(5), 4–13.

Thompson-Hoffman, S., & Hayward, B. J. (1990). *Students with handicaps who drop out of school*. Tempe, AZ: Conference on Preventing Rural School Dropouts.

Teichmann, D. (1994). Connecting through e-mail and videoconferencing. *Technology and Learning, 14* (8), 49–66.

Uroff, S., & Greene, B. (1991). A low-risk approach to high-risk students. *NASSP Bulletin, 75*, 59–66.

VanTassel-Baska, J., Patton, J. M., & Prillaman, P. (1991). *Gifted youth at-risk: A report of a national study*. Reston, VA: Council for Exceptional Children.

Warschauer, M. (1999). *Email for English teaching: Bringing the Internet and computer learning networks into the language classroom*. Burlingame, CA: Alta.

Chapter 12

EDUCATING ALL CHILDREN GLOBALLY

FERNANDO ALMEIDA DINIZ

The world is being transformed by new rules, new tools and new actors into a vast global marketplace. Human freedoms face new threats from transition, conflicts, xenophobia, human trafficking and religious fundamentalism. And all over the world people with HIV/AIDS face serious threats to their human rights. Along with these new issues, persistent poverty and wider inequality are now treated as a denial of human rights and thus emerge as continuing human rights challenges. (United Nations Development Program [UNDP], 2000, p. 42.)

At the start of this millennium, humankind is being encouraged to think "globally." The terms "globalization" and "global politics" have found expression in the vocabularies of the world's major languages, though they have come to encompass everything from financial markets to information and communications technology, popular culture to criminal activity, and fashion to spiritual trends. Yet, there are some who warn that the idea lacks precise definition and is in danger of becoming another cliché of our times; they contend that beyond a general acknowledgement of a real or perceived intensification of global interconnectedness, there is substantial disagreement as to how the phenomenon is to be conceptualized. Neither is there universal support for the merits of the approach as a means of achieving a socially just society.

Held, McGrew, Goldblatt, and Perraton (1999) distinguished between three broad schools of thought in an attempt to understand and explain this social phenomenon; they called these the "hyperglobalizers," the "sceptics," and the "transformationalists" (p. 2). The first school sees nation-states as unnecessary and celebrates the emergence of the global market and competition as the harbingers of human progress. Perhaps the most prominent political leaders who have been associated with this politics of "competition and consumption" are Margaret Thatcher and Ronald Reagan, both of whom presided over a period when the national income gap between rich and poor in their respective countries rose by more than 16% (UNDP, 2000, p.6). It was the British Prime Minister who infamously proclaimed in an interview in a women's magazine: "There is no society. There are only individuals and families." The reaction to this was a swift and powerful debate led by the Commission for Social Justice which counter-argued that, "a good society depends not just on the economic success of the individual, but on the 'social capital' of the community. Communities do not become strong because they are rich; they become rich because they are strong" (Commission on Social Justice, 1994, p. 10).

The second school maintains that the above thesis is fundamentally flawed and politically naïve since it understates the power of national governments to regulate and actively promote continuing economic liberalization. It sees "regionalization" as central as the world economy evolves in the direction of three major financial and trading blocks: Europe, Asia-Pacific and North America. The exclusion of Africa, Central and South America and a large part of Asia from the equation is, in my view, significant. The final school sees "globalization" as a powerful transformative force that is responsible for a "massive shake-out" of societies, economies, institutions of governance and world order. It is the only thesis that explicitly recognizes that the reconfiguration of global power relations has resulted in new patterns of global stratification in which some states, societies and communities are becoming winners while others are increasingly marginalized. To a great extent, these two schools account for the "Third Way" economic policies adopted by the Blair and Clinton administrations; their approach accepts the economic logic of capitalist globalization but constructs the nation-state as partner or enabler in empowering individuals and disadvantaged groups to "help themselves" (Blair, 1998; Giddens, 1998). This shift towards the pursuit of national social capital as a means of combating social exclusion has certainly brought benefits, though Britain and other countries continue to experience serious social divisions, triggered by unpredictable external forces, as globalization weakens the nation-state's powers, including those over economic management. Reich (1992), in a book appropriately titled, *The Work of Nations*, argued that all that will remain within national borders are the people who comprise the nation; each nation's primary assets will be its citizens' skills and insights. About 10 years later, this view seems outdated, as the notions of "nation" and "nationals" are under strain in the United Kingdom (Diniz, 2000).

The main conclusion for optimists and pessimists alike is that, at this stage of human history, there is still uncertainty about the underlying causes of "globalization" and its connection with wider debates about modernity. The only certainty is that virtually all nation-states have to some extent become enmeshed in and are functionally part of this larger pattern of global transformation and global flows. Alongside this is the increasing evidence of the intense patterns of exchange, power, hierarchy, and inequality that have surfaced in social divisions across the world (UNDP, 2000). It is these questions of the social impact of economic, ecological and social security on human communities, rather than traditional geopolitics, that are increasingly gaining the attention of governments and citizens alike (Held et al., 1999). Whether world governments and educators are equally committed to human rights remains a central question. In this chapter, my premise is that human rights do matter locally, internationally, and globally. It is the extent to which these intricacies are infused in global education and school programming that I seek to explore.

THE STRUGGLE FOR HUMAN RIGHTS

The twentieth century has brought unprecedented advances in human progress and betterment, including the defeat of Hitler, the end of colonial rule, the struggles against the legacy of slavery by the civil rights movement in the United States, the rights achieved by women, and the end of apartheid. There is a greater consensus over the concept of "human rights" and, since the end of the cold war, the relationship between "human rights" and "human development" is no longer in dispute; the notion of civil and political rights on the one hand and economic and social rights on the other are regarded as two sides of the same coin (Department for International Development, 1997). Civil society has increasingly played an active role in promoting the idea of "human rights" itself and individuals are much more confident about using the phrase to express what they find important; for example, people across the globe understood what they considered to be abuses of human beings when shown television footage of the terrible violence of genocide in Rwanda and were instrumental in forcing the issue on to the political agenda (Shaw, 1999). And as the events surrounding the World Trade Organization Ministerial Conference in Seattle, Washington in 1997 showed, there is public reluctance to rely on governments and institutions to bring about changes and a desire, particularly by articulate young people, to take direct responsibility for the struggle for human rights. In other words, the emerging human rights culture is capable of being strengthened from below, as is demonstrated by the explosion of nongovernmental organizations that now champion human rights concerns at local and global levels (UNDP, 2000).

However, as UNDP (2000) documented, there is a downside of persistent "human wrongs," of gross violations of human dignity and life, both loud (e.g., genocide) and silent (e.g., poverty, child labor, and sexism) that continues to present a global challenge in all societies and cultures, rich and poor. The report also strongly suggested that it would be futile to assume that there is an universal commitment to human rights issues and to ignore the reality that there are many groups, governments, institutions, and individuals in positions of power and superiority who still see the promotion of human rights for some groups—children, women, ethnic minorities, immigrants, poor people—as a threat; their opposition is often camouflaged with distorted claims of cultural relativism, or political necessity, or some make the lack of resources the reason for inaction. Even in times of prosperity or in more economically rich societies, there is evidence of outright hostility or indifference to sections of communities.

GLOBAL RESPONSIBILITY AND GLOBAL AWARENESS

The question of the relationship between global responsibility and global awareness was brought home to me a short time after being invited to contribute to this book. Consider my fascinating but sad experience! I had traveled to Boston, Massachusetts, to attend an important national seminar concerning the problematic question of "Minority Issues in Special Education," and I chose to attend, mindful of the failure of the British and European special education establishments to address this issue (Diniz, 1999). Here, in effect, is a problem of inequality and human rights in education systems across continents (Artiles & Larsen, 1998). Just before the seminar, I paid my first visit to one of the city's internationally famous institutions of higher education and unexpectedly had the following encounter with a member of the academic staff whom I met.

Q: represent the White American academic.
R: represents me, Black British visiting academic.

    Q: "Are you at (Names his university)?"
    R: "No, I'm from the University of Edinburgh."
    Q: "Oh, Scotland! But you don't look Scottish to me?"
    R: (Maintaining British etiquette) "Why do you say so?"
    Q: "Because you look like from much further away" . . . (gestures)
    R: (Politely persists) "I don't get your meaning . . ."
    Q: "You're not originally from Scotland!"

The stage was set for a negotiation of meaning about traditional distinctions between domestic/international, insider/outsider in conventional politics. In the current discourse it might also be about "inclusion" and "exclusion." See further discussions below:

> **R:** "How similar we are, both 'outsiders' aren't we! You are not originally from here either, are you?"
> **Q:** (Looks sharply at R)
> **R:** "My apologies if I've not recognized your Native American roots."
> **Q:** (Walks away with more gestures)
> **R:** (Continues in reflection and somewhat ashamed at self!)

I do not believe my racial, ethnic, or cultural identity was the central point, though this may have triggered events; and whereas the incident is one that I am well used to as a Black man living in a radicalized Britain, it did catch me offguard. (Note: I use the term Black to refer to people who are associated with the African, Asian or Latin American diasporas and acknowledge that this term is contested in discourse on "race" and ethnicity in Europe; the equivalent term in the USA is "people of color"). What might this tell us about our capacity to take responsibility for the common human heritage envisaged in the raft of UN Charters and Declarations of Human Rights? Is it possible to escape responsibility for those "other people" in spaces distant from those that govern our daily lives in "nation-states" or "discrete civilizations," to which "Q" may have believed only he rightly belonged to? I was reminded of a term "space invaders," that Puwar (2001) coined to characterize the situation of Black senior civil administrators employed in the British Civil Service, "an institution that is deemed to be at the absolute apex of disembodied, neutral professionalism." She argued that "an engagement with the interview accounts of these 'space invaders' allows us to grasp some idea of what it is like for them to coexist in a place that is built on a 'racial contract' which has demarcated spaces in accordance with radicalized corporealities" (p. 1). This in turn made me question whether I was a radicalized space invader in "Q's" thinking, incapable of having a claim to being Scottish or European? It raises further dilemmas about the status to be accorded to the increasing numbers of displaced persons and refugees currently escaping from state disintegration, ethnic tensions, and poverty in Africa and Asia or seeking a better life in the rich industrial "free" world; conservative estimates have suggested that there were 70 countries with an excess of 10,000 refugees, a gross underestimate today (UNHCR, 1995). Should we as individuals be concerned with the human rights of these new space invaders? Can "Fortress Europe" or "Fortress USA" stem the flows and what are the consequences for world peace?

Some might suggest that I was reading too much into this encounter with "Q" and that I should have dismissed it as an unfortunate example of dysfunctional interpersonal or international relations. I felt so too, but could not help thinking that the prism that "Q" had adopted so naturally might have something to do with the substance of the seminar I was to attend. It was not surprising therefore that the next item that came to my attention was a report, in the *Boston Herald*, decrying the failure of African American and Latino students in the Massachusetts state exams, despite the billions of dollars that are being spent (Hayward, 2000). Nor were the complaints that I heard about incidents of institutional racism experienced by "minority" students at the two high-status universities or that both institutions had an underrepresentation of minority academics in their faculties. Such experiences are not solely confined to the United States. Recently, within the university in which I work, an electronic message to all academic staff contained details of the United Kingdom Trade Union Congress' meeting concerned with the rights of Black workers. It provoked this response from a university colleague I call "E."

> Enough is enough! I have heard about conferences for Women Engineers. Now, Black Workers? If there were to be a conference for white, middle-class male staff there would be havoc. This is not what I pay my union subscriptions for. (Signed: White, middle-class and comfortable, thank you!)

What does the above episode tell us about individual and group solidarity for human rights in employment? Was "E" actually expressing genuine objections at being excluded for being White, middle-class and male? Writing about the ethics of global responsibility, Midgley (1999) suggested that people who view the language of "rights" as inappropriate, whether for humans or animals, may simply label it as empty rhetoric and dismiss the whole claim without even asking themselves about the moral issues behind it. Ominously, she concluded that for academics, "this confusion between the verbal and the substantial levels is surely rampant" (p.168). The behaviors of "Q" and "E" have been a powerful reminder that, despite the rhetoric of "diversity" and "inclusion" often heard in academic discourses, institutionalized attitudes remain powerful barriers to change across the education system.

Meanwhile, at a structural level, the notion of global responsibility faces governments in the rich world with ethical and political dilemmas as they walk the tight rope between being guardians of their "national economic interest" and members of the new age "global village"; the trade war between the United States and European Union over bananas from the Caribbean is illustrative of this conflict. Schools and universities in Europe and the United States are similarly in the front line of contradictory pressures in attempting to contribute to the nation's competitiveness, while claiming the accolade of being inclusive global institutions (Apple & Zenk, 1996). In a significant research report on current education practice in Britain, Gillborn and Youdell (2000) concluded that "the wider education system, policymakers, head teachers and teachers are currently remarkably busy remaking and reinforcing inequality, especially in relation to "race" and social class (albeit that they are frequently unaware of these particular "fruits" of their labours). It is time that this level of activity was refocused toward the achievement of social justice" (p. 222). Given the systemic challenges facing us at all levels, I believe our priorities as educators must be to refocus our attention towards educating future generations so that they are prepared to live in a socially just global community. We need to develop a praxis of human rights education that is capable of liberating all learners from attitudes that "imprison human rights potentialities in a static, particularistic and regressive discourse, reproducing prevailing patterns of power rather than the reinvention of the politics of human possibility" (Booth, 1999, p. 32).

MAPPING AN AGENDA FOR "HUMAN RIGHTS EDUCATION" IN SCHOOLS

There can be no justifiable discussion about the nature of schooling or educational experience unless crucial concerns about the "right" to education and the extent to which this has been met across the globe are first acknowledged and addressed. According to UNESCO (1995), there has been a dramatic increase in participation rates with over one billion children in formal education globally. However, the number of adult illiterates is also reported to be one billion and in some industrial countries one person in five is functionally illiterate (UNDP, 2000). In the rich world, the barriers to providing a "right" to education relate to the retention of pupils and the attainment of equality of educational outcomes in school performance; in the poor world, it is the lack of finance to provide access to basic education. Thus, whereas universal education in the industrial countries is taken as a "right," (some would say *for granted*), it is a precious resource for children in the poorer majority world. The perennial debates in rich industrial countries about the shortages of resources for education are a conundrum that educators in the developing world find bewildering! In the remainder of the chapter, I explore how education in school can act as a vehicle for fostering, what Rorty (1993) termed, a "global human rights culture." What might the agenda for Human Rights education look like?

The UNDP (2000) placed a high priority on education as a force for human development and advocated a comprehensive agenda to secure the well-being and dignity of all people everywhere. Its "7 Freedoms," listed below, offer a potential descriptor for a school curriculum for human rights education:

- Freedom from discrimination—by gender, race, ethnicity, national origin or religion.
- Freedom from want—to enjoy a decent standard of living. Freedom to develop and realize one's human potential.
- Freedom from fear—of threats to personal security, from torture, arbitrary arrest and other violent acts.
- Freedom from injustice and violations of the rule of law.
- Freedom of thought and speech and to participate in decision-making and form associations.
- Freedom for decent work—without exploitation.

The belief in the link between education and human rights has also been mentioned earlier in the World Conference on Human Rights Program of Action, which called on "states and institutions to include human rights, humanitarian law, democracy and the rule of law as subjects in the curriculum of all learning institutions in formal and informal settings" (UN, 1993, pp. 78–80). How have education systems throughout the globe responded to this call? What is happening in schools in Europe and the United States?

Within the education systems of the member states in the European Union, there is broad political agreement on major social policy issues, such as the issue of "citizenship" and "citizenship education." However, this does not mean that there is uniformity of approach in implementation for there are significant differences in the philosophical traditions and administrative systems of the 15 nation-states that form the European Union. For instance, whereas British schools have not been encouraged until recently to offer anything considered a "political education," schools in Germany, the Netherlands, and France explicitly do so, though they do not share a common approach or value-base (Torney-Purta, Schwille, & Amadeo, 1999). Not surprisingly, government-inspired curriculum definitions of "citizenship education" are themselves contested outside these circles (Ichilov, 1998). In the case of Britain, "citizenship education" is now a mandatory designated subject in secondary education (ages 11–16) and recommended for primary schools (ages 5–11) in England. The curriculum has been set at a national level and aims to "make secure and to increase the knowledge, skills and values relevant to the nature and practices of 'participative democracy' (my emphasis); also to enhance the awareness of rights and duties, and the sense of responsibilities needed for the development of pupils into active citizens; and in so doing to establish the value to individuals, schools and society of involvement in the local and wider community" (Department for Education and Employment, 1998, p. 6). Since Britain is a member of the European Union, it is also obliged to respond to calls for the promotion of "European citizenship" and educational initiatives to foster closer political integration. One of these is concerned with the inclusion of the "European dimension" in schools and university level education, in order to "strengthen in young people a sense of European identity and make clear to them the value of European civilization" (Council of Ministers of Education, 1988).

There are, in my view, a number of reasons for treating the British government's affirmation of the notion of "participatory democracy" with caution for it is unclear whether this is no more than a call to support traditional British political structures, procedures, and power relationships. Whereas its definition of citizenship education mentions human rights, diversity issues, and the world as a global community, the focus appears heavily weighted towards being an upright and active citizen, in line with "Third Way" politics, an approach that has failed to engage young adults in the 2001 British parliamentary elections. The concept of a "European identity and civilization" advocated by the European Union is equally questionable and sits uneasily with the experiences of substantial numbers of newer "immigrants" who do not share heritage origins in the continent of Europe. It appears that, in this case, British educators have been given the task of mobilizing their students' passive acquiescence in the traditional interests of Europe as a major economic power block in the global world. One is left to ponder two questions. Where, in the curriculum, is there room for an education *in* human rights of the type that addresses the "7 Freedoms" advocated above? What experience of participative democracy do children, teachers, and citizens have in determining the curriculum that fosters a human rights culture in Europe's schools? In a related fashion in the United States, not more than five months into his presidency, George W. Bush announced an aggressive pursuit of the Missile Defense Project with the claim of protecting America from foreign attack. How does this policy correlate with the United States' global responsibility for the search for world peace and its social responsibility for the world's poor nations? What message does this send to young people in schools and classrooms in the United States?

A PERSPECTIVE ON UNIVERSITY EDUCATION

Bearing in mind the dilemmas posed by "Q" and "E" in the previous sections of this chapter, what role can universities play in educating their students? Booth and Dunne (1999), two leading academics in International Politics, identified key systemic limitations against and opportunities for promoting human rights education in universities across the globe. They argued that the main barriers stem from (a) the meritocratic nature of the university system, in which access to education is still contingent on institutional barriers that determine the ability to benefit from higher education; (b) opposition from academics who say that universities should not address human rights issues but should be value-free, objective, and apolitical in their teaching and research; and (c) the "culture of contentment" that has shaped the outlooks of the young and their elders in the rich world, those with the social capital, and a more comfortable political tendency. Nevertheless, Booth and Dunne argued that while issues of human rights and economic justice in the wider world may not hold an immediate attraction in the lives of university students, university educators should hold on to the positive changes that are evident in their students' growing cosmopolitan awareness of human rights abuses and their support for transnational social movements. Optimistically, they advocated a form of "cosmopolitan education" that builds on this latent awareness in young people, giving them the tools to critically evaluate the underlying causes of oppression in the world and to decide what part each can play as active global citizens. From my perspective, such a move would require a significant institutional change in educational cultures if students are not only to hear about human rights issues but also routinely experience democracy in classroom pedagogy.

CONCLUSION

In this chapter, I have presented global education as an important worldwide phenomenon. We are in this "game" together, so we must play it as a family. I believe human rights education must be practiced from preschool through university levels. In fact human rights education has a much wider relevance to other areas of education, for example, that of teacher education in universities. As we advance in this millennium, we as educators and citizens still must answer an important ethical question, How do we all heed San Suu Kyi's (1997) call to "Please use your liberty to promote ours?" We cannot afford to ignore global challenges that face us today. In the words of Obiakor (2001):

> There is no doubt that race, ethnicity, tribalization, and national pride will continue to matter. The good news is that we have all the weapons to make better our communities and our world. Our schools and our universities have roles to play. It is counterproductive to continue traditional responses that have failed to yield fruitful dividends in global collaboration and consultation. We must be valued as global stockholders as we empower each other. Empowered people do not feel threatened by others—empowered people value human differences and energies in their collaborations and con-

sultative ventures. Our cultural paradigms must be shifted to create new avenues for global collaboration and consultations. If we fail to value individual differences in this age of change, we will continue to increase our *blindness* on how we interpret our ideals and realities in our global world. Education must continue to be the key to global understanding! (pp. 8–9)

REFERENCES

Apple, M. W., & Zenk, C. (1996). American realities: poverty, economy and education. In M. Apple (Ed.), *Cultural politics and education.* Buckingham, Great Britain: Open University Press.

Artiles, A. J., & Larsen, L. A. (1998). Learning from special education reform movements in four continents. *European Journal of Special Needs in Education, 13*(1), 5–9.

Blair, T. (1998). *The third way: New politics for the new century (Pamphlet 588).* London, Great Britain: Fabian Society.

Booth, K., & Dunne, T. (1999). Learning beyond frontiers. In T. Dunne & N. J. Wheeler (Eds.), *Human rights in global politics* (pp.303–328). Cambridge, Great Britain: Cambridge University Press.

Commission on Social Justice (1994). *Social justice: Strategies for national renewal.* London, Great Britain: Vintage Books.

Department for Education & Employment (1998). *Education for citizenship and the teaching of democracy in schools* (Crick Report). London, Great Britain: Qualifications & Curriculum Agency.

Department for International Development. (1997). *Eliminating world poverty: A challenge for the 21st century.* London, Great Britain: Her Majesty's Stationery Office.

Diniz, F. A. (1999). Race and special educational needs in the 1990s. *British Journal of Special Education, 26*(4), 213–217.

Diniz, F. A. (2000). Commission on the future of multiethnic Britain: A personal perspective on the progress report. *Multicultural Teaching, 18*(3), 45–48.

European Union (1988, May 24). *Meeting of the Council of Ministers of Education.* Brussels, Belgium: Office of the European Union.

Giddens, A. (1998). *The third way: The renewal of social democracy.* Cambridge, Great Britain: Polity Press.

Gillborn, D., & Youdell, D. (2000). *Rationing education: Policy, practice, equity and reform.* Buckingham, Great Britain: Open University Press.

Hayward, E. (2000, November 14). Racial gap haunts MCAS. *Boston Herald,* p. 3.

Held, D., McGrew, A., Goldblatt, D. & Perraton, J. (1999). *Global transformations: Politics, economies and culture.* Cambridge, Great Britain: Polity Press.

Ichilov, O. (1998). *Citizenship and citizenship education in a changing world.* London, Great Britain: Woburn Press.

Midgley, M. (1999). Towards an ethic of global responsibility. In T. Dunne & N. J. Wheeler (Eds.), *Human rights in global politics* (pp.160–174). Cambridge, Great Britain: Cambridge University Press.

Obiakor, F.E. (2001, March). *Working together in our global village: Beyond rhetoric.* Position paper presented as a Visiting Scholar, Brigham Young University, Provo, UT.

Puwar, N. (2000). *The radicalized somatic norm and the senior civil service.* Northampton, Great Britain: University College Northampton.

Reich, R. (1991). *The work of nations*: New York: Simon and Schuster.

Rorty, R. (1993) Human rights, rationality and sentimentality. In S. Shute & S. Hurley (Eds.), *On human rights: The Oxford amnesty lectures.* New York: Basic Books.

San Suu Kyi, D. A. (1997, February 4). Please use your liberty to promote ours. *International Herald Tribune.*

Shaw, M. (1999). Global voices: civil society and the media in global crises. In T. Dunne & N. J. Wheeler (Eds.), *Human rights in global politics* (pp. 214–232). Cambridge, Great Britain: Cambridge University Press.

Torney-Purta, J., Schwille, J., & Amadeo, J. (1999). *Civic education across countries.* Amsterdam, The Netherlands: Eburon/International Association for Evaluation and Educational Achievement.

United Nations (1993). *The Vienna Declaration and program of action* (pp.79–80). New York: Office of the United Nations.

United Nations Development Program [UNDP] (2000). *Human Development Report 2000.* New York: Oxford University Press.

UNESCO (1995). *World Education Report.* New York: Oxford University Press.

UNHCR (1995). *The state of the world's refugees*: In search of solutions. Oxford, Great Britain: Oxford University Press.

Chapter 13

EDUCATING ALL CHILDREN: FUTURE PROSPECTS

Don Drennon-Gala, Festus E. Obiakor, and Patrick A. Grant

Today, it is obvious that to maintain a strong nation, we must maintain a well-educated populace. To this end, we find scholars and educators scrambling to find the holy grail of education in America. Therefore, to this point these attempts have led to mere mediocrity and failure. The success stories that we have read about in journals, local newspapers, and periodicals are found to be attributed mainly to education programs that draw in the student who would succeed under any condition that the student experiences (Obiakor, 2001). Various buzzword programs that educators and scholars grasp at repeatedly have shown little or no success whatsoever (Utley & Obiakor, 2001). One is left to ask the popular question, "Where is the beef?" We argue, in this chapter, that we can no longer continue with business as usual. We also conclude that we must focus on the comprehensive approach to teaching and learning as we look for new ways to educate our future generation.

SOCIAL SUPPORT AND THE COMPREHENSIVE SUPPORT MODEL

If the society is interested in having all children educated, we must begin to determine what we can do (including the "self," family, schools, communities, and government entities) to make this happen. We need to desist from pointing fingers and looking for scapegoats to blame. We also need to begin to redirect our energies toward correcting the problem and looking forward to the future. The successes that await the society with the Comprehensive

Support Model (CSM) (Obiakor, 1994) are plentiful, and general and special educators must remain focused on these initiatives.

Social support by parents and teachers have been found to have a direct impact on the strength of the social bond between the youth and these significant adults. The existence of this social bond could have an impact on the student's decision to remain engaged or disengaged in the educational process (Drennon-Gala, 1994,1995; Sarason, Pierce, & Sarason, 1990; Sarason, Pierce, Shearin, Sarason, Waltz, & Poppe, 1991). In general, social support has been operationalized as contacts, relationships (direct and indirect), or behaviors of parents and teachers toward early adolescents as they undergo life cycles (see Drennon-Gala; Sarason and associates). Social support is expressed in many different ways through the direct positive involvement of parents and teachers with the child's life; and it is supposed to be experienced at varying degrees by early adolescents regardless of family structure (Drennon-Gala, 1997). Social support, as expressed through the involvement with the early adolescent, will lead to the feeling of being cared for and loved, as a co-member of a network of mutual obligations (Cobb, 1976; Drennon-Gala, 1995). Social support, as expressed through indirect involvement, includes the verbal and physical encouragement and the adult presence that a child perceives that he or she receives from parents or teachers, or both (see Drennon-Gala; Sarason and associates). Some notable effects of the breakdown of social support within the family unit and within the classrooms in American schools and the harshness of those repercussions have evidenced student violent behaviors, high school dropouts rates, disruptions, disasters, and deaths (Gegax & Bai, 1999; Obiakor, Mehring, & Schwenn, 1997).

Obviously, the concept of social support is a microsocial concept where particular social phenomenon can be examined. The CSM responds to various social problems and examines various social phenomena by applying this macrosocial concept. This is especially true when looking at the various dynamics of the "self," school, home, community, nation, and globe, and how these various entities affect and motivate the student during the educational process (McDonald & Howard, 1998; Obiakor, 2000). In this book, its various authors introduced a multifaceted model represented by various social institutions that support the goals of one social institution, that is, education. When examining the concepts associated with the CSM, we observe terms used, such as resilience, buffering, and other terms that describe the social impact and effects that various social institutions have in the form of a support system on the individual as a result of a modification of the approach to a social dilemma. In fact, we find that family cohesion and social support are associated with resilience (Carbonell, Reinhertz, & Gianconia, 1998). When considering the CSM, it is important to acknowledge the benefits of collaborative educators at national or global level. For education to work, the *whole village must be at work.*

As we can see, the social breakdown in schools has resulted in violence, poor test scores, and the low number of new teachers entering the teaching profession in light of the exodus of senior tenured teachers (Kantrowitz & Wingert, 2000). These sad situations have brought about national attention to the problem without the actual problem being properly identified–this has only caused additional confusion. Whether it be a 14 year old student in Puducah, Kentucky; a 16 year old in Pearl, Mississippi; a 15 year old student in Springfield, Oregon; a 14 year old student in Panoma, California; an 11 year old student in Jonesboro, Arkansas; a 16 year old in Bethel, Alaska; or two middle school students in Littleton, Colorado; one common factor found in each of these cases is the fact that they attend schools that downplay emotional intelligence and highlight only the 3 Rs (reading, writing, and arithmetic) or scores in standardized tests (Obiakor, 2001). In a *Newsweek* article entitled, "Designing Smarter Schools" McGuigan and Foote (2000) revisited what a school should look like rather than what occurs within school buildings. Historically, we have focused on the architecture of a building instead of the architecture of our learning environment. Violence still occurs within round buildings as well as square buildings. Funny enough, utility bills are greater for round buildings than square buildings; and history tells us that it is more difficult to expand the size of the round building than the square building when the population of students increase.

THE CSM: FUTURE PERSPECTIVES

Today, policy-makers and educators are moving toward a comprehensive support approach. This is a departure from what we have done in the past. Apparently, we are moving away from buzzword programs that retard creativity in order to introduce pedagogy that will effectively deliver a comprehensive curriculum to students. We are beginning to acknowledge what we need and what we do not need. What is not needed is a program that sounds nice but fails to produce results. Seeking innovative ideas to enhance the education process is crucial to bring together the "self," parents, schools, local businesses, community groups, churches, and government agencies. Surely, this will make the CSM work–the CSM requires the involvement of all these social institutions within our society.

When considering the "self" and the concept of resiliency, we believe resiliency goes beyond the ability to thrive, mature, grow in the face of adverse conditions, and successfully adapt to life tasks in the face of adverse conditions (Carbonell et al., 1998; Finn & Rock, 1999; Gordon, 1995). We are convinced that the student who has successfully bonded with family members will undoubtedly be socially stronger when engaged in activities in other social institutions, such as schools (Drennon-Gala, 1995). This binding process also would make it easier for students to be responsive to the school environment and take proactive steps to maximize their learning potential. To succeed, the "self" must grow stronger when confronted with problems. In fact, to enhance the future of the "self," parents, schools, communities, and governments must be very involved.

Parents' interactions go beyond the attendance at Parent Teachers Association (PTA) meetings or sporting events (Begley, 1999; Drennon-Gala, 1994; Leland, 1999; Manetti & Schneider, 1996). In fact, these functions do not afford the needed social support, but rather fulfills the parents' belief that they are doing something that supports their child. We believe families must become an integral part of the CSM and provide the foundation from which students evolve from within social institutions. In the future, significant adults must become part of the process (e.g., getting involved in the child's homework). In short, parents must feel that they are a part of the education process, not just mere participants. Programs to buttress parental empowerment must be instituted and intensified–these programs must view parents as equal partners.

It is important to note that schools play a dominant role in building students' academic and social lives. Teaching styles and curricula must respond to students, and not the other way around. School buildings must provide environments that are conducive to learning, and school officials must get parents to volunteer within the school. For instance, parents can volunteer as tutors in mathematics, history, sciences, and English. Not only can they work with their own children, they can also work with other students. For decades, many school administrators have been keeping parents out of the educational process based on insensitive and unrealistic expectations. In the future, we must convince and compel these administrators to accept parents into the school as equal partners (Obiakor, 2001). Also, in the future, schools must be learning environments that maximize the fullest potential of students. General and special educators must properly identify, assess, categorize, place, and instruct students without prejudice and illusory assumptions.

There are many communities within the United States and the world, and each community is considered the macrocosm of the family. Watts-Jones (1997) stated that this relationship is reciprocal and intertwined. Today, it appears that in our neighborhoods, we have seen the actual involvement of families with other families lessen to the point of near total disappearance. This social phenomenon has been fostered by the Eurocentric individualistic orientation that does not lend itself to collaboration, consultation, and cooperation. Eurocentrically, when there is a problem, the solution is to avoid it until it disappears. The critical question is—How can we build emotional intelligence when we fail to come together as a community? Our communities have spent our resources building more jails rather than more schools. Just as we can "adopt a road" to clean-up litter, we must "adopt a school" and help with the growth of young people (Howell, 1999; Smith, 2001). We believe in doing so, the community will accept the commitment to take on the responsibility to raise the child. It truly takes a responsible village to raise a responsible child. We are convinced that we can treat all children the same while respecting their differences. We dream of a day when (a) community leaders would ignore ethnicity, race, and socioeconomic status and treat everyone equally with equal concern and effort; (b) no child would be treated better than the next; and (c) all children would be provided with the same opportunities as the next child. We must avoid *fraudulent* multiculturalism and be open-minded on the discourse on race, ethnicity, and socioeconomic status in our respective communities. In addition, we must stop viewing differences as defects. As a consequence, we have to positively change what we do as adults—this positive change will stimulate positive social changes. We strongly believe communities that act in a positive manner to address and resolve differences that have plagued their society will foster social growth. Such a paradigm shift will lead to collaborative involvement of community leaders and businesses in the intellectual and emotional growth of all children.

Regardless of the case law that has been procured through the United States Supreme Court, unless the government takes a proactive approach to assist state and local governments in the implementation of programs within communities, progress will be stifled and destroyed in the future. We hear common cries for new laws to protect disadvantaged individuals, however, what we have not seen is a more aggressive enforcement of laws that already exist in the United States Code. Not only are there civil remedies available for those discriminated against (see 29 U.S.C. §2000-e et al.), but there are remedies available in Title 18 of the United States Code (see 18 U.S.C. §241 et al.). The problem is that the existing statutes that protect individuals from discriminatory practices have not been used to their full extent possible—this has allowed many violators to abuse people on bases of race, ethnicity, physical, and psychological disabilities without fear of accountability. When the government becomes a part of the process to improve the conditions of communities by enforcing the laws that exist, then we will see students' potential maximized. We must revisit the quality of enforcement of the government to fight injustices to enhance educational quality for all learners. In the future, innovative programs that work can be shared more readily through State and Federal governments—this will allow for time saving and the quality of education to be shared with all learners within all communities. The Goals 2000 program was a start in the right direction toward providing assistance to improve some programs, but it is viewed by many as having a band-aid effect with no follow-up. It is important that we enforce existing legislation to assure equitable education programming, make school systems accountable, and create alternative programs to maximize the potential of *all* students.

CONCLUSION

In this chapter, it is our position that a strong nation must maintain a well-educated populace. To this end, we must strongly advocate for a departure from traditional programming and failure that we have observed in education thus far. In addition, we must move toward a comprehensive curriculum to enrich and teach all students. Educators and scholars must focus on programs that work, not on those programs that are politically convenient. We believe to educate all learners there must be a CSM that incorporates the "self" (i.e., student), family, school, community, and government. The collaborative involvement of all these entities is necessary to make this comprehensive support process work. We must redirect our energies proactively to create innovative programming for our future generation.

We must continue to recognize that social support by parents and teachers is critical in establishing a strong foundation in which to build a strong social structure. Based on this structure, an adequate engagement of constituencies must be an imperative if we are to solve multidimensional crises that confront today's children and youth. As it appears, current educational programs do not fit all children at all times. *We need programs that respond to the unique needs of all students, all parents, all schools, and all communities.* It is not impossible to treat all children with respect and integrity. We believe we must respond to the differences and energies that students bring to school programs. In other words, we must value their ethnicity, race, and socioeconomic status. We are convinced that the failure to value these variables might create the much dreaded "victim" mentality, which consistently results from misidentification, misassessment, miscategorization, misplacement, and misinstruction.

As we conclude this book with this futuristic chapter, our eyes must be on the prize, and no child must be left behind. Our traditional blame game will not work in this new millennium. We must look for new ways to solve problems! We are convinced that social growth can be realized when communities act in a proactive manner to address and resolve differences. Families, schools, community leaders, and government agencies must be held accountable. As set-forth in the CSM, we need innovative programming that involves all collaborative forces. The need for each element of the CSM to work simultaneously together is critical to the success of any general and special education program. Our commitment must be an imperative because in the end *if we do not pay now, we will pay later.* We must continue to believe education has the power to change our children, our parents, our schools, our communities, our governments, and our world.

REFERENCES

Begley, S. (1999, May 10). When teens fall apart. *Newsweek,* pp. 42–43.

Cannon, A., Streisand, B., & McGraw, D. (1999, May 3). Why? *U.S. News & World Report,* pp. 16–19.

Carbonell, D.M., Reinhertz, H.Z., & Gianconia, R.M. (1998, August). Risk and resilience in late adolescence. *Child and Adolescent Social Work Journal, 15* (4), 251–272.

Drennon-Gala, D. (1994). *The effects of social support and inner containment on the propensity toward delinquent behavior and disengagement in education.* Unpublished doctoral dissertation, University of Rochester, New York.

Drennon-Gala, D. (1995). *Delinquency and high school dropouts: Reconsidering social correlates.* Lanham, MD: University Press of America.

Drennon-Gala, D. (1997, October). *Myth or fact: The relationship between family structure and delinquency–some implications.* Paper presented at the meeting of the American Sociological Association, Toronto, Ontario, Canada.

Finn, J.D., & Rock, D.A. (1999). Academic success among students at risk for school failure. *Journal of Applied Psychology, 82,* 221–234.

Gegax, T.T., & Bai, M. (1999, May 10). Searching for Answers. *Newsweek,* pp. 30–34.

Gordon, K.A. (1995, August). Self-concept and motivational patterns of resilient African-American high school students. *Journal of Black Psychology, 21,* 239–255.

Howell, W. (1999, June). Philadelphia's "adopt-a-school" partnership to prevent delinquency. *Corrections Today,* pp. 26–28.

Kantrowitz, B., & Wingert, P. (2000, October 2). Who will teach our kids? *Newsweek,* pp. 36–47.

Leland, J. (1999, May 10). The secret life of teens. *Newsweek,* pp. 45–50.

Mahoney, K.A. (2000, November). New times, new questions. *Educational Researcher, 29* (8), 18–19.

Manetti, M., Schneider, B.H. (1996, January–March). Stability and change in patterns of parental social support and their relationship to children's school adjustment. *Journal of Applied Developmental Psychology, 17* (1), 101–115.

McDonald, L., & Howard, D. (1998, December). Families and schools together. *OJJDP Fact Sheet #88.* Washington, DC: Justice Clearing House.

McGuigan, C., & Foote, D. (2000, November 27). Designing smarter schools. *Newsweek,* pp. 68–69.

Murline, A. (1999, May 10). Once bullied, now bullies—with guns. *U. S. News & World Report*, p. 24.

Obiakor, F.E. (1994). *The eight-step multicultural approach: Learning and teaching with a smile.* Dubuque, IA: Kendall/Hunt.

Obiakor, F. E. (2001). *It even happens in "good" schools: Responding to cultural diversity in today's classrooms.* Thousand Oaks, CA: Corwin Press.

Obiakor, F. E., Mehring, T. A., & Schwenn, T. O. (1997). *Disruption, disaster, and death: Helping students deal with crisis.* Reston, VA: The Council for Exceptional Children.

Sarason, B.R., Pierce, G., & Sarason, I.G. (1990). Social support: The sense of acceptance and the role of relationships. In B.R. Sarason, I.G. Sarason, & G.R. Pierce (Eds.), *Social support: An interactional view* (pp. 97–128), New York: Wiley.

Sarason, B.R., Pierce, G., Shearin, E.N., Sarason, I.G., Waltz, J.A., & Poppe, L. (1991). Perceived social support and working models of self and actual others. *Journal of Personality and Social Psychology, 60,* 273–287.

Smith, M. (2001, Spring). Creating community in the classroom. *Kappa Delta Pi Record, 37* (3), 111–115.

Utley, C.A., & Obiakor, F. E. (2001). *Special education, multicultural education, and school reform: Components of quality education for learners with mild disabilities.* Springfield, IL: Charles C Thomas.

Watts-Jones, D. (1997). Toward an African-American genogram. *Family Process, 36,* 375–383.

NAME INDEX

A

Aber, J. L., 8
Alexander, K., 101
Algozzine, B., 11, 55, 157
Allen, L., 8
Allington, R. L., 120
Alston, E., 143
Amadeo, J., 186
Anderson, E. A., 70–72
Anderson, R. S., 167
Apple, M. W., 184
Aquan-Aassee, J., 10
Arllen, N., 106
Artiles, A. J., 117, 118, 151, 182
Arvidson, H. H., 166, 167
Ascher, C., 7

B

Baca, L., 159
Bai, M., 192
Bainbridge, W. L., 53
Baker, D. P., 41, 44
Bakken, J. P., 90
Banks, C. A., 39, 41, 42
Banks, I. W., 172
Banks, J. A., 32, 33, 35, 41, 52, 57, 114, 160
Barrett, J. M., 138
Baruth, L. G., 56, 59
Bassler, O. C., 43
Bassuk, E., 66, 67
Beck, M., 68
Begley, S., 194
Bell, T. L., 138
Benard, B., 20, 28
Bennette, K., 133

Benson, C. S., 133
Bergin, A. E., 69
Bess, S., 77
Bianchi, S. M., 34
Bielema, K. A., 69
Bigge, J. L., 173
Bitter, G. G., 173
Blair, T., 180
Blando, J., 167
Bogenschneider, K., 34, 36, 38, 44
Bomby, M., 100
Booth, K., 185, 187
Borman, K. M., 131
Borquez, J., 9
Boydell, D., 92
Boykin, A. W., 3, 4, 49
Bransford, J. D., 168
Braun, L., 169, 171
Brazil, N., 121
Bricker, D. D., 102
Brinly, B., 143
Brissie, J. S., 43
Brody, G. H., 41
Bronfenbrenner, U., 102
Brooks-Gunn, J., 9
Brophy, J., 26
Brosnan, P. A., 173
Brown, B. B., 45
Brown, B. L., 24, 28
Brown, J. H., 20, 21
Brown, J. S., 168
Brunner, C., 168
Bryk, A. S., 116
Budoff, M., 90
Bukowski, W. M., 10
Bull, G. L., 173
Bull, K. S., 138
Burdge, M., 140

Burn, B. B., 131, 132, 143
Byrd, D., 91

C

Calabrese, R., 39
Camburn, E., 116
Campbell, R. F., 131
Carbonell, D. M., 192, 194
Carlucci, C. M., 90
Carnine, D. W., 88
Caston, M. D., 20
Catalano, R. F., 69
Ceballo, R., 9
Cervantes, H., 159
Chandler, S., 118
Chang, J., 8
Chasee-Lansdale, P. L., 9
Chaskin, R. J., 106, 109
Chatters, L. M., 34
Chavkin, N. F., 41, 107
Cheney, D., 106
Clayton, J., 140
Cobb, 192
Cockran, P. S., 173
Coley, R. L., 9, 10
Collins, A., 168
Collins, M., 58
Comer, J. P., 6, 33
Cookson, Jr., P. W., 131
Cooper, H., 41, 44
Coots, J. J., 32
Cornbleth, 160
Coutinho, M., 140
Crosswait, D. J., 137
Cruickshank, D., 86
Cummins, J., 56, 153, 158
Cunningham, L. L., 131
Cunningham, P. M., 120

D

Darch, C., 88
Darling-Hammond, L., 115, 132
Davis, B., 113
Davis, J. E., 6
Davis, P. C., 138
De Li, 70
Deaton, S., 143

DeCoste, D. C., 166
Deem, R., 35
Delagado, B. M., 8, 9
Desimone, L., 34, 44
Dev, P. C., 25, 26
Devaney, B. L., 37
Diamonti, M., 92
Diniz, F. A., 180, 182
Dinsmore, J., 93
Dolan, L. J., 72
Dornbusch, S. M., 44, 45
Douvanis, C., 73, 79
Douvanis, G., 73, 79
Drennon-Gala, D., 192, 194
Drew, C. J., 60
Duguid, P., 168
Dunne, T., 187

E

Edel, A., 50
Eifler, K., 93
El-Hindi, A., 169
Elliott, J., 140
Elliott, S. N., 39
Ellis, M., 22
Ellwood, M. R., 37
Elmore, R. F., 136, 137
Engel, M., 130, 133–35
Engelman, S., 88
Enwefa, R. L., 172
Enwefa, S. C., 172
Epstein, J., 7, 32, 38, 42, 108
Erickson, R. N., 139, 140
Eskay, M., 9, 137
Espe-Sherwindt, M., 43

F

Feinman, J., 8
Feldman, S., 91
Fensternmacher, G. D., 117
Fernandez, A., 158
Field, S., 19
Field, T., 22
Finn, J. D., 6, 68, 69, 194
Flood, J., 169
Flor, D., 41
Foote, D., 193

Ford, B. A., 121, 122, 124
Fordham, S., 40
Forness, S. R., 88
Foxx, S., 91
Fuhrman, S. H., 136, 137, 145
Fuller, D. R., 166, 167
Fuller, E., 137

G

Gabert, G., 51
Gallego, M., 169
Garcia, R. L., 124, 125
Gauze, C., 10
Gay, G., 120
Gegax, T. T. 192
Gersten, R., 88
Ghatak, R., 44
Gianconia, R. M., 192
Giddens, A., 180
Gillborn, D., 185
Giordano, G., 173
Gittell, M., 106, 108
Glasser, W., 53
Glennen, S. L., 166
Glickman, N., 106
Goldblatt, D., 179
Goldman, S. R., 168
Good, K., 173
Goodlad, J. I., 33, 91
Goodman, R. M., 106
Goor, M. B., 8
Gorder, 71, 78
Gordon, K. A., 6, 68, 194
Gow, H. B., 87
Grant, C. A., 39
Grant, P. A., 56
Grant, P. B., 56
Gras, A., 90
Graves, M., 169
Greene, B., 171
Gretchen, B. R., 146
Griffith, A., 33, 34, 41, 44
Grossman, H., 68
Guerrero, M., 124
Guetzloe, E., 68, 71
Guillaume, A. M., 8
Gunsalus, C., 69
Gutek, G. L., 50–52

H

Haberman, M., 8
Haigh, J., 140
Hall, D., 143
Hamilton, M. L., 116, 118
Hamilton, S. F., 171
Hammen, C., 66, 67, 70
Hammitte, D. J., 55
Haney, W., 153
Hanson, S. M., 34
Hardman, M. L., 60
Hargreaves, A., 113
Harris and Associates, 76
Harris-Obiakor, P., 9, 137
Harry, B., 42, 124, 151
Hausman, B., 66, 67, 70
Hawkins, J. D., 69
Hayward, E., 184
Heflin, L. J., 65
Heims, M. L., 34
Held, D., 179, 181
Helge, D., ,138, 139
Henderson, A. T., 42
Hilliard, A. G., 56
Hilton, C. N., 29
Hoffman, A., 19
Hollingsworth, S., 169
Hollins, E. R., 116
Holzberg, C. S., 173
Hoover-Dempsey, K. V., 38, 43
Horn, W. F., 33
Hovat, E. M., 40
Howard, D., 192
Howard, J., 103
Howard, V. F., 56
Howell, W., 195
Hyle, A. E., 138

I

Iannaccone, L., 137
Iazzetto, D., 93
Irvine, J. J., 9
Ivarie, J., 43

J

Jackson, A., 76

Jacob-Timm, S., 101
Jain, P., 105
Jaklitsch, B., 66
Jamison, P. J., 90
Jang, 70
Jayarante, T. E., 9
Jenkins, P. H., 69
Johnson, J. F., 70, 71, 75, 76
Jordan, W. J., 6
Julian, D. J., 34

K

Kaiser, K., 92
Kantrowitz, B., 193
Katkavich, J., 124
Katz, L. G., 25
Kauffman, J. M., 65
Kavale, K. A., 88
Kearns, J., 140
Keating, T., 88
Kelley-Laine, K., 32, 43–45
Kennedy, S., 140
Kercher, M. H., 90
Kerka, S., 21, 22
Kim, S., 117
King, T. W., 166, 167
Kirst, M., 131, 133, 145
Kleine, P. F., 64, 71–73
Kleiners, H., 140
Kleinert, H., 140
Klopfer, L. E., 168
Knoll, J., 140
Knowles, J. G., 91–93Cole, A. L., 91–93
Koblinsky, S. A., 70–72
Kong, S. L., 56
Kozol, J., 3, 4, 6, 7, 12, 44, 54, 78, 134
Kreitzer, A. E., 153
Kuykendall, C., 59, 61

L

Ladson-Billings, G. J., 8
Lai, A., 8
Lapp, D., 169
Lareau, A., 40
Larsen, L. A., 182
Larson, 70
LeCompte, M. D., 133

Lee, V., 117
Leeper, L., 173
Leland, J., 194
Leppert, C., 56
Leshner, A. I., 67, 80
Leu, D., 169
Levin, J., 69
Lewis, A. C., 132
Lewis, E., 34
Lewis, J., 56
Lieber, J., 90
Lifton, R., 28
Lindsay, J. J., 41, 44
Linehan, M. F., 65, 67, 73–75
Lino, M., 34
Little, J. W., 118
Lively, K. L., 64, 71–73
Lloyd, L. L., 166, 167
Louis, K. S., 116, 117, 119
Love, J. M., 37
Lumsden, L., 26

M

MacMillan, D. L., 89
Madaus, G. F., 153
Madden, N. A., 72, 169
Madsen, C. K., 92
Malley, J., 68
Malouf, D. B., 90
Malous, D., 140
Manetti, M., 194
Manning, M. L., 56, 59
Marburger, C. L., 42
Mazurek, K., 67, 77
McAllister, G., 9
McCroskey, J., 155
McDonald, L., 192
McDonnell, J., 138
McDonnell, L. M., 137
McGee Banks, C., 52
McGinn, N., 151
McGrew, A., 179
McGrew, K. S., 139, 140
McGuigan, C., 193
McGuire-Cockrell, P., 142
McIntyre, J., 91
McLaughlin, M. W., 136, 137
McLoyd, V. C., 9

McNamara, 40
McNeil, L., 153
Means, B., 167
Mehring, T. A., 69, 192
Messmore, P., 94
Middleton, T., 167
Midgley, M., 184
Miller, C., 94
Miller, J. Y., 69
Miller, R., 50
Mitchell, C. C., 8
Montgomery, D., 138
Moore, D. R., 116
Moore, J., 173
Morocco, C., 167
Morrison, J., 103
Muller, C., 44
Murphy, J., 33

N

Neil, D. M., 35
Newman, K., 106, 108
Newman, R., 65, 77, 78
Nieto, S., 117
Nikolovska, L., 100
Nixon, C. J., 68
Noddings, N., 87
Noguera, P. A., 10
Nolan, J. F., 69
Nye, B., 41, 44
Nystrand, R. O., 131

O

O'Shea, D. L., 55
O'Shea, L. J., 55
Obi, S. O., 8, 9, 137, 138, 140
Obiakor, F. E., 4, 7–9, 11, 13, 11, 18–20, 25–28, 33, 35, 38, 4969, 71, 72, 76–78, 114, 137, 138, 188, 191–84
Odom, S. L., 102
Ogbu, J. U., 40
Olenick, M., 155
Olian, C., 64, 72, 74, 80
Oliva, P., 153
Olson, K., 167
Ooms, T., 42
Orfield, 151

Ortega, I., 106, 108
Osborne, R. E., 18–20, 23, 25, 27

P

Pascual-Leone, J., 56
Payne, I. R., 69, 70
Pearson, J. M., 137
Peck, C. A., 102
Perraton, J., 179
Persell, C. H., 36
Peterson, R., 10, 75
Pierce, G., 192
Pinson-Millburg, N. M., 34
Pisapia, J., 68, 69
Placier, P., 116, 118
Poppe, L., 192
Port, P. D., 56
Porter, M., 8
Portz, J., 105
Potthoff, D., 93
Poulos, G., 44
Poussaint, A. F., 6
Powers, J. L., 66
Prater, L. 34, 42, 43
Pratte, R., 50
Pryor, C. B., 100
Purkey, S., 93
Puwar, N., 183
Pyle, M., 34

Q

Quint, S., 76, 78

R

Reed, S., 71, 78
Reimers, F., 151
Reinhertz, H. Z., 192
Reinking, D., 169
Remz, A., 167
Renchler, R., 25
Resnick, L. B., 168
Reynolds, C., 121
Richardson, G. E., 68
Richardson, V., 117
Riley, R., 91–94, 153, 154
Ritter, P. L., 44

Robbins, P., 143
Roberts, D., 9
Robinson-Zanartu, C., 153
Rock, D. A., 6, 68, 69, 194
Roderick, M., 116
Roeder, P. W., 146
Rogers, J. F., 171
Rogers-Adkinson, D., 8, 9
Rorty, R., 185
Rosenshine, B., 88
Rosenthal, A., 145
Rossman, M., 22
Rotatori, A. F., 8
Rothman, J., 66, 69, 78, 79
Rountree, M., 70
Royse, D., 10
Rubin, L., 66, 67
Rudy, K., 65
Rueda, R., 117
Rumberger, R. W., 44
Ryder, R., 169

S

Sagor, R., 68
Sakai, A., 87
Samuda, R. J., 56
San Suu Kyi, D. A., 188
Sarason, B. R., 192
Sarason, I. G., 192
Sarri, R. C., 100
Sautter, R. C., 71, 78
Schiller, K. S., 145
Schlossberg, N. K., 34
Schneider, B. H., 194
Schnunk, D. H., 44
Schwenn, J. O., 69, 114, 192
Schwille, J., 186
Sconzert, K., 93
Scott, D. L., 140
Scott, R., 121
Sebastian, J., 138
Sebring, P. B., 116
Seidman, E., 8
Seligman, M. E. P., 89
Semmel, M. I., 90
Servon, L., 106
Shafer, D. R., 6, 7
Shaw, M., 181

Shearin, 192
Sheridan, S. M., 39
Shimahara, N. K., 87
Shimizu, W., 8
Shriner, J., 140
Siegel, J., 173
Simich-Dudgeon, C., 38, 56
Sippola, L. K., 10
Slavin, R. E., 7, 72, 169
Smith, D., 33
Smith, J., 117
Smith, M., 195
Smith, T., 76
Solo, L., 37
Soltman, S. W., 116
Sparks, S., 9
Speck, B. W., 167
Spiegel, A. N., 139
Spillane, J. P., 146
Springate, K. W., 101
Standing, K., 35
Stegelin, D. A., 101
Steinberg, L., 45
Stevenson, D. L., 41, 44, 145
Stevenson, H. C., 7, 10
Stirtz, G., 93
Stoneman, Z., 41
Storer, J. H., 137
Strickland, D. S., 7
Strike, K. A., 86
Stronge, J. H., 64, 65, 70, 71
Sussman, M. B., 34

T

Talbot, E. M., 56
Tanner, M., 42
Taylor, R. D., 9
Taylor, R. J., 34
Taylor, S., 22
Thomas, M. D., 53
Thormann, M. J., 90
Thurlow, M. L., 139, 140, 146
Torguson, C., 124
Torney-Purta, J., 186
Tower, 67, 68, 70, 75
Trent, S. C., 151
Tucker, M. B., 34
Turnbull, A. P., 36

Turnbull, H. R., 36
Turner, M. D., 140
Tyler, W., 59

U

Uroff, S., 171
Utley, C. A., 11, 114, 122, 191

V

Vanderwood, M., 140
Varner, W., 72, 74, 80
Vega, W. A., 34
Voltz, D., 121
Vye, N., J., 168

W

Waggoner, K., 34, 41, 44
Wakschlag, L. S., 9
Walsh, T., 93
Waltz, J. A., 192
Warger, C., 106
Wasik, B. A., 72
Wattas-Jones, D., 10, 194
Waugh, 160
Way, W., 22
Weiner, B., 89
Wells, L. A., 42
Westfall, A., 68, 69
Whedon, C. K., 90
White, W. A., 67, 68, 70, 75, 88

Widenhaus, C., 171
Wilder, L. K., 68, 69, 76, 78
Will, M., 139
Williams, B. F., 56
Williams, D. L., 41
Williams, R., 140
Wilson, B. L., 146
Wilson, K. G., 113
Wilson, W. J., 6, 7, 10
Wingert, P., 193
Winzer, M. A., 67, 77
Wirt, F., 131, 133, 145
Wise, A. E., 132
Wong, K. K., 105, 143
Wraga, W. G., 152

Y

Yee, I., 8
Yell, M., 140, 156
Yeo, F., 8
Youdell, D., 185
Ysseldyke, J., 139, 140, 157

Z

Zeichner, K. M., 114, 117
Zenk, C., 184
Ziebarth, J., 93
Ziebarth, T., 105
Zimmerman, B. J., 44
Zorfass, J., 167
Zuniga-Hill, C., 8

SUBJECT INDEX

A

Academic achievement
　community involvement, 10
Academic presentation
　underprepared teachers, 114
　　demographics, 115
　unequal representation, 114
Academic programs objectives, 55
Accessibility, 54
Accommodation, 60
African Americans
　black pride movement, 52
　civil rights movement and education, 52
　extended family parental roles, 56–57
　overrepresentation in special education, 8, 12, 25, 151
　post Civil War education in trades and service, 51–52
Anglocentric values, 3
Assessment, 55–56
　criteria, 56
Assistive technology in learning theory, 90, 166–75 (*see also* Computer-assisted instruction)
At-risk students
　cash, care, computers, coalitions, 171–72
　computer literacy education, 169–72
　computer technology applications, 172–74
　individualized instruction, 171–74, 196
　language barriers, 171
Attribution orientation in learning, 89–90
　avoidance behaviors, 90
　challenge or deterrence, 90
　failure, behaviors of aftermath, 90
　four attitudes for success, 89
　ability, effort, luck, task, 89
　learned helplessness, 89
　success or failure internalization, 89

B

Behavioral learning, 88
Bernard, Henry, 50
Bilingual education, 158–59
Black pride movement, 52
Blame game, obsolescence, xiii, 4, 13, 45, 191
Braille, 167 (*see also* Assistive technology; Technology)
Brown v. Board of Education, 3, 8, 51
Borderline communities, 104–6
　governmental fiscal responsibility, 104–6
　minimal citizen participation, 104
　role of elected officials in school viability, 105–6

C

Cash, care, computers, coalitions, 171–72
Children
　depression influences, 10
　emotional development and community interactions, 10, 194
　extended family parental roles, 34, 56–57
　self-esteem, influences, 10
Civil rights movement
　and education for African Americans, 52
　Black pride, 52
　initiative away from industrial trades, 52
Common schools, 50–52
　African Americans and trade schools, 51–52
　immigration and assimilation, 51

Subject Index

rationale and value system, 50–52
state-sanctioned pubic school system, 51
Community
  academic development, environmental interactions, 10, 194
  behavioral deviancy, community interactions, 10, 194
  definition, 99–101
  educational core statement, 4, 10
  it takes a village, xiii, 4, 10, 99, 192
  macrocosm of family, 10
  resources, self-initiative to access, 22–24
  rural, definition, 100–1
  school and community interlock, 10–11, 99–110 (*see also* Schools)
    support systems considered essential, 10
  self-initiative to access resources, 22–24
  service learning opportunities, 24
  suburban, definition, 100
  urban, definition, 99–100
Community and educational role, 101–10
  comprehensive development of students, 102–3
  ecological systems theory, 102 (*see also* Ecological systems theory)
  neighborhood reform movements, 103–10
    borderline communities, 104–6
      minimal citizen participation, 104
      governmental fiscal responsibility, 104–6
      role of elected officials in school viability, 105–6
    dysfunctional, struggling communities, 103–4
      absence of change movement participation, 103
      school board accountability, 104
  restructuring, 106–10
    conscientious communities' dynamics, 106–9
    proactive community/school dynamics, 109–10
    recommendations, 109–10
  sanctuary, lack of feeling of, 103
  values, mores, belief embedding in school systems, 101–2
Comprehensive Support Model, xiii, 4–13, 33, 159–63, 191–97
  federal legislation context, 159–63
    bilingual education, 159–63
    disability access, 159–63
    multiculturalism, 159–63
    teacher preparation for culturally diverse populations, 159–63
  functional components, 6–13, 159–63, 191–97
    community, xiii, 3, 10–11, 22–25, 191–97 (*see also* Community)
    education, 25–28, 191–97 (*see also* Education)
    family, xiii, 3, 7–8, 19–22, 33–45, 191–97 (*see also* Family)
    government agencies, xiii, 3, 11–13, 191–97 (*see also* Government)
    school, xiii, 3, 8–10, 191–97 (*see also* School)
    self, xiii, 3, 6–7, 18–19, 191–97 (*see also* Self)
  goals and objectives, 13–14, 159–63, 191–97
  operational definition, 4–5
    elements and objectives, 5, 191–97
Computer-assisted instruction, 90 (*see also* Assistive technology)
  at risk students, benefits for, 170–72
  language barriers, 171
  instructional technology, 166–75
  literacy in technology, 169–70
  teacher preparation, 169
Constructivist learning, 88
Culturally diverse schools
  demographics, 114
  intelligence tests
    multicultural student's results, 12
  multicultural education, 35–37
    literature focus on white traditional family, 36
    socioeconomic impact on parental involvement, 36, 56–57
  multicultural socioeconomic status, 33, 35–37
  multicultural view of self and independence, 25
    impact for professional development, 114
  professional development challenges, 114

D

Demographic changes, 3
Direct instruction, 88–89
   accommodation, 54, 60
   CSM objectives, 60
Disabled
   ability not based on traditional IQ test, 157
   accessibility, 157
   equal access to free appropriate public education, 157–58
   inclusion vs. exclusion, 157
   individualized education plan, 157–58, 196
   least restrictive environment, 157
Dysfunctional, struggling communities, 103–4
   absence of change movement participation, 103
   school board accountability, 104

E

Ecological systems theory
   exosystem, 102
   macrosystem, 102–3
   mesosystem, 102
   microsystem, 102
   role of community, 102–3
Educate America Act, 54
Education Act of Homeless Children and Youth, 79
   state funding for direct services to homeless students, 79
Education for All Handicapped Children, 12, 157–58
Education, overview
   extended family parental roles, 56–57
   failure syndrome, 26
   family conditions promoting child success in school, 37
   multicultural education, 35–37
      literature focus on white traditional family, 36
      socioeconomic impact on parental involvement, 36, 56–57
   multicultural view of self and independence, 25
   self and education, 25–29
   student motivation
      school goals and objectives, 25
      teacher perceptions and expectations, 26
      urban schools and student potential, 26
         expectations based on stereotypes, 26
         racial, economic distribution and teacher perception, 26–27
         stereotypical perceptions, 26
Elementary and Secondary Education Act, 154–55, 163
   Title I programs, 154–55
Equality vs. quality issues, 3, 11–12, 53
Ethnic students
   bilingual education, 158–59
   cultural mismatch, 153
   language barriers via vernacular, 171
   socioeconomic status, 36, 56–57, 155–56
   testing tools inadequacies, 151–54
   translations for values and behavior on assessment tools, 153
Exosystem, 102

F

Failure syndrome, 26–28 (*see also* Education)
   resiliency and overcoming poor expectations, 11, 28
   societal influences, 28
Family
   bridge between student and school, 7
   career development influences, 21
   community-family partnerships, 10
   cornerstone of CSM, 7
   educational core statement, 4, 32
   extended family parental roles, 56–57
   family conditions promoting child success in school, 37, 56–57
   family empowerment, 8
   family functioning and impact, 21–22
   home schooling, 32
      parent-child relationships and career development, 21–22, 33
      parenting styles, 21–22
   parental involvement, 41, 55–56
   participation in student life, 7, 32–33
      definition, 32–45
      parental involvement vs. interest, 38
   proactive family characteristics, 22

self-determination model components, 22
traditional picture and today's picture, 33–34
   behavior management, 34–35
   English not primary language, 33–34
   extended family environment, 34, 56–57
   father as primary caregiver, 34
   female-headed households, 34
   grandparent as caregiver, 34, 57
   multicultural, 33, 56–57
   never-married mother, 34–35
   single parent, 34–35, 56–57
   stepparents, 34, 35
Field training for teachers, 91–94
   Genesis program goals, 94, 95
   quality preservice elements, 92
   innovative programs, 94
   standards for experience, 91
   supervisory instructors, 92–93
   urban or poverty setting, 93
Funding
   apportionments, 12

G

Genesis program goals, 94, 95
Globalization, 179–89
   human rights, 181–89
      agenda for education programs, 185–88
         barriers, 188
         seven freedoms, 186
      global responsibility, awareness, 182–85
      historic overview, 181–82
   hyperglobalizers
      nation-states as unnecessary, 179–80
         global markets and competition, 179–80
   skeptics, 179
      regionalization of 3 major blocks, 180
   transformationalists, 179–81
      globalization, 180–81
Goal-oriented behavior, 19–21, 23, 24
Goals 2000
   goals and influences, 12, 54, 151–54
   objectives, 152
Government, federal
   affirmative action, 12
   assessment and testing, 152–54
   bilingual education, 158–59, 195
   Brown v. Board of Education, 3, 11, 150, 151, 156
      equal but not equitable, 3, 11, 150, 155–56, 195
   disabled, 157–59, 195 (*see also* Disabled)
      accessibility, 157
      free and appropriate public education, 157
      inclusion, 157
      least restrictive environment, 158
   discrimination, educational policies to remedy, 150, 156
   education as local government responsibility, 130–32, 155
   educational core statement, 4
   English proficiency, 158–59
      bilingual education programs, 158
      cultural mismatch, 153
      Lau v. Nichols, 158–59
      socioeconomic status, 36, 56–57, 155–56
      testing tools inadequacies, 151–54
      translations for values and behavior on assessment tools, 153
   ethnic students, testing assessments, 152–54
   federal education policies, 150–63, 195
   funding initiatives, 12, 139–46, 195
   Goals 2000, 12, 54, 151–54
      objectives 152
      standards-based reform, 152
   legislation via litigation for equality, 12, 195
   Plessy v. Ferguson, 3, 11
      separate but equal, 3, 11, 53, 150
   social segregation via
      funding differentiation, 4, 12, 151
      ethnic neighborhoods, 4, 12, 151
      language and culture, 12, 151
      social status, 4, 12, 151
      urban flight, 4, 12, 151
   special education
      overrepresentation of ethnic and African Americans, 8, 12, 25, 151, 156
   state vs. national influence, 130–36, 139–46
      resources, 130–36
   Title I programs, 155, 156

Government, millennium initiatives
  assessment measures, 140–46
  disabled, education services, 140–46
  equal opportunity to education opportunities, 139–46
  Individuals With Disabilities Education Act amendments, 140
  quality educational opportunities, 139–46
  special needs students, attention to, 139–46
  state responsibilities to education, 143–46
  testing standards for disabled, 140
Government, state, 130–46
  accountability standards distribution, 132
  administration of school districts, 132–36
    authority, 133
    centralization, 133–34
    curriculum development, 133–34
    equal vs. equality, 135–36
    multicultural emphasis, 135–36
    multilevel governance, 136
    overview, 133
    regulatory authority for professional credentials, 133–34, 141–42
    social segregation issues, 135–36
    tax and financing authority, 134
    technology and work force preparation challenges, 136
  assessment and testing standards, 139–46
  constitutional sovereignty over education, 131–32
  federal aid, conditions for, 131–32
  functions and policies, 132–36
  higher education fiscal responsibilities, 144
  local districts' trickle down effect, 131
  multilevel governance, 136–39
    rural areas, 137–39 (*see also* Rural areas)
    overview of challenges, 137–39
    school district consolidation, 137
    urban areas, 13
  obligation as determined by national, 131
  role
    determination of purpose of public education, 130
    financing, administration of school systems, 130
    racial, ethnic, gender, religious differences, 130
  state responsibilities to education, 143–46

H

Habitat for Humanity, 78
Health care
  insurance coverage for all children, 53
  mainstreaming special needs children, 54
Hispanic Americans
  bilingual, bicultural education, 52
  cultural heritage, 52
  extended family parental roles, 56–57
  pride movement, 52
Holmes Group of Education Deans, 115
Homeless, 64–80
  abuse, 65–71
  academic support services, 76
  anxiety 67, 70
  barriers to school attendance
    guardianship, 79
    immunization records, 79
    school fees, 79
    transportation, 79
  barriers to school success
    health and nutrition deficiencies, 79
    inadequate food, clothing, school supplies, 79
    transience, 79
  basic needs, self attempts to meet, 65–70
  behavioral patterns, 65
  boundaries and limits, setting, 69
  clothing needs, 75
  community relationships
    advocacy, 77
    efforts to assist with basic needs, 77–78
    mentoring programs, 77–78
    housing programs, 78
    tolerance, 77
  counseling needs, 69, 70
  demographics, 65, 70
  depression, 67
  developmental delay, 67
  educational environment, 65–80
    emphasis on positive relationships, 71
    parental involvement, acknowledgement, 72
    recognition of student strengths, 71

teacher awareness of individuals, 72
failure factors, identification, 69
familial portrait, 65–67, 70–71
family dysfunction, 79
government role in assisting, 78–80
   protect and support individuals, 78
   Runaway and Homeless Youth Act, 79
health care needs, 68, 69, 75
invisibility, 64–65, 80
language disabilities, 67
mentoring, 76
nutritional and meal needs, 76
peer relationships, 67–68
religious involvement, 70
resiliency, 68
school attendance, 64–67, 72–74
   compliance strategies, 73–74
   special schools on site, 74
   transportation, 74
substance abuse, 70
teacher in-service training, 75
transient living, impact of, 65, 67, 72–73
Human relationships in school, 119
Human rights, 181–89
   agenda for education programs, 185–88
     barriers, 188
     seven freedoms, 186
   global responsibility, awareness, 182–85
   historic overview, 181–82

I

Immigration and assimilation, 51
Improving America's Schools Act, 154
   priorities, 154
Individualized Education Plan, 157–58, 196
Individualized instruction
   computer technology applications, 172–74
Individuals With Disabilities Education Act, 12, 140
Informational age, 3
Instructional technology, 167–68
   barriers to use, 168
   classifications, 167
     application, 167–68
     communication, 167–68
     exploratory, 167
     tutorial, 167
Intelligence tests
   disabled, unreliable measurement, 157
   multicultural student's results, 12
It takes a whole village, xiii, 4, 10, 99, 192

J

Jim Crow era, 3, 11–12

K

Kentucky Education Reform Act highlights, 141–43

L

Lau v. Nichols, 158
Learned helplessness, 19
   behavioral responses, 19
Leave no child behind, xiii, 45, 53, 61

M

Mann, Horace, 50
Macrosystem, 102–3
Mastery learning, 89
Mesosystem, 102
Microsystem, 102
Motivation
   operational entities of CSM, 5
Multicultural students
   bilingual education, 158–59
   educational environment portrait, 35–36
   equality vs. quality of education issues, 36–37, 53
   extended family parental roles, 34, 56–57
   family conditions promoting child success in school, 37, 56–57
   fraudulent efforts, 11, 195
   inclusive educational programming, 35–37
   research, focus on white traditional family, 36
   resiliency in educational pursuit, 6
   socioeconomic status, 33, 35–37
   teacher objectives for diverse populations, 9
     literature, absence of multicultural focus, 36

Multicultural training model for partnerships, 120–26
  phase one: personal attitudes, 121–23
    competency, 122–23
      common core of knowledge and skills, 123
      Local Professional Development Committees, 123
      performance-based assessment, 122
    exposure and experiences, 122–23
  phase two: knowledge base, 123–26
    critique of current partnerships, 125
    participation-observation format, 124
    significant community resources, 121–26
    school and community team, 125
    thematic community resource calendar, 124
  phase three: collaborative networks, 126
    facilitation of collaborative activities, 126

N

National Board for Professional Teaching Standards
  teacher training goals and objectives, 85–86
National Network for Educational Renewal, 115
National Runaway Switchboard, 79
National Standards for Parent/Family Involvement Programs, 57
Neighborhood reform movements, 103–10
  borderline communities, 104–6
    minimal citizen participation, 104
    governmental fiscal responsibility, 104–6
    role of elected officials in school viability, 105–6
  dysfunctional, struggling communities, 103–4
    absence of change movement participation, 103
    school board accountability, 104

O

Operational elements of CSM, 5

P

Parental participation in school
  extended family parental roles, 56–57
  family conditions promoting child success in school, 37, 56–57
  family structure, 33–35
  involvement vs. interest, 38, 56–57, 194
  proactive families, 22, 57
  socioeconomic status and time availability, 35–37
  teacher initiatives for involvement
    broaden view of involvement possibilities, 41, 55–56
    homework, 44
    initiatives for nonparticipating parents, 42
    options to develop, 40–42, 57–58
    parental involvement vs. parental interest, 38
    parental reasons for desiring involvement, 43
    parenting workshops, implied meanings, 38–39
    positive strategies for relationships, 42–43
    PTO involvement and student success predictors, 44, 56–57, 194
    racial skepticism re legacy of discrimination, 40
    technology avenues for communication, 43
    volunteering based on time and lifestyle flexibility, 43
Parent Teachers Association, 57
Parent Teacher's Concerned With Children, 57
Partners in Action, 78
Plessy v. Ferguson, 3, 159
Poverty
  ethnic populations, 36, 56–57
    socioeconomic status, 36, 56–57, 155–56
  rural education challenges, 101, 137, 138
  Title I programs, 154–55
Preservice training for teachers, 91–94
  Genesis program goals, 94, 95
  quality preservice elements, 92
  innovative programs, 94

standards for experience, 91
supervisory instructors, 92–93
urban or poverty setting, 93
Proactive community/school dynamics, 109–10
    recommendations, 109–10
Proactive family characteristics, 22
Professional development, 113–26
    academic field representation, 114–15
    assessment strategies, 113
    impact of multiculturalism, 114
    in-service training, 113
    multicultural responsiveness, 120–26
        training model, phases, 121–26
            phase one: personal attitudes, 121–23
            phase two: knowledge base, 123–26
            phase three: collaborative networks, 126
    rationale, 114
    school elements for successful programs, 120
    successful programs, conditions for, 118
    teacher beliefs re classroom practices, 116–17
        ethnically diverse students, 117
        learning potential of students, 117
    teacher engagement, 119
    teacher thinking, 117–18
        constructivist, sociocultural approach, 117
        urban school construct, 118
    teacher responsibility vs. school district, 115–16
Professionals, educators
    multicultural awareness development, 39
    parental involvement
        broaden view of involvement possibilities, 41, 56–57
        homework, 44
        initiatives for nonparticipating parents, 42, 57
        options to develop, 40–42
        parental reasons for desiring involvement, 43
        parenting workshops, implied meanings, 38–39
        positive strategies for relationships, 42–43
        racial skepticism re legacy of discrimination, 40
        technology avenues for communication, 43
        volunteering based on time and lifestyle flexibility, 43
        vs. parental interest, 38
    PTO involvement and student success predictors, 44, 56–57
    racial prejudgment re potential and success, 38, 40
    research focus on middle-class population, 44
    school environment for parental involvement, 39–45, 56–57
    socioeconomic portrait and teacher expectations 38

R

Racism
    disproportional special ed population, 8, 12, 25
    disproportional incarceration, 24
    expectations and responsibility to overcome, 25
    perceptions and teacher expectations, 25
    police profiling, 24
Religious indoctrination via school, 50
Resiliency, 6
    capability to live despite life, 6, 28
    definition, 6
Runaway and Homeless Youth Act, 79
    state funding for direct services to homeless students, 79
    criticisms, 79
Rural communities
    challenges, 101, 137–39
    definition, 100–1
    demographics, 100
    disabilities, services to, 138
    dual education systems, 101
    compensatory funding programs, 139
    poverty, 101, 137, 138
    professional development obstacles, 137–38
    professional isolation, 137–38
    special education programs, 136–38
    staff turnover, 101, 138

S

School
- community and school interlock, 10–11
  - support systems considered essential, 10
- educational core statement, 4
- failure syndrome, 26
- instructional program, 10
- leadership, 10
- learning environment emphasis, 10
- multicultural students, special needs, 8
- multicultural view of self and independence, 25
- objectives for diverse student population, 9
- PTO involvement and student success predictors, 44, 56–57
- racial prejudgment re potential and success, 38, 40
- research focus on middle-class population, 44
- school environment for parental involvement, 39–45, 56–57
- socioeconomic portrait and teacher expectations 38
- self and education, 25–29
- staff development, 10
- student motivation
  - school goals and objectives, 25
- tailoring curriculum to student, 8, 10
- teacher initiatives for parental involvement
  - broaden view of involvement possibilities, 41
  - homework, pros and cons, 44
  - initiatives for nonparticipating parents, 42
  - multicultural awareness development, 39
  - parental reasons for desiring involvement, 43
  - parenting workshops, implied meanings, 38–39
  - participation options to develop, 40–42
  - positive strategies for relationships, 42–43
  - racial skepticism re legacy of discrimination, 40
  - technology avenues for communication, 43
  - volunteering based on time and lifestyle flexibility, 43
  - vs. parental interest, 38
- teacher perceptions and expectations, 26
- urban schools and student potential, 26
  - expectations based on stereotypes, 26
  - racial, economic distribution and teacher perception, 26–27
  - stereotypical perceptions, 26

School and community team, 125

School, objectives (CSM), 53–61
- academic programs, 55
- accessibility, 54
- accommodation criteria, 60
- assessment, 55–56
  - criteria, 56
- community and support services objectives, 58–59
- criteria for appropriate learning environments, 53–54
- critical, political buzz words
  - accommodation, 60
  - accountability, 53
  - grade-level testing, 53
  - no child left behind, 53
  - vouchers, 53
  - zero tolerance, 53, 60
- financial management, 54–55
  - minority school funding priorities, 54–55
- governance objectives, 60–61
- parental involvement objectives, 56–57
- safety criteria, 60
- school environment objectives, 59–60
- student responsibility objectives, 58
- support services, must haves, 59
- teachers and staff objectives, 57–58

School, public school philosophy, 50–54
- accessibility, 54
- African Americans and trade schools, 51–52
- common schools, 50
- education as expression of culture, 50
- historical perspectives, 50–54
- immigration and assimilation, 51
- national ideological consensus, 50
- rationale and value system, 50–52
- religious indoctrination, 50
- state-sanctioned pubic school system, 51

Subject Index

School-to-work vs. service learning, 24
Segregation, 3–4, 12, 151–63
  separation via
    ethnic neighborhoods, 4, 12, 151
    funding differentiation, 4, 12, 151
    language and culture, 12, 151
    social status, 4, 12, 151
    urban flight, 4, 12, 151
Self
  centerpiece of CSM, xiii, 3, 6, 18–29
  community role, 22–25 (*see also* Community)
    it takes a whole village, xiii, 4, 10, 99, 192
    self-initiative to access resources, 22–24
    service learning opportunities, 24
  concept definition, 19
  deprivation of basic necessities, impact, 6
  dream of future potential, 19–20
  education
    racial, cultural, economic profiling, 26
    school objectives to increase student motivation, 25
    self-initiatives to overcome expectations, 26
    teacher expectations and prophecies, 25–26
  educational core statement, 4
  failure syndrome, 26–28 (*see also* Failure syndrome)
  family role, 19–22 (*see also* Family)
    career role for future, 19–20
  multidimensional development, 19–29
  resiliency, 6, 20–21
  role in determining educational success, 18–29
  self-responsibility, 4, 6–7
Self-determination, 18, 20, 21, 23, 27
  dream of future potential, 19–21, 23
  goal-oriented behavior, 19–21, 23, 24, 27
  resiliency, 19–24
  self-reflection, 22, 27
  victim mentality absence, 21, 23, 196
Self-Determination Model, 22
  components for fostering self-success, 22
Self-empowerment, 7, 18, 27
Self-esteem
  community influences, 10
    special ed disproportional population, 24
    negative advertisements, 25
    racial profiling, 24
  construct of self, 18, 27
  dream of future potential, 19–21, 27
  poverty, determination to rise above, 20–21
    poor in materials, rich in spirit, 20–21
  victim mentality, 21, 23
Self-ideal, 18, 27
  self qualities desired to achieve, 27
Self-initiative, 22–23
  access community resources, 22–23
Self-knowledge, 3, 6, 18, 22
  beliefs and values structure, 19
  definition, 19
  initiative to rise above expectations, 27
Self-loving, 7, 22, 27
Self-perception, 18, 22, 27
  behavioral responses, 19
Self-reflection, 22, 27 (*see also* Self-Determination Model)
Self-responsibility, 4, 6–7, 18–29
Service learning opportunities, 24–25
  work-based initiative, 24
Significant community resources, 121–26
Single parents (*see also* Family)
  parent, child, school interactions, 34–35, 194
Social behavior
  community influences, 10
Social norms and family structure
  English not primary language, 33–34
  extended family environment, 34
  father as primary caregiver, 34
  female-headed households, 34
  grandparent as caregiver, 34
  multicultural family, 33
  never-married mother, 34
  school outcome and behavior management, 34–35
  single parent, 34–35
  stepparents, 35
Special education
  assessment standards, 139–46
  coordinated services provision, 140–46
  overrepresentation of multicultural students, 8, 12, 25, 151
  overrepresentation of African Americans, 8, 12, 25, 151

testing requirements, 140–46
underrepresentation in gifted programs, 8, 12
Special needs children
   mainstreaming classroom curriculum, 54
Spirit of teaching, philosophy of, 84–96
Standards-based reform
   Goals 2000, 12, 54, 151–54
Stewart B. McKinney Act, 79
Student safety, criteria, 60
Suburban communities
   challenges, 100
   definition, 100
   demographics, 100
   dual education systems, 101
   ego, materialism, lack of unity, 100
   political ambivalence, 100
   youth centers, 101
Success-oriented behaviors, 29
   Conrad Hilton philosophy, 29

T

Teach the unteachable, reach the unreachable, xiii, 3, 12
Teacher engagement in school, 119
   human relationships, 119
      school as social unit, 119
      students as individuals, 119
   teaching and learning, 119
      academic achievement, 119
      body of knowledge, 119
Teacher preparation, 84–96 (*see also* Professional development)
   body-spirit-mind connection, 84–85, 94
   character and competence, 87, 95
   coaching strengths, 87
   critical thinkers, 85, 95
   curriculum development, 85, 95, 115–16
   field experience, 92–96
   knowledge-based models, 85–86
   moral philosophy, 86–87, 95
   multicultural training model, 121–26
   NBPTS goals and objectives, 85–86, 94
   problem solvers, 85, 95
   professional development programs, 116–21
   reflective practitioners, 85–86, 95
      traits, 86
   self-reflection, 86
   society, participation as models, 84
   teaching/learning process intertwine, 84, 95
   theories of learning, 88–90 (*see also* Theories of learning)
Technology
   assistive devices, 166–75
   assistive education theory, 3, 90, 165–69
   at risk students, benefits for, 170–72
   barriers to use, 168
   cash, care, computers, coalitions, 171–72
   individualized instruction applications, 172–74, 196
   instructional technology classifications, 167
   literacy skills in technology, 169–70
   peer tutoring, 174
   school-based technology support system
      equalization of opportunities, 169–72
      essential elements, 168–69
   special needs students, 166–75
   teacher preparation, 169–70
Tests and measurements
   assessment tools for ethnic students, 151–54
   disadvantaged students, language, 153–54
   teaching to the test, 153
Theories of learning
   assistive technology, 90
   attribution orientation, 89
   behavioral learning, 88
   computer assisted instruction, 90
   constructivist learning, 88
   direct instruction, 88–89
   mastery learning, 89

U

Urban communities
   challenges, 100
   crime, gangs, 100
   definition, 100
   demographics, 100
   dual education systems, 101
   homelessness, 100
   political ambivalence, 100
   racism, ethnic prejudice, 100

violence, 100
Urban school construct, 117–18
   sociocultural approach, 118

V

Victim mentality absence, 21, 23, 196

W

Winners vs. losers, definition, 28

Z

Zero tolerance, 53, 60

Charles C Thomas
PUBLISHER • LTD.

2600 South First Street
Springfield, IL 62704

Forthcoming releases from Charles C Thomas, Publisher!

COMMON TERMINOLOGY, ABBREVIATIONS AND SYMBOLS FOR THERAPEUTIC RECREATION AND OTHER ACTIVITY THERAPIES
A Glossary and Workbook
To be published 2002, 160 pages
David L. Jewell
$23.95, paper ISBN 0-398-07266-3

IMPROVING SCHOOLS FOR AFRICAN AMERICAN STUDENTS
A Reader for Educational Leaders
To be published 2002, 264 pages
Sheryl J. Denbo & Lynson Moore Beaulieu
hard ISBN 0-398-07281-7
paper ISBN 0-398-07282-5

EDUCATING ALL OUR CHILDREN
To be published 2002, 210 pages
Festus E. Obiakor, Patrick A. Grant & Elizabeth A. Dooley
cloth ISBN 0-398-07264-7
paper ISBN 0-398-07265-5

BEHAVIOR MANAGEMENT STRATEGIES FOR TEACHERS
Achieving Instructional Effectiveness, Student Success, and Student Motivation - Every Teacher and Any Student Can!
To be published 2002, 278 pages
Joan C. Harlan & Rowland T. Sidney
hard ISBN 0-398-07326-0
paper ISBN 0-398-07327-9

ENDING DISCRIMINATION IN SPECIAL EDUCATION (2nd Ed.)
To be published 2002, 150 pages
Herbert Grossman
paper, ISBN 0-398-07304-X

FULL SERVICE SCHOOLS
A Place for Our Children and Families to Learn and Be Healthy
To be published 2002, 196 pages
Robert F. Kronick
paper ISBN 0-398-07294-9

CONSTRUCTIVIST TEACHING STRATEGIES
Published 2001, 210 PAGES
Jessie C. Brown & Arlene Adams
$54.95, hard ISBN 0-398-07221-3
$36.95, paper, ISBN 0-398-07222-1

PHYSICAL EDUCATION RECONCEPTUALIZED
Persons, Movement, Knowledge
Published 2001, 268 pages
Saul Ross
$58.95, hard ISBN 0-398-07124-1
$39.95, paper ISBN 0-398-07125-X

BEST PRACTICE IN MOTIVATION AND MANAGEMENT IN THE CLASSROOM
Published 2001, 240 pages
Dennis G. Wiseman & Gilbert H. Hunt
$49.95 hard, ISBN 0-398-07237-X
$33.95 paper, ISBN 0-398-07238-8

TEACHING ENGLISH CREATIVELY (3rd Ed.)
Published 2001, 260 pages
John H. Bushman
$61.95, hard ISBN 0-398-07206-X
$44.95, paper ISBN 0-398-07207-8

EFFECTIVE RESPONSE TO SCHOOL VIOLENCE
Published 2001, 266 pages
Tony L. Jones
$61.95, hard ISBN 0-398-07188-8
$39.95, paper ISBN 0-398-07189-6

ESSENTIAL STRATEGIES FOR SCHOOL SECURITY
A Practical Guide for Teachers and School Administrators
Published 2001, 268 pages
Richard A. Haynes & Catherine L. Henderson
$54.95, hard ISBN 0-398-07177-2
$36.95, paper ISBN 0-398-07178-0

WHAT PRINCIPALS SHOULD KNOW ABOUT . . .
A Primer on School Subjects
Published 2000, 216 pages
Sandra Tonnsen
$43.95, cloth ISBN 0-398-07009-1
$29.95, paper ISBN 0-398-07010-5 (displayed)

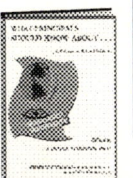

PROCEDURES FOR STRUCTURING AND SCHEDULING SPORTS TOURNAMENTS
Elimination, Consolation, Placement, and Round-Robin Design (3rd Ed.)
Published 2000, 192 pages
Francis M. Rokosz
$29.95, paper ISBN 0-398-07050-4

Contact us to order books or a free catalog with over 811 titles
Call 1-800-258-8980 or 1-217-789-8980 or Fax 1-217-789-9130
Complete catalog available at www.ccthomas.com • books@ccthomas.com

Books sent on approval • Shipping charges: $6.95 U.S. / Outside U.S., actual shipping fees will be charged
Prices subject to change without notice